On PERFORMING

Also by David Craig

On Singing Onstage

On PERFORMING

*A Handbook for
Actors, Dancers, Singers
on the Musical Stage*

David Craig

Foreword by Robert Lewis

McGraw-Hill Book Company

New York   St. Louis   San Francisco   Auckland   Bogotá   Hamburg
Johannesburg   London   Madrid   Mexico   Milan   Montreal   New Delhi
Panama   Paris   São Paulo   Singapore   Sydney   Tokyo   Toronto

1 2 3 4 5 6 7 8 9 F G R F G R 8 7

ISBN 0-07-013341-7

LIBRARY OF CONGRESS CATALOGING-IN-PUBLICATION DATA

Craig, David.
    On performing.
    1. Musical revue, comedy, etc.—Instruction and
study.   2. Singing—Vocational guidance.   3. Acting—
Vocational guidance.   4. Dancing—Vocational guidance.
5. Entertainers—United States—Interviews.   I. Title.
MT956.C7   1987   782.81′07′1   86-21010
ISBN 0-07-013341-7

To Miranda,
who taught me that the generation gap
can be a fiction

CONTENTS

FOREWORD

How do you break into show business? What's the best way to audition? How does one choose the best teacher? Questions. Questions. Questions.

Well, here's a practical how-to book from a master teacher who has long been giving bright answers to a host of grateful musical performers from the well-known to the hope-to-be-well-known.

We get dividends, too: advice from experienced players who are questioned by David Craig. Of course, the distance between what an artist does and what he thinks he does can be the widest chasm in geography. But here the interviewer struggles to keep the interviewees on as practical a plane as possible. The answers Craig seeks in his questions to the performers lie in the balancing of the three components of the craft: acting, dancing, and singing, the combining of which makes up a complete musical statement. The author never serves just one field to the exclusion of the others. When, for example, he speaks of *acting*, he means the acting of a performing singer, and he dwells on the problems that arise from the combined effort of the two disciplines. The same goes for the other combinations. The book is about the mutual goals of a theater experience that embraces acting, dancing, and singing.

Here you'll find a nurturing contribution from Robert Preston, a prime example of what Craig defines as a modern actor-dancer-singer (and in that order). How's this for a three-word hint at how to avoid playing the cliché by finding the essence of a specific character? When Shelley Winters saw Preston's creation of the part of the eighty-seven-year-old Ben Franklin, she told him, "You're sure as hell not playing an eighty-seven-year-old man." Preston's terse reply was, "Neither was he." There are equally fascinating nuggets from eight other worthies in the musical field.

If David Craig sometimes betrays a longing for the great musical performers of the past, we can take solace in the fact that he analyzes what made them great and so lays the groundwork for what has to be a brighter future.

Robert Lewis

AUTHOR'S
ACKNOWLEDGMENTS

I want to thank Gary Carver for fifteen years of professional friendship and contribution to the functional life of my classes in Los Angeles and New York; Kate Billings, whose perceptions of the work she recorded and transcribed presented me with an ongoing source of feedback; Lou Keay, who transferred interviews from an often inaudible tape into clear copy; Betty Barto, who rendered further secretarial services with ceaseless good humor; Paul Gemignani, distinguished Broadway music director, who shared valuable, personally held opinions; Donna DeSeta and Rick Pagano, who helped me define the east- and west-coast casting scenes; Eddie Weston, who helped me define union policies of the Actors Equity Association; the nine eminent actors, dancers, and singers who found the time, in schedules that barely permitted it, to talk about their work; and the hundreds of men and women who, in the classes I taught, taught me.

OVERTURE

*This is a book that attempts to deal with the performance of songs in general and their performance in the musical theater in particular. In a previous volume, *On Singing Onstage*, I endeavored to describe the techniques of performance and discovered that it is a far easier task to trap the how-to of a subject than to discuss it in the abstract. That book presented to the actor, the dancer, and the singer a defined pedagogical system that would enable the budding performer to get a song off the page and on to its feet. Even as I wrote it, I knew I was evading the abstraction. To write about what is correct and incorrect is simpler by far than to deal with what is good and bad; one man's value judgments are arguably no better or worse than those of the next persons in line. But the reaction of readers was clear: "Enough evasion. Now that I know how to do it, what do I do now?"

It was inevitable that the form of this second volume would be a catchall, with only one goal: to shed light, in as many ways as I could, on the art of performing on the stage when sing you must.

The first essay, in Act One, Scene One, is on the subject of style, which, it truly can be said, never stops changing and always stays the same. Without it the performer is unidentifiable in the crowd, and with it his or her recognition factor is unique and preeminent. For me it is number one on the list of what one must not only comprehend but come to grips with and, throughout a lifetime's career, attempt to cultivate.

Act One, Scene Two, "The Audition Process," holds its number two position for the obvious reason. You cannot be seen until you get a job, and you cannot get a job without enduring the rites of passage: an audition. It is important to know that the experience, rarely more than five minutes (albeit it seems an eternity) long, has nothing to do with the marketplace of show business. It has its own ground rules for both opposing teams—those who want work and those who do the hiring.

The second part, "Entr'acte," rambles through "where we were and where we are" in the country of musical theater.

Act Two, Scene One, "The Twenty Most Often Asked Questions . . . Answered," consists of those questions posed most often, whether I teach in New York, in Los Angeles, in seminars around the country, in Canada, or in academia. I bring up this geography to underline the universality of the puzzlement. Each answer is a mini-essay designed to resolve confusion.

Act Two, Scene Two, "The Interviews: How They Did It and Do It," consists of nine interviews that are an antidote to the type of subjectivity that pervades books of this kind. Subjectivity remains, but it belongs to each of the subjects rather than to me. The nine performers are recognized artists on the musical theater stage. Each has appeared on Broadway, but each arrived by a different route and from a different provenance. They include actors who sing, dancers who sing, and singers who sing, and they can be seen as a distinct and demographic group characteristic of the American musical theater. The reader may rest secure in the knowledge that those who are in the know do very well know.

The final part, "Exit Music," reprises the themes that run through the book and attempts to speak of the future and where we may be going.

I began teaching in 1948. My work was then described as coaching. In the early fifties I realized that, although coaching is a valuable service, it does not and cannot teach anyone to perform. The student works in the coach's living room and not on a stage. The warmth of a one-on-one relationship is distinctly more tropic than the climate found in the theater and at an audition. There are coffee, shared gossip, and shared jokes and no threats, all of which adds up to no terror. But show business is mercantile and not social, and coaching was clearly not an ideal learning environment for a career in a competitive marketplace.

The classes were conceived at a time when they were unheard of as a mode of training for the musical theater. This may strike the reader as having taken place in some prehistoric age, because singing classes today are as commonplace as acting and dance classes. From the beginning, I have had the good fortune to attract professional actors, dancers, and singers. They taught me how to teach the subject they were so eager to study. I barely have time to express to them my gratitude, for I see the house lights are dimming. The overture is at an end. The conductor turns for a hand—not a big one—and faces the orchestra once again as the curtain rises on . . .

On PERFORMING

ACT ONE
SCENE ONE

❦

Style

*S*tyle is a word that is not disposed kindly to definition. Whether it refers to fashion or, in the case of performing, to the singular mark of an artist's work, it remains a descriptive that resists being nailed down. In that sense it resembles the quality ascribed to certain lucky souls who possess it—that quality called *charm*. Charm and style are essences or the sum of the parts of some of us that makes us what we are. Someone *is* charming and, getting closer to home, a performer *has* style and is therefore considered to be *stylish*. What makes the label so difficult to define is that one person's notion of what constitutes a charming personality may be deemed by another to be saccharine self-consciousness. Similarly, too, *style* refuses to sit still long enough for everyone to come to universal agreement on its image. To define *style*, the *Oxford English Dictionary* (OED) requires five categories comprising twenty-eight delineations of the word, with the following definition the most apt for our purposes:

> Style: A particular mode or form of skilled construction, execution or production; and the manner in which a work

of art is executed, regarded as characteristic of the individual artist or of his time and place.

I have chosen to examine musical performing styles in two distinct and separate places—on musical theater stages and in the marketplace (all other arenas in which performing takes place—and to go further back in time to the beginning of this century. Styles in the marketplace change at a dizzying rate, while stage performing, restricted as it is to the demands of book, character, and staging, moves with more restraint. It is this disparity of style that has a profound effect on young people in the musical theater today, for never before has popular culture moved so far from that particular quality of theater performing that still informs what we see on the stage and, even more important to the performer, what is required of him or her at an audition.

The Marketplace

There is no question that singing performers in the very early years of this century were vastly more competent than those who enjoy any degree of success today. John McCormack and Richard Tauber, two stars of that time, were trained singers whose voices were hailed by connoisseurs as well as the "man in the street," since they could, and did, sing anywhere and everywhere. They were as comfortable in operetta and opera houses as they were singing Irish ballads or Lehar waltzes on the vaudeville stage. Because they were audible singing wherever they chose to sing and because whatever they chose to sing was what everyone wanted to hear, there was no need for the specialization that exists today. In other words, the "serious" singer fulfilled a dual role by servicing the "pop" scene as well. But the years immediately before and just after World War I were hell-bent on cutting those ties that bound Americans to anything European. Jazz was the annihilating agent that condemned to death all music and styles of performing that didn't recognize its sovereignty. Everyone one-stepped, two-stepped, and bunny-hugged, and the waltz . . . well, the waltz went the way of the Hapsburgs.

The twenties can be said to have been the last years in which performing styles in the marketplace and on musical theater stages were recognizably the same. Tin Pan Alley* embraced the likes of the Gershwins, Berlin, and Kern, and their words and music were danced to and sung by the entire nation in much the same manner that they were performed in their original presentation on musical theater stages.

In the thirties, radio wed science to the lively arts, and show business has never been the same since. For the first time there was a mass audience for Tin Pan Alley—one that was hungry for entertainment that it could, and did, call its own. Thereupon, the musical theater began its life apart from the mainstream, moving further and further away from what once had been a homogeneous public—at least as far as taste in styles of performing was concerned. Theater stars might be radio stars, but radio stars need not ever have stepped foot on a stage. For those of us who grew up with the radio as the entertainment center of our home lives, it was difficult to understand that the theater was not something to be considered precious, in the sense of being uncommon and highbrow. Just as television has obviated the need to go out to see a film, a ball game, a concert, or a ballet, so did radio make it possible to listen to a show business that, before radio's invention, could be seen and heard solely by attending the theater. The advent of film in the late twenties, with its even greater power to entertain millions and with the added advantage that one could get out of the house, gave rise to a newer audience, and this young audience was not only born but catered to. Youth was finally to have not only its day but its say.

What of the performers? It was clear that changing times would create changing styles. The troubador, epitomized by Al Jolson (who had replaced John McCormack and Richard Tauber in the public's affections) was himself pushed aside, not out of contempt but out of the eagerness of new generations to worship their own and not their parents' idols. Jolson, although far more "pop" than *his* predecessors were, was, nevertheless, open-throated, capable of filling the Palace Theater without a microphone, and stylish, indeed. However, it was

*According to H. L. Mencken, "A geographical region in New York City in which publishers of popular songs have their offices." Edward B. Marks says the term was invented by Monroe H. Rosenfeld. It is now less a place than a catchall reference to all popular music, just as *Broadway* is used to define all theater in New York City.

a new tyro, exemplified by Bing Crosby, dubbed a *crooner*,* who may be regarded as the father of all performers whose style has been reduced down to the needs not of the audience but of an electronic device. Radio created—and in its early days required—its own kind of singing sound. The following, perhaps apocryphal, anecdote was told about Ethel Merman. It illustrates how the world of the theater in those early days had, out of necessity, formed an uneasy alliance with radio and its confining conditions before the latter was ready for the partnership. Miss Merman was a preeminent theater star with a voice that could shatter more than glass. She was booked as the guest star on the prestigious *Bell Telephone Hour*, and as she began to rehearse her first song, she was interrupted by the man in the booth in charge of sound control. "Miss Merman," he said, deferentially, "I wonder if you would step back a little from the microphone?" Miss Merman did so and began again, only to be stopped a few bars later. The voice of the gentleman in the booth could be heard over the loudspeaker, "That's fine, Miss Merman, but would you step back a little more?" Miss Merman, ever game, did so and started in for the third time when, again, she was halted. The gentleman's voice had lost none of its courtliness, but once more he requested she stand farther back from the microphone. This time, Miss Merman, who was known to tolerate foolishness not at all, walked over to her coat and hat, picked them up, and crossed to the door. "Listen, fellas", she said, "call me when you get this f_ _ _ _ _ thing invented." And with that, she exited.

Jolson's movie *The Jazz Singer*, although a milestone in cinema history,§ did not erase the image of the man as vaudevillian extraordinary. Indeed, when his film career began to dip, he returned to the stage and, in his late years, even enjoyed success on his own radio show. The films of *his* preemptor, Bing Crosby, were further along the road to modern film as we know it and were many more in number. Crosby had begun, on radio, as a member of a singing group called the Rhythm Boys, and he became a full-fledged movie star without ever working on a vaudeville or a musical theater stage. Was

---

OED definition of *croon*: To sing in a low, smooth voice into a closely held microphone.

§It was the first "talkie," and its advertising campaign proclaimed: "Jolson Sings!"

he a man of possessed style? His voice was surely less interesting
by far than his screen persona, but the combination of his ease and
homegrown American good humor was irresistible. The black-faced
Jolson singing "Swanee" had evolved into an alumnus of Gonzaga U.
(a reference to Mr. Crosby's alma mater, which was coupled with his
name as often as Hoboken is with Mr. Sinatra's) and was now singing
without a trace of racial overtone, but suffering a distinct loss of vocal
dynamic and "theatrical style."

Those performers lucky enough to get into films have always had
a worldwide audience. Big as Crosby's success was, the pre– and
post–World War II years brought *his* successor even greater numbers
of idolators. Frank Sinatra, a vocalist with the Tommy Dorsey Orchestra, ascended through recordings, films, nightclubs, and
concerts—the whole range of today's world of show business—to
become the undisputed crooner-king of pop performers. His career
spans many generations, and his audiences still retain their affection
for him despite, or perhaps because of, the deterioration time has
worked on his voice and the biography of the man. His life is every
man's fantasy: An enormous success that began from humble beginnings, many marriages and each with a woman of great beauty, and
more money than can be dreamed of. He is surely the most accomplished male singer we have. His voice is as much a part of the
national collective unconscious as the taste of Coca Cola and, like
Lena Horne, he is always many times more interesting than anything
he sings. For me, this is the sine qua non of *style*. There were dozens
of crooners who fronted big-name bands, and many of them appeared
in films, but only Crosby and Sinatra achieved the kind of success
that leaves its indelible imprint on the popular history of its time.
Their staying power can be attributed not only to their personal gifts
but to their undeniable charm—that quality that, like style, creates
its own tyranny over our attention.

The fifties began not only the second half of the century but a
revolutionary slate-cleaning. Everything that was "old" was out, and
the "new" preempted the "old" with a new sound, a new look and,
more to the point, a new style of performing. It was not to look like
anything that had gone before it until, years later, nostalgia was to
be called back for a return engagement. The crooner was summarily
retired into history. (Sinatra, in defiance of the fashion, has managed
to keep his footing but not without an early struggle. Show business

careers in America have always been obstacle-course runs until the performer reaches an age when all is forgiven. The race still goes on, but elder citizens, although still required to run, are not weighed down with the old handicaps). The new young performer possessed energy—the inverse of crooning—and sang, with little to no vocal distinction, less of love than of friendship, equality of both genders, and about something "blowin' in the wind." *Beetles* was no longer only a reference to an order of insects but, along with a change of spelling, described a new species of four extraordinary performers out of Liverpool. And what of style? It went the way of all flesh before it, gone in the fortissimo sound of rock and roll. A distinct lack of style, as I have previously defined it, was now evident—a "style-lessness" that has been the major pop statement for over thirty years. The predominant number of successful performers, both soloists and group members, appear to be shaped by cookie cutters and, as soon as the cookie jar is empty, are replaced with facsimiles created from the same old rock and roll recipes.

But time-honored show business rules are never out of style. As the quality thins, the wrapping it comes in grows gaudier. Ziegfeld's show girls and George M. Cohan's unfurled American flags are still with us. Laser beams, fireworks, and the latest screen technologies are the basic tricks of the MTV trade. It is true that sometimes the cookie can be made to look like a cake but the cost in dollars and cents to the performer and the recording companies has skyrocketed, and today nothing less than a platinum record can hope to amortize their investment. The smell of decay is setting in. Nostalgia is already in second position and moving in fast. In many pockets of the marketplace it can even be considered a hot ticket. Kinescopes from the *Ed Sullivan Show* of the Beatles look disturbingly as dated as Al Jolson's *The Jazz Singer*. Presley is gone, Jagger and Stewart are middle-aged, and transvestitism and unisex have abrogated the revolution. What was once the "new" sound has become a sociosexual statement, and who is singing what to whom—and why—is not always clear.

Before moving over to the musical theater to see how the passage of time has brought it, for the first time in almost fifty years, into the same orbit traveled by the marketplace, let's look at the offshoots of the pop musical scene that have created and are still creating their own brand of exceptional stylists who cannot be ignored.

Vaudeville was but no longer *is* held to standards of the highest artistry. It was the Camelot of a golden age, when great performers became greater still by performing on hundreds of stages across the country until their work was polished to a glittering sheen. The great vaudeville singer-stylists were often associated with signature songs: Harry Richman ("Puttin' On the Ritz"), Ted Lewis ("Me and My Shadow"), Bert Williams ("Nobody"), Nora Bayes ("Shine On, Harvest Moon"), Fanny Brice ("My Man"), Ruth Etting ("Mean to Me"), Kate Smith ("When the Moon Comes over the Mountain"), Eddie Cantor ("Making Whoopee"), the last of the red-hot mamas, Sophie Tucker ("Some of These Days"), and, of course, the eminent Al Jolson ("Swanee"). These are but a few of the illustrious stars of their day. I have omitted, and not without considerable pain, the comics in vaudeville, but the category of singer-stylist makes for harsh exclusions. These performers achieved their success in a time when one song, unaided by gold or platinum record sales, reached across the entire country fueled only by the force of the artist's expended energy. Is it any wonder that their style was their signature? When any one of them sang a song, it was imprinted on the American mind with the total identity of the performer. Great vaudevillians were not only idolized, as even today all successful pop singers are, but, more important, they were beloved as well. When we speak of *style*, *that* kind of style is out of style.

Film provides us with its own stylists. The briefest of rosters includes the astonishing Mickey Rooney, Judy Garland, Fred Astaire, Gene Kelly, Donald O'Connor, Martha Raye, and Bill Robinson.

Jazz is exempt from time's killing power, since its sound is far more important than its performance. A unique voice and a special ability to hear the variations and changes within the melodic and harmonic structure of a song excuse the absence of any discernible performing style (unless bad style can be considered its own style). Jazz, like opera, has always lived in a world where sumptuous sound and sophisticated musicality preempt everything else. For this reason, the jazz singer's ability to sing with the extraordinary superiority of an Ella Fitzgerald or a Sarah Vaughan allows for a nonperforming style audiences are more than willing to accept. It is my guess that great jazz singers, like great opera singers are, with rare exception, far more comfortable in the recording studio, where their work is targeted into a microphone and where they do not have to concern themselves with attendant spectators. Stunning vocalism, under these conditions, does not require "selling" to an audience. It is for this reason that jazz concerts are better attended with ears open and eyes closed. There are, of course, exceptions to this judgment. Maria Callas was as stunning to see as she was to hear and Mel Tormé can both sing and swing with evident elegance.

Foreign imports have added their own particular spice to prevailing concepts of performing style, and Americans have welcomed the English and French music hall and cabaret entertainers with their customary open-armed embrace. From England: the inimitable Noel Coward, Jack Buchanan, Stanley Holloway, and Gracie Fields (again, I have omitted sending in the clowns), and from France: Yvonne Printemps, Maurice Chevalier, Charles Trenet, the unforgettable Piaf, Charles Aznavour, and the late and lamented Jacques Brel.

Until the fifties revamped our notion of what performing was about, there was only one recognized style within which an infinite variety of expression was to be found. Whether one observed an entertainer on a stage, in a club, or on the screen, the methods employed to stand up and sing were the same. Since only one style serviced all of show business, emulation was relatively easy. The new generation copied the style of the old in much the same way that Junior was expected to wear a scaled-down version of Dad's blue serge suit. There was no need for audiences to choose from many styles, only the place in which they cared to attend the only one extant. For them, Al Jolson was as recognizable on the vaudeville stage as he was in musical theater or on the shadowy silver screen. Junior, harboring a dream to go into show business, was, like the audience, spared choice and, accordingly, was privileged to work comfortably in all three arenas. This must seem, for young performers in the eighties, a time out of fiction. Today, it would be inconceivable to think that any one performer could 'do his or her number' and rest assured that it would be fitting and suitable to all aspects of show business and, at the same time, suit the tastes of all audiences. As show business has grown into a major industry, so has the variety and tastes of audiences multiplied. Songwriters who have always sung their songs with well-intentioned but unmusical sounds now find favor with a less demanding public. Country-western balladeers, once banished to a parochial audience, are nationally acclaimed. Folksingers who, only yesterday, were tainted with a leftist stigma sing here, there, and everywhere with impunity, and Boy George plows his androgynous fields before appreciative heterosexual audiences.

It is not my intention to make a blanket denunciation of the marketplace and the performers who enjoy the enormous acclaim that today's high-powered show business affords the chosen many. Nor would it be possible to claim that there is no excellence to be found. Michael Jackson, although his gender may be fuzzy, is an eminently talented young man who corroborates my thesis that only constant work shapes an artist's style. He has been toiling away since he was a child, and it is evident in his every move. He is, as all stylists are, unique because he is uniquely himself.

Today the young neophyte can choose from an array of performing styles and, having made his or her choice, work solely within the borders of that particular show business that sanctions it—and, with luck, have a very good friend at the Chase. I make this objective observation not out of contention but to illustrate the diversity of the marketplace and how far it has come from those early years when "When Irish Eyes Are Smiling" and "Vienna, City of My Dreams" were on the Hit Parade and, more important, required a voice to sing them.

M usical Theater

While the musical theater has changed, it has done so far more slowly and far less radically than the common marketplace that is its kin. True, the "down-front" style of performing that was popular in the first decades of the century seems as innocent and alien to our eyes as the acting in silent movies, but the verismo acting style effected by the advent of the Method and its various versions has not influenced musicals as much as it has the legitimate theater and film. There are many reasons for this apparent lack of interest in bringing what purports to be "reality" onto the musical stage.

To begin with, the harder we try to bring the techniques taught by the late Lee Strassberg to the performance of a musical, the more it resists the effort. The truth is that there never was, is not now, and never will be a scintilla of reality in a performer's standing on a stage and singing what must be sung instead of spoken. If there was, every actor worth his or her reputation would move from speech into song with the grace of Astaire. I use the gentleman's name because it has always been my opinion that dancers, rather than actors, make better singing performers (if they can sing at all) for the very reason that they live in a world where music and the corset of rhythm are integral elements of their art. Actors waste time, at the start of their singing studies, searching for the comfort they experience in simply acting. The act and art of singing with technical proficiency draws on too many alien skills. Only when actors come to realize that they must learn a language they have never known before, do they begin to make progress toward finding their own singing style.

However, it would be folly to suggest that no qualitative change has occurred. The wedding of a proper singing technique to an organic stage life is not shotgun, nor is it a union that cannot be, to some degree, achieved. But the intricate network of sets and the movement of them on and off the stage, all timed to split-second lighting cues, destroys any environment the performer may need to create the "real world." One need only bear witness to the sheer numbers of stage-hands, stage managers, and their assistants backstage who are there to work, with great effort, to make certain that audiences will see an effortless rendering of the show. We like to think we have come a long way from the days when the performer belted out a song with no effort made to relate it to the person standing on his left or right who was supposed to be on the receiving end of the number. And, in many ways, we have. Yet, even today, in a time when we are all agreed that the old style is downright silly, I can think of dozens of instances on Broadway in which down-front singing can now be seen and audiences, God love them, are cherishing every show biz moment. Why?

Musical performing not only resists change but appears to be most comfortable when it is most Elizabethan. In a musical, upstage is a dimly discerned Siberia. The entire theater is the show, and though the proscenium arch establishes the border that separates those on stage from the audience out front, most great performers seem impelled to move forward in order to give the illusion of "embracing" the audience. I have often heard performers describe with affection a theater that, when they were on its stage, gave them the feeling they could reach out and touch the mezzanine.

Change is most noticeable, however, in the book and the score. Today's musical books have very little to do with the insipidity of their antecedents of the twenties and thirties. That is why they are unreviveable. It is ironic that the standard repertoire for which all of us have so much affection studded "books" that defy reprise. And yet, *Forty-Second Street* and *Me and My Girl* in all their inanity, run on and on, without so much as one suppressed giggle from the ticket buyers who flock to see them. So much for progress.

Today's musical theater comprises two factions. One, unkindly dubbed "the tired-businessman's show," assures the audience that it will not see anything too deep, too meaningful, and too lacking in good tunes and good-looking girls. In this group—and it has always been with us—appearances have changed but little since the beginning of the century. Sequins and bugle beads abound, and while "choreography" has replaced "dance routines," the difference is not enough to scare away the buyer. In the other corner, struggling to survive and sometimes doing a good job of it, are the musicals that attempt to bring into a musical context an amazing variety of subjects. Stephen Sondheim has sung about marriage and its trials, Japanese emergence into the twentieth century, smiles of a summer night, and the birth of a celebrated Impressionist masterpiece. He has been awarded prizes and has been applauded by everyone—but the tired businessman—and, in his future work, he can be depended upon not to reprise yesterday's tired formulas or, for that matter, anything he himself has already investigated. His goal is clear: to explore the outer limits of what can be sung on the musical theater stage. Performances in musicals in this second category tend to be more organic. This is facilitated by the very nature of the subject matter, since its motive is not so much to entertain as to engender emotional responses. Actors who sing (rather than dancers who can only dance and singers who cannot act or move) tend to feel a sense of belonging in this kind of musical theater, since it does not call for "star turns" and, as we have seen, actors are not, by definition, entertainers. The irony is obvious. Mr. Sondheim requires voices to the same degree that Puccini does. As a result, singers scurry to pull up their acting qualifications, dancers take on both a singing and an acting teacher, and the actor runs to his or her singing lessons with renewed determination—as all three groups strive to realize a crossover.

When aspiring entertainers choose the musical theater from the many options available, they are thrust into what can only be described as a time warp. Not only is it strange music they will be asked to sing, but it might as well be coming from the spheres. Contemporary theater music, with the exception of Sondheim and one or two lesser lights, is at a dead standstill. What is heard in the theater is very like what has always been heard—and, sadly, not as good a version of it as was scored by others who are now long gone into the hall of fame. Those "thirty-two bar" tunes presented to us are but pale copies. But what is more important is that those show tunes do not sound like anything the young beginner has heard in his or her own backyard. Nor does the style in which these songs must be sung and performed mirror the current performing style that beginners see on television and at a Bruce Springsteen concert. Faced with the distressing truth that their knowledge of what pop singing is all about does not make them fluent in the language they are asked to sing in when they enter the musical theater, young neophytes must turn to a teacher who, they hope, will act as a guide into the musical theater world. This world is just as it has more or less always been: vacuum-packed. Very little circulation of air is allowed in, and the necessary levels of oxygen required to maintain life are dropping with each new theater season. But teachers are a second-best alternative since they are once-removed from the musical theater marketplace and because, more often than not, they are pianists who are not able to perform what they teach any better than the beginner student. Even when the teacher is able to show and tell, it is a lean method for passing on the elements of style because style, as we have defined it, is better learned by watching, working, and stealing from those established performers who were, in more extravagant times, demonstrating it at every turn.

The musical theater and the marketplace meet at a moment in time when they have much in common. As of today they have become strange bedfellows. In the theater, an almost dead halt in original material has occasioned a long string of revivals just as the newest wrinkle in the pop recording industry is to string together a dozen of the oldest pop standards, deck them out with a forties orchestration and . . . turn on. Linda Ronstadt, the return of the big band sound, the shifting of jazz into the mainstream, and Rampal "swinging" are no less indications of a "closed for inventory" state of the art than are revivals of *South Pacific*, *The King and I*, *Brigadoon*, and *My Fair Lady*. All betray the famine in the musical theater and in the marketplace.

It has taken almost fifty years for this convergence between the musical theater and the marketplace to occur. During that time, the theater has found it more and more difficult to replace the passing parade of great performers with new echelons of young entertainers. Once, in the long long ago, it was possible to see Marilyn Miller, Bert Lahr, Jack Haley, Helen Morgan, Gertrude Lawrence, Noel Coward, Ethel Merman, Bea Lillie, Mary Martin, Dennis King, Bobby Clark, the Astaires, Josephine Baker, James Barton, Fanny Brice, George M. Cohan, Harrigan and Hart, Willie and Eugene Howard, Frank Fay, Billy Gaxton and Victor Moore, Nancy Walker, Eddie Foy Sr. and Jr., Danny Kaye, Joe Weber and Lew Fields, Sid Caesar and Phil Silvers, each of them, at one time or another, singing, dancing, and making audiences laugh, and doing it all in a most stylish manner. The profligacy of those times, when seen in the light of today's musical theater, testifies to the poverty that has set in. There is not just one explanation for the hard times, but certainly the number one reason would have to be: A beginning performer today does not have the opportunity to get up on one stage and then another and another and another and work to shape a singularity of performing style. Without that continuum, not even one of the above stellar artists would have had the skill to cross a stage, let alone "fill" it. As a teacher who has been witness to a not unimpressive lineup of young, gifted performers, I know that it was attrition that narrowed down their numbers and unemployment that finally did a goodly number of them in.

There are other factors that mitigate against the young performer cultivating an authentic personal style. It is important to remember that style, by definition, can be good or bad. Good style is recognized by everyone. It needs no lesson from a critic to instruct even the least informed members of an audience that what they are looking at is good—not when it is palpably evident that it *is* good. But bad style is not so readily labeled. Today, drama and music critics seem, at times, to have struck up a secret partnership with management. The most commonplace performers are greeted, extolled, and presented to the public with the same high-powered advertising campaigns as the ones that sell soap. In consequence, there are singer-performers whose celebrity, although great, cannot disguise the fact that they are incapable of even an adequate performance on a stage. Stripped of all the brouhaha, how many of today's putative stars would be capable of holding a stage without the trappings that accompany them wherever they perform? Harold Pinter has said that "this is an age of . . . overblown publicity and overemphatic pinning down." When young people are told that what is bad is good, the cultivation of a polished style becomes almost impossible.

Theater music, or at least its unwillingness to move away from the confines of yesterday's show tunes and the formulas that fashioned them, is another aspect of the problem. Very little of what we hear in the musical theater has absorbed the sound of contemporary music, and when, in the case of a Sondheim, it does aspire to something more than an AABA or an ABAB tune (the two standard thirty-two bar song forms), it is declared unmelodic, or worse, better heard in the opera house. The time has come to speak and sing out about anything and everything that informs our lives before and after the theater curtain rises and falls. It is possible that this kind of score will not be greeted with affection by older audiences, but if we do not begin to concern ourselves with more youthful ones, we may find ourselves, at some future point of time, with no audiences at all. Before the split occurred between the musical theater and Tin Pan Alley, Berlin, Gershwin, Kern, Porter, and Rodgers all wrote songs that were danced to and sung by people all over the world. The melodies written for 1,500 people to hear every time the curtain went up were soon heard by millions when they went out dancing or turned on their radios. The border was always open. Today that border is closed and guarded and rarely does theater music slip through. When a song does find a broad-based audience, it does so because it either recognizes the ground rules of the commercial marketplace or comes from a hit show of gigantic celebrity. In order for it to find its new life, it must be put through the mills of MTV or receive hefty plugging from deejays around the country. Its derivation, where it came from, even the name of the musical and the composer's identity are of no interest to the members of this audience, but with clever television advertising, they can be made aware of that origin. "Don't Cry for Me, Argentina," popular long before the production of *Evita*, began a new and efficient merchandising scheme. It is impossible to know how many theater tickets were sold because of the song's popularity, but the old procedure—outward *from* the show—had reversed itself. Outward *to* the show was seen to be inarguably effective. Does this kind of music vocalize itself stylishly in the theater? It does when it is put back into the service of the play and the character and performed by a singer—with style.

I have said that style, both good and bad, can be recognized, and even at first sight. The same can be said for a performer who possesses neither and may be described as styleless. For instance, the physical aspect of Fred Astaire, when he is singing, is always effortless and elegant—the purest example of Samuel Beckett's claim that "all true grace is economical." His "thinking" is not only pleasing to the eye but, somehow, surprising. He is a performer of great style. On the other hand, Ginger Rogers, when she is singing and dancing on her own, is not. Her language is vulgar and obvious, leaning as it does on gestures that indicate "you," "yours," "me," "mine," "my," and "I." And yet, style is a fickle quality, for when Rogers joins Astaire, she not only becomes possessed of style but somehow brings her partner out of his supraelegant world into one which all of us can feel we might be a part of—if only we could dance. There is no question that, together, Astaire and Rogers epitomize style, and not only are they stylish, but they refute one characteristic suggested by the dictionary—they transcend their time and place. This is rare, indeed, for style changes, and very little in show business does not suffer when viewed outside its own time and place.

Were the musical theater and contemporary Tin Pan Alley locked in a struggle to determine which deserves preeminence, all of this talk about style would have great value, since their performances are disparate in the extreme. But the truth is that disinterest in each other is the only emotion they share in common. One has the podium, no mistake about it, and the other has history to sustain its right to be. This peace permits young performers whose tastes lie in one or the other court to choose their own particular playing field. For a span of two decades after its incursion into the pop marketplace, rock and roll demolished anything that stood in its way. The theater, by virtue of its historic majesty, and because it was impelled to allow entrance to a minor invasion of a relatively small faction of composers, lyricists, librettists, avant-garde directors, and incipient producers, was tolerant enough. The success of *Hair* turned tolerance into a runaway love affair, until, quite suddenly, it was demonstrated that there was not an ensured lode in them thar hills. Audiences who cared for the music of the streets could seldom afford the ticket price to hear it in a Broadway environment, and the critical gauge designed to measure the worth of the product did it in in the same fashion in which other more conservative lambs were slaughtered. At the moment when wiser Broadway heads realized rock and roll was not to be the guaranteed money maker that would end the theater's blight, everything returned to business as usual. The theater returned to what it knew it knew, and Tin Pan Alley went back to where it came from. As of today, there seems to be no sign of rebellion, and new generations of record buyers have long ago forgotten, if they ever knew at all, that once upon a time there was a genuine attempt at a revolution. The "new" theater music I hear is either recycled old theater music or sounds from the school of Sondheim. (I exempt the music of Andrew Lloyd Weber because it is not natively American and it is not rock and roll.)

However, the sharp diminution of musical theater product has had little effect on suppressing the interest so many young people have in its songs. Wherever I teach I am struck by their determination to learn how to perform its music more skillfully and in the style to which it is accustomed. Those young would-be performers, so intent on invading the hallowed precincts, have too few *genuinely professional* playing grounds on which to play. For them, I offer this advice, no matter the difficulty involved in bringing it to pass: perform wherever you can, yes, but work to blend the love you have for theater music with the technical proficiency that illumines its performance. These two elements are the parental heating agents that create personal style. It is as true of the singer as it is untrue of the actor that style informs everything he or she does. A play may obfuscate the actor's personal identity, but no song can ever erase the singer's self. Singers will always be described not by *what* they sing but by the adjectives that characterize them *when* they sing. When a performer is styleless, he or she is unreadable, not "there," merely an instrument through which the song is vocalized. This is the reason why all great performers are always more interesting than anything they sing. This may be less true in the case of the singer of serious music because dazzling sound can arrogate other aspects of the singer's art. But in the musical theater—and in the marketplace—style is, and will always be, the calling card of all great performers.

SCENE TWO

❦

The Audition Process

I have written about auditions in my previous book, *On Singing Onstage.* The do's and don't's of operating within the system have been catalogued by me as well as by others. What interests me here is the process itself and why all of us have to settle for what is generally agreed to be a flawed method for casting a show.

It must be obvious that show business, like any other business, is a pregnable fortress. How you attack it and gain entrance is an indication not only of your military skill but of your right to be inside. There are some people who make good soldiers for attacking and some who do not, and there are those who can stage a successful offensive but, once the victory is achieved, ultimately fail to demonstrate why they fought the battle. In my own experience, I have been fooled at least once by someone whose audition was splendid but who could not be relied upon to perform adequately after the job was secured, and I have known performers who cannot audition or "read" but who, had they been given the job, would have been first-rate.

Much of the audition process is a puzzlement and both sides know it. Why one person gets the part and another does not is often mystifying. The staff will insist that they have chosen wisely, but one need only attend the final production to see that their choices were, at least some of the time, wrong. The staff will also maintain that they know what they are looking for when, more than likely, they agree only on what they are *not* looking for. On his or her part, the actor-dancer-singer can be absolutely convinced that the audition was "right-on," while those who watched it would better have described it as a "write-off." It is this element of things being seldom what they seem that makes the audition process inadequate and, at the same time, so fascinating to observe. I have stood on both sides of the hiring and the firing line, and I am still struck by how little each side comprehends the other.

*F*rom the Point of View of the Performer

The "suicide" rate at auditions is high, and the weapon that does the job as efficiently as a handgun is ignorance—ignorance of how best to comport oneself to make an effective attack against that pregnable fortress.

To begin with, it is sad but all too true that an audition is judged to be a success or a failure within the short time it takes you to enter from the wings onto the stage or into a room and not much further than the first sixteen bars of whatever song you have chosen to sing. Many negative factors can conspire to lead you to suicide: an air of failure before the fact can do it; a demeanor that implies that you do not know your worth, or worse, that you know it too well; becoming a victim of the event; an awkwardness in handling yourself as the moment-to-moment circumstances of the experience play themselves out; ill-chosen clothing; an ill-chosen song; and finally, demonstrable evidence that you do not know how to perform the song you have elected to sing. Some or all of these are the weapons that annihilate and what is so sad about the whole sorry performance is that you may very well remain unaware that your death has been self-inflicted.

An entrance onto the stage or into a room cannot be performed naturally. It must have the appearance of what is defined as normal behavior, but unless you create its illusion, what is normal becomes abnormal. There are many reasons for this. Self-esteem results from being assured, beforehand, that you will know what to do when the time comes to do it and that you will know how to do it well. Ogden Nash spoke of the "sound of escaping esteem." An audition is a place where it escapes with a vengeance. In Paul Scott's novel, *The Towers of Silence*, one of his characters remarks, "My father once said to me, 'Barbie, there is a conspiracy among us to make us little'." Mr. Scott must have known the world of auditions as well as he knew India. It is not that those who are holding the auditions have conspired to dwarf those who are auditioning. It is the process itself that tends to diminish. Merely to recognize that this is so is to take arms against it. Remember: you are not the first one up there (see page 00). Many have walked the plank before you, and they have left the smell of failure behind them. The air is charged with a negative voltage with which you must do battle. Doing so takes an enormous amount of positive thinking on the instant of your entrance, since you must not only erase it but turn it into a positive field of energy.

In order to accomplish this massive inversion of the ambient atmosphere, you will need to do the three things listed below. The only people who are exempt from the following advice are those who, for one reason or another, do not need it. Performing well in any environment is an art, not a science. In show business, two and two can add up to five if you can get away with it. If you are fortunate to be who and what you are, with no discomfort living in the particular skin that encases you, any cautionary advice may very well damage you by making you conscious of the one thing that is your prize asset—your lack of self-consciousness. For those who are less cozy with themselves and their persona:

1. Do not fill the time before you are called with social chat. If friends and acquaintances are there, make it clear that you do not tolerate any intrusion into your "space." Center and quiet yourself. You will need all the concentration you can bring to bear not to trip at the starting line. I cannot emphasize strongly enough this element of your audition. Remember, you are not coming on alone. You are bringing your worst enemy with you. You. Unless you take the time to rid yourself of that inimical part of you that breeds in the swamps of distraction, it will do you in.

2. The song you will be singing should not be sung for the first time that day. Vocal warm-ups learned from singing teachers should be reviewed before you leave your home. You and the pianist you bring with you (always a better plan than using the one who is there to play for those unfortunates who will possibly be murdered by him or her) should have rehearsed the material at least twice on your piano or in the pianist's studio before your arrival at the casting place. This will mean that the performance of the song the staff will hear you sing at the audition will be, as far as you are concerned, the third one you will be singing that day. The first two should precede the third in an order as close as you can arrange. To go through them the day before is of no more significance than going through them the previous month. The element of one, two, three is the equivalent of ready, get set, go!

3. This rule is my own, and I can justify it only on empirical grounds. The rule? Never drop your eyes to the floor from the moment you enter. This is less simple to achieve than you might imagine but practicing it until it is second nature will have great value. Dropped eyes read negatively. They imply unsureness, loss of concentration, and a short-circuiting of the flow of electrical energy that should exist between you and the audience, no matter their number (see "The Twenty Most Often Asked Questions . . . Answered," number 5). The negative direction—"Don't drop your eyes"—is not valuable until it is replaced with a positive suggestion. Do, then, give yourself tasks that must be done. Begin to deal with your reality as soon as you enter. Check out the space in which you will be performing— its width, its height, and its depth. Where is the ideal spot to stand? It is agreed that downstage center will always be the best of all possible worlds, but often, in a room, glare from windows directly behind you and/or poor indoor lighting can make the task of seeing your work difficult for those who are auditioning you. If you believe this may be so, ask. No one will think you a fool if your concern or your confusion is justified. Your question will advertise adult behavior under stress.

Remember that you are trying to pull up the drop in the energy around you that has been caused by those who went before you. When vaudeville was a vital part of show business, the running order of the acts on the bill was the primary concern of each artist. The dream was not just to "play the Palace," but to headline it. This meant that each act building to the headliner was better than the one before it.

The tension was created by increasing the standard of excellence and this, in turn, guaranteed the audience a closing act that would be even better than the penultimate one. If it wasn't, it didn't hold the spot for long. The same reasoning can be applied to a full day of auditions, except that the act before yours was probably worse than it should have been and no better than what it followed.

Again, from the performer's point of view, those who are auditioning you appear to be seen through refracted light. The military metaphor still applies. These cannot be people, can they? They are the enemy! Of course, this is nonsense. The heightened tension and the pressure generated by the need for a job can do strange things to your perception of the environment. Sometimes you will read their behavior toward you as hostile, and sometimes you may even be right. An understanding heart and a kind and gentle spirit are not possessed by those who cast musicals any more than they are built-in character components in any one of us. They may get up and leave while you are working and, worse, do it in full view. They may stop you with a precipitate "thank you" and a peremptory "don't call us, we'll call you." They may talk among themselves while you are performing and display what appears to be a disinterest in your work. I have heard of a Broadway producer who watched the Super Bowl football game on a small television set during the auditions. A request from the director only induced him to turn down the volume control. These, and other acts of apparent rudeness, can be explained away. Either they *are* rude, in which case you drew a bummer, or you are misreading their behavior. Someone who leaves while you are working may have business to do, in which case the departure has no relation to your performance. Or you may be stopped in the middle of what you are doing because the song you chose to sing is inappropriate. The ensuing chat with you will ascertain whether you have something else more fitting for the occasion. "Thank you's" and "we'll call you's" may be nothing more than they seem. An end to the whole affair. There is always the positive side: they may very well call you. But that is not the point. You are there to show your work, and you can do no more than show it at its best. Whether your best is what they are looking for is not for you to know. Whether it is or whether it isn't is out of your hands. A good audition is one that, when it is over, does not leave you humiliated and ashamed of your performance. Those feelings are unbearable in the aftermath of an audition, and there is no one who has not endured them at one time or another. You have only to make certain it never happens more than once.

It is important to remember that, in one way or the other, many members of the staff have had to audition before you. The writers have had to do it to obtain a producer, a director and a choreographer, and they have most likely done it many times. Under circumstances equally humbling they have all had to woo backers away from their wallets. Still to come, after you and everyone else has auditioned, will be the creative input of the director and the choreographer as they put *their* work on the line during rehearsals and the out-of-town run. At your audition, they are the judges, but their turn is just around the corner. No soul in show business is free from being judged, and the hell of it is that judgments will be made by people who may not have a particle of knowledge of the subject and what you are trying to do. That's show business, and we all know there's no business like it. If your audition was a good one, you can always say—to yourself, of course—"I hope you all know how to do *your* work as well as you have just seen me do mine." This may be small solace but it need not be cold comfort.

Some performers think of an audition as a place in which their work will never be seen in a favorable light. Their line of defense is historic: "If they'd only give me the part, I know I could do whatever is called for. But I can't stand up and sing out of context and with no point of reference." This is blatant balderdash. If you don't know how to sing a song, you don't know how to sing a song. When you are in a musical, a song cue indicates that you are going to be singing a song, and no amount of self-willing and self-convincing will enable the character you play to sing it better than you can, for *you* are the character you are playing and it is you who will be singing that song.

This is the one abiding factor that separates the actor from the actor-singer. In their real lives, actors can be awkward, shy, and socially inept, but put them in a play and they will be transformed before your eyes. They become as graceful as Ariel, as verbal as Cyrano, and as stylish and socially adroit as Ernest. How well he or she performs this disappearing act is the testimony of the actor's skill. It can be argued that this would be manifest during the book section of a musical, but when that song cue is heard, the ball game has new ground rules. If the actor is shy, awkward, and socially inept, you will see it all when he or she sings, and the character will not, in any way, be able to help the actor dissemble his or her shortcomings. The basic difference between acting and singing is that we *are* the songs we sing and we can no more change that than tamper with our fingerprints. Whether they are conscious of it or not, actors know that they themselves are not up for assessment when they read for a play. The director and the playwright want to hear and see what they can bring to the character and to the play. Musicals, like commedia del l'arte, are cast to the vocal sound required and an appearance that defines the role. A pretty girl will be the ingenue; a handsome man, the leading man. That heavyset lady waiting in the wings to audition is up for the part of the character woman. The one thing they will be asked to demonstrate is: Can they sing well enough to fulfill the requirements of the score? Only after that question is resolved, will they have an opportunity to read.

The book of a musical is not as lengthy as the manuscript of a play. Room must be left for the score, the dances, and the orchestral contributions. An evening in the theater consumes the same number of hours whether a musical or a play is on the stage. In the case of the musical, the first to be sacrificed at the altar of brevity is the book. It will be tightened and cut until every word in it has a function.

The purpose of the score is not to reprise what has been said, although some musicals fail to heed this. It is there to move plot lines, delineate character, and/or most important of all, reveal the conflict within a character's inner thoughts by allowing the character to sing them out and, better still, by so doing, to work them out. And all this must be executed in an entertaining manner, for if the song fails to "work," it will be cut ruthlessly and, with luck, replaced with superior material.

The reductive nature of the book rarely permits offbeat casting. There is no time to explain it away. That pretty girl will *be* the ingenue, that amusing middle-aged man auditioning a comedy song will *be* the character-comic, and that lovely lady will *be* the leading lady. It is a lost cause to try to fight this typecasting. It is built into the system. How well you might be able to interpret a role will always take third place to how you look and how well you sing. When the part is yours, *you* are the part. That is why you have been cast in it. If your performance is brilliant, the image of you in that role, once seen, will forever be associated with the role and with you in it: for example, Yul Brynner as the Siamese king; Robert Preston as the "music man";

Ethel Merman as Annie Oakley and Gypsy's mother; Mary Martin as Nellie Forbush. A success in a musical can explode and advance an actor's career more rapidly than a dozen appearances in plays. Musicals are painted in primary colors. They shun pastels. They are bigger than life because they do not pretend to dramatize the reality of life. Is it any wonder that actors grapple with the terror of singing as they work to learn whatever they must in order to be in a musical?

I have met some lucky souls who profess to enjoy auditions. They maintain an amused attitude toward them and manage to stay above the emotional involvement that makes the experience so self-destructive. For most of us, however, auditions will never be a pleasant experience. But the more knowledge and expertise you bring to them, the more their power to destroy is neutralized.

Further suggestions:

1. Once you are ready, do as many auditions as you can. There is a certain skill in doing them that can be cultivated. In the beginning you will probably bungle it. Practice auditioning for jobs you would not take if they were offered to you. Somehow not wanting a job allows you to surrender to a loss of interest in getting it. As soon as you are liberated from caring, you will probably do well and may even have it offered to you. You can always refuse it.

2. Dress for an audition. At least, do not dress unwisely or in any way that will make you unrecognizable or unbelievable in the role. And most important of all: If you are asked to return, do not alter what you wore the first time. Do not change your hairdo. Unless otherwise informed, do not change the song you performed. Further callbacks eliminate guesswork. You will be told what to sing and, in some cases, given something from the score to prepare. Then, and only then, will you be certain you are singing what they wanted to hear. If what you sang the first time achieved the callback and you are *not* advised otherwise, reprising what you sang is a good tactic. If it worked the first time, it is safe to assume that the song you chose was close or right on target.

3. Since those who cast musicals have, in their mind's eye, a fantasy of what the character should look like, I think it unwise to audition too early. You will always be seen to be less than the fantasy. There comes a time in the casting of a show when it is apparent to everyone that they will never find someone with three eyes. At the moment when fantasy surrenders to reality, you should come on the scene with two good eyes. Try, then, to get your audition scheduled as late as possible. Agents may tell you that they cannot tamper with your scheduled appointment or that you may lose the chance to audition if you hold out for a later hour or, better still, a later day. Don't you believe it. I have known performers who landed in shows because of thirteenth-hour compromise. Had they appeared at the start of auditions, they would not have made it through a song.

4. The debate between the east coast and the west coast (which one is the better place to call home) still continues long after what gave it credence is no longer demonstrable (see "Exit Music . . . The Future Tense). Years ago, actors went to New York because they wanted to be actors. They went to Los Angeles because they wanted to be stars. Simplistic as this may read, it is nonetheless true that the New Yorker's chauvinism still exists, even when those choices have long since been abandoned for more realistic ones. Forty years ago an ever-diminishing show business was the prodding agent that metamorphosed the actor, the dancer, and the singer into the actor-dancer-singer. Those who refused, or were not able to effect the change, took their chances and were threatened with declining sources of income. Along with product shrinkage came product location changes. Today, the line of demarcation between the east and west coasts no longer exists. One can live in New York and do a television sitcom, live in Los Angeles and work on the stage and be in film, and live and work everywhere. The performer who auditions for a musical in New York may very well be seen a day later reading for a television show, or more to the point, for another musical, in Los Angeles. To maintain, as some creative people still do, that you cannot find *real* talent on the west coast is not only nonsense but a declaration of tunnel vision. At the moment of this writing, a west coast actress-singer in a Broadway musical that was given murderous reviews by the critics was the only cast member—all the rest were New Yorkers—to be singled out for unmodified praise. Performers can and do elect to live where they want to live, but when the possibility of work is presented to them, the shuttle plane from east to west and back is now procedural. The assumption that those who audition in New York live there and that those who audition in Los Angeles live *there*, is pure presumption. I have been told by reliable casting sources that a performer seen on the east coast who subsequently gets the job would have barely been permitted half a chorus and received a "thank you . . . next" had he or she auditioned for the same role in Los Angeles. If this is so (and my experience tends to corroborate it), and you want to be in musicals, my advice is not only to audition late but to "Go east, young man."

A sorry footnote: If the director, the music director, and one or even two writers *do* hold auditions in Los Angeles, anyone who is given a callback will have to fly to New York to sing for those who were absent or unwilling to make the westward trip. The cost of the flight (more often than not) is incurred by the performer. You must be willing to take the risk. If you get the job, those costs (including hotel and living expenses in New York) will be amortized by the subsequent salary. If the callback counts you out, the high price must be marked up to experience. To do or not to do the callback is a decision you must make. There are justifications for going or staying put. These decisions will always be personal as well as professional, and each person makes the choice that must be made. It is just one more example of how the audition process hurts.

From the Point of View of Those Who Audition You

Let us first identify who they are and then talk about why they are there. One might imagine that the writers of a musical are always present at all auditions, but this is not so. They may not appear until the finals, after the weeding-out process has separated the supposed wheat from the chaff. Holding auditions, despite what you may think, is a tiring and tiresome business. Although this may strike you as heretical, third-rateism is as prevalent in show business as it appears to be wherever else one looks. Auditions bring one face-to-face with that awful truth: there is not a vast pool of talent out there waiting to be discovered. It takes the patience of Job to remain amiable, curious, and forever hopeful. The number of people who will want to be heard is astonishing, especially considering how many among them should have stayed home. This is said sadly. If ever you want corroboration for how good you are (if you are good), get to your audition early and stay late to see your competition. You will walk taller once you have ascertained how negligible it is.

The refracted light that fogs the vision of performers and turns those for whom they audition into the enemy is, in fact, the same light in which those who cast musicals view each performer: "This is not a human being. This is my cross." The tedium of sitting through days upon days of auditions can very well blind as well as deafen the auditioner. The fight is to stay alert and, in all fairness, to give each performer who enters the benefit of the doubt before the fact. This is a fight that gets fought every minute of the day.

When the writers are not present, delegates act as proxies and make the early decisions. In the beginning this may be a small or a large group. As the weeks go by, a large group will become a small one as the reality of the labor erodes the patience and curiosity of those who are not integral to the audition. Those who count *will* be there. Of that you can be sure.

1. *The music director:* This person is in charge of all the music in the production and to him or to her will flow everything that is relevant to that domain—conducting the orchestra, choosing the vocal ensemble (in partnership with the vocal director if the music director does not choose to do, or cannot do, the vocal arrangements), listening to the dance ensemble audition if they will have to sing (this time in partnership with the choreographer), and carrying out the wishes of the composer and the lyricist as he or she understands them. These are complex chores and not every music director performs them equally well. There are some music directors who are not very good conductors and some who are brilliant. There are those who know next to nothing about performing and there are some who are surprisingly well-informed. There are some who know what singing is all about and how the voice is resonated and there are some who are startlingly ignorant of correct vocal production. Whether the music director is or is not competent at any one or all of these tasks, he or she will be sitting out front during the decisive audition period.

2. *The casting agent or director:* The middleman or -woman between the performer and the hirer. The casting agent's job is not to cast the piece, as the title implies, but to bring to the attention of the producer(s) and the creative staff the best and most appropriate available talent. There are those who believe that the casting agent can be more of a barrier than a conduit, and, from at least one vantage point, this may appear to be true. What must not be overlooked is the simple fact of who employs whom. You must remember that casting agents are hired hands who are on the payroll to perform a specific function. They do not cast the show. What may pass as obstructive behavior may be a manifestation of orders received and acted upon. In some cases, the office of the producer(s) or the producer-director can afford its own casting department. However, rising costs and falling numbers of productions in various stages of progress—not to mention the proliferation of the number of producers who jointly produce a musical—have sharply diminished those offices still able to afford this luxury. Today, the more general practice is to hire on an independent casting director or agent. This member of the team joins the production office later than his or her in-house equivalent, but auditions cannot begin until the casting agent is hired. Conferences then follow during which the composer, the lyricist, the librettist, and the director outline what they are looking for. (As I have said, this may be more a delineation of what they are *not* looking for.) The casting director is now able to create a breakdown list of the casting requirements and send it on to talent agencies who will match their clients to the list and arrange for audition time. Casting agents' input can be of great value, since they are conversant with almost all the talent available. That is their job. They, or their proxies, see every film, attend every play and musical, frequent nightclubs and reconnoiter television programming in an endless effort to stay informed. Their knowledge of new and established actors can be prodigious. Out of this vast store of information, and with the added aid of the talent agencies who service the breakdown list, the imperatives of supply and demand are met.

The scene today is homogenized. Because there is so little show business, actors, singers, and dancers mix, merge, and go out for anything they think they can handle. Actors who once would not think of doing commercials are now only too ready to sell soap. Singers who would not allow themselves to sing anything but the best, welcome the opportunity to record jingles. Dancers, too, are able to read for parts and to sing for their suppers when once they lived only in a mute world. When each group stayed its own backyard, the work of the casting director was less complicated. Are today's casting directors qualified to know so much about so much? Yes, if possession of all that information can be said to validate them. No, if you are asking for real cognition. Some of them are ex-actors and know what they are looking at. Some of them continue to work as part-time actors and are all too aware of the pain of auditioning for work. Some of them only know what acting appears to be and some of them only know what they like. In all cases, they should be expected to know what the creative staff will like and, even more important, they must know what the business likes.

What all casting directors have in common is their humanness. It is almost impossible to remain completely objective when someone comes before you. You may tell yourself that you will keep your mind, as well as your eyes and ears, open, but none of us can do it. You see someone and, in a split second, small judgments turn you away from or toward whom you are looking at. They rise up from very personal feelings about what turns us on or off. We may not even be conscious of their origins, but this is of no importance. It takes a superhuman effort to ignore these irrelevant and often devastating assessments. But remember that the performer is the Casting Agent's bread and butter. The partnership may be unholy and seldom fifty-fifty, but each cannot endure without the other. This mutual dependency can breed contempt on both sides, but every once in a while a Casting Director will speak thrillingly of someone who performed that day and a performer may walk away from an audition and affirm that he or she was treated fairly and with compassion. In the final analysis, the team needs to cast the show. Why not with you?

3. *The writers:* The first echelon whose presence, along with the Director, indicates that real bullets are being used. All final casting decisions are made by them. Are they competent to make these decisions? Again, in a reply confessedly general and impersonal: Most composers are not performers, but most lyricists can deliver their own material with skills ranging from the simple and effective to the stunningly proficient. I personally know of one great composer who knows little about what he is watching and I have seen an eminent lyricist perform with such stylish facility one would have wished he played the role.

There are added roadblocks: A pianist(s) will be hired to play accompaniments for those who unwisely came without one. Pianists have been known to be dangerously inadequate and able to play only the simplest material placed in front of them (see "The Twenty Most Often Asked Questions . . . Answered," number 6). They can be obstructionist and refuse to play what you have handed them in order to cover up their lack of skill. It is only fair to add that their refusal may be justified for quite another reason—that you have chosen to sing a song they know is inappropriate. This may result in an effort on the accompanist's part to check out your repertoire and put you on the right track. But any performer who meets his or her doom at the hands of an inept pianist can never be assured that those out front will know the reason for the murder. They will see what they see.

Audition schedules are sometimes treated with the same unconcern as airline departures. Again, this may be due to human error. But three, four, five, and even six hours behind? This is another act of attrition that may prevent you from doing anything near your best work.

I have seen casting directors talk throughout a performance, and I have seen them leave in the middle of one . . . and in all cases do it in full view of the artists at work. I have seen them dismiss people who chose to sing what they could not have known was material of no value for the occasion when a word to the performers could have elicited a change of song more apt to display what they wanted to see.

Furthermore, the business at large can be awesomely ignorant of the nature of talent and what it can reasonably be expected to do. The following is a direct quote from an eminent west coast trade publication. It appeared during the third week of September 1983:

OPEN CASTING CALL

Syndicated TV series is seeking an attractive female singer with the following qualifications: Ability to sing fluently in French & English; at least 4 years combined experience in domestic and international film, stage and TV, including extensive experience in co-hosting a musical/variety show; must have excellent musical pitch with vocal range of more than 2.5 octaves, ability to sing jazz, rock, new wave and cover tunes as a solo artist and back-up artist, read music, compose original music, plus recording studio experience. Prior improvisational experience in comedy sketches also required.

Please bring photographs and résumé to audition.

If this were not funny, it would be tragic. Did this casting call uncover someone who fulfilled all these requirements? And if it did, where had this nonpareil been hiding? And what salary was offered to compensate such a paragon?

It has become more realistic to expect performers to be more protean than in the past. The numbers of dancers in the many companies of *A Chorus Line* who not only pass the stringent dance requirements but also sing and act competently enough are testimony to this prolifigacy. Artists like George Hearn, who can sing opera and play Skakespeare, unlike hen's teeth, do exist. This is true even among instrumentalists. The lines of young pianists and violinists and cellists who debut every year and display almost preternatural skills would have been unheard of a century ago. Like Olympic athletes who break records as soon as they are made, the new generation of performers in the musical theater will be more and more able to fulfill the creative writer's wildest dreams. There was a time when the singer had to be cleared by the director or the director-choreographer to allow the song to be danced. And both the singer and the dancer were never taken seriously as actors. Today, the actor-dancer-singer can be a truly triple-threat performer.

Just as there are splendid actors, dancers, and singers, there are compassionate and qualified casting directors, musical directors, composers, lyricists, librettists, directors, and choreographers. It is true that performers who think they were not given a fair shake may be correct in thinking the other side is the enemy. On the opposite side of the line, *they* may be justified in blaming their bad behavior on the tedium induced by so much that is unqualified and incompetent. I doubt whether the situation will ever change unless both sides undergo competency tests. As in the case of government and big business—a synonym for show business—that is highly unlikely to occur.

ENTR'ACTE

❧

The Musical Theater: Where We Were and Where We Are

The Past

Young people who choose to commit themselves to a career in the musical theater have little to no comprehension of the terrain and even less opportunity to attend it for purposes of study. With a minimum of musicals to absorb a maximum of eager performers, the anguished cry, "Where am I going to put it?" (*it* being a collective noun encapsulating talent, energy, and a determination to pursue the dream) becomes a question of the first magnitude. It is not my intention here to reprise the symptoms of the malaise that have brought the musical theater to its present-day plight. The high cost of producing today's musicals and the soaring price of tickets to see the few shows that do achieve a run are known even to those who are uninterested in the problem. But there was a glittering time when the question, "Where am I going to put it?" never—well, hardly ever—needed to be asked. From the turn of the century down into the decade of the sixties, the gifted performer had a relatively simple goal: getting a job in one of a considerable number of musicals (comedy, operetta, and revue) that were produced each season. Now it is not unreasonable to wonder whether there is a job out there to get.

Nay sayers to the contrary, however, we are in an ongoing business (you had better believe it!) and it is important that young performers understand that continuum. Where we were informs where we are and the allure that it holds for all of us is understandable and condonable in the light of the musical theater's golden past. Here, then, is where those who went before us "put it."

In the one year 1924–1925, thirty-nine musicals opened on Broadway, and albeit some of them are forgotten (and with good reason), the following productions, all memorable, were seen in that one twelve-month season!

1. *The Ziegfeld Follies.* With Will Rogers.
2. *George White Scandals.* Gershwin's "Somebody Loves Me" was introduced in this edition.
3. *The Dream Girl.* Victor Herbert's last operetta.
4. *Rose Marie.* By Rudolph Friml and Oscar Hammerstein, it was the first musical to bring in over a $1 million profit.
5. *Be Yourself.* George Kaufman's and Marc Connelly's first collaboration on a score, for which Ira Gershwin wrote some of the lyrics.
6. *Earl Carroll's Vanities.* With Sophie Tucker.
7. *The Greenwich Village Follies.* The sixth edition of a series of notable revues.
8. *Dear Sir.* With a score by Jerome Kern.
9. *The Grab Bag.* With the great clown, Ed Wynn.
10. *Artists and Models.* With a Sigmund Romberg and J. Fred Coots score.
11. *Dixie to Broadway.* The last appearance of the memorable Florence Mills.
12. *Annie Dear.* A Ziegfeld musical that starred his wife, the unforgettable Billie Burke.
13. *The Magnolia Lady.* With Ruth Chatterton in a rare appearance in a musical.

14. *Lady Be Good.* The Gershwin brothers and Fred and Adele Astaire in a musical with "standard" hits by the bushel.

15. *The Music Box Revue.* An Irving Berlin score sung by Grace Moore and, clowning together, Fanny Brice and the great Bobby Clark and his partner, Paul McCullough.

16. *The Student Prince.* The premiere performance of the Sigmund Romberg classic.

17. *Big Boy.* With the formidable Al Jolson.

18. *Puzzles of 1925.* With the legendary Elsie Janis.

19. *Sky High.* With another great clown, Willie Howard.

20. *Tell Me More.* With, again, a Gershwin score.

21. *The Garrick Gaieties.* A new revue that introduced the team of Rodgers and Hart to Broadway.

22. And lastly, three Gilbert and Sullivan full-scale revivals: *Princess Ida*, *Patience*, and *The Mikado*.

Leaving aside the issue of abundance, I present below an abridged and admittedly subjective listing of great shows, beginning with the year 1914, when Jerome Kern's music was first heard on Broadway, and extending through 1985. The list illustrates how far the musical theater has evolved from *The Black Crook* (first produced in 1866 and generally accredited as the progenitor of the American musical) to the present time, when composers, lyricists, and librettists are liberated from the constrictive formulas of the past and free to score any subject they care to sing about.

1914: *The Girl from Utah.* Ina Claire had appeared in the London production, but the producer, Charles Frohman, made musical history by interpolating into his New York re-production seven added songs (among them the historic "They Didn't Believe Me") by a very young Jerome Kern.

1916: *The Passing Show of 1916.* The first time George Gershwin's name ever appeared in *play-bill.* He was nineteen years old, and he contributed one song: "Making of a Girl."

1919: *A Lonely Romeo.* The first time Rodgers and Hart's name ever appeared in *play-bill.* The song? "Any Old Place with You."

1919: *Yip Yip Yaphank.* Irving Berlin's revue of army life. The success of this World War I production was reprised again in World War II with *This Is the Army.*

1920: *Poor Little Ritz Girl.* Rodgers and Hart's first full book score.

1921: *Two Little Girls in Blue.* Vincent Youmans's first score, in collaboration with Ira Gershwin, still hiding behind the name Arthur Frances (an invented alias created from the first names of his brother and sister.

1922: *For Goodness Sake.* Fred and Adele Astaire had make their debut in *Over the Top* in 1917, appeared again in 1919 in *Apple Blossoms* and in 1921 in *The Love Letter*, but in this musical they achieved stardom.

1924: *Lady Be Good.* As listed above, this Gershwin musical brought the Astaires back after their success in *For Goodness Sake* and *The Bunch and Judy* in 1922. The score was innovative and, for the first time, indicated that if one's voice was no better than it should be, songs could still be sung with no apparent harm done to them. Gershwin had slain the operetta dragon.

1927: *A Connecticut Yankee.* The musicalized tale of Mark Twain's modern man thrust, by circumstance and dramatic license, into the world of Camelot. The score was written by Rodgers and Hart, now beginning their lustrous career after their debut in *The Garrick Gaieties.*

1927: *Showboat.* Jerome Kern's and Oscar Hammerstein's watershed musical based on the Edna Ferber novel.

1930: *Strike Up the Band.* Again by the Gershwins, this musical crossbred Savoy opera with American jazz and perfected the form the following year . . .

1931: . . . with *Of Thee I Sing.* The first musical to win a Pulitzer prize.

1935: *Porgy and Bess.* By the Gershwins and DuBose Heyward; the first American opera produced on and for Broadway. Since 1985, it has been listed permanently in the repertory of the Metropolitan Opera Company.

1936: *On Your Toes.* The world of ballet placed within a musical context. "Slaughter on Tenth Avenue," in the second act, was a full-length ballet choreographed by George Balanchine. A first.

1940: *Pal Joey.* John O'Hara's tale of seedy show people in Chicago. The first verismo musical, with a score by Rodgers and Hart that included the lovely "Bewitched, Bothered and Bewildered."

1941: *Lady in the Dark.* Ira Gershwin and Kurt Weill (his new collaborator after the tragic death of his brother) scored Moss Hart's book about a lady "who could not make up her mind." Psychoanalysis had not only found its voice, but could now sing about it.

1943: *Oklahoma!.* Rodgers and Hammerstein's first opus was a watershed musical.

1944: *On the Town.* Leonard Bernstein, Betty Comden, and Adolph Green—along with Jerome Robbins's choeography and Nancy Walker's unforgettable cabdriver. A debut for the writers and a new generation's voice.

1945: *Carousel.* Rodgers and Hammerstein's second musical, this time based on Molnar's *Liliom.* An enduring masterwork.

1946: *Lute Song.* A ravishing production of a Chinese tale, scored by Raymond Scott with stage designs by the eminent Robert Edmond Jones that put the lie to the old chestnut that "you can't go out whistling the sets."

1946: *Annie Get Your Gun.* Merman's greatest role and Irving Berlin's great score. A "10" for both.

1947: *Street Scene.* Kurt Weill's last score, with Langston Hughes's words, an operatic rendering of Elmer Rice's 1929 play about tenement life in New York City. Now a part of the repertory of the New York City Opera Company.

1947: *Finian's Rainbow.* The exception to the rule that Broadway abhors whimsy. This enchanting musical about the haves and the have-nots, racism, Irish elves, and American corporate greed was scored by Burton Lane and E. Y. (Yip) Harburg.

1947: *Brigadoon.* Alan Jay Lerner's and Frederick Loewe's first major success. A grand "modern" operetta.

1948
and
1949: *Kiss Me Kate* and *South Pacific*. The two distinguished musicals of their time. An example of opposites attracting. Cole Porter at his wittiest and Rodgers and Hammerstein at their romantic best.

1950: *Guys and Dolls*. Frank Loesser's masterpiece based on Damon Runyon's beloved New York characters.

1956: *My Fair Lady*. Lerner and Loewe's magnum opus. No musical ever possessed a wittier book but that may be due to the fact that no musical ever had George Bernard Shaw as the librettist. The score was a worthy partner for the master's words.

1956: *The Most Happy Fella*. Frank Loesser's classic work. A daring, if imperfect, treatment of Sidney Howard's *They Knew What They Wanted*.

1957: *Candide*. Based on Voltaire's novel, with Leonard Bernstein's dazzling score and a book and lyrics by Lillian Hellman, Richard Wilbur, John Latouche, and Dorothy Parker. A failure in its first incarnation, it was successfully restaged by Hal Prince with a new libretto by Hugh Wheeler and added input by Stephen Sondheim in 1974.

1957: *West Side Story*. Leonard Bernstein and Stephen Sondheim in collaboration with Arthur Laurents and Jerome Robbins. This definitive musical, out of *Romeo and Juliet*, must be considered another Broadway opera.

1957: *The Music Man*. Meredith Willson's valentine to his home state of Indiana. Pure 24-karat golden corn.

1959: *Gypsy*. Jule Styne's and Stephen Sondheim's musical about Gypsy Rose Lee that turned out to be about her mother because Ethel Merman sang her.

1959: *Fiorello*. A musical biography of New York City's beloved mayor, Fiorello LaGuardia, with a score by Jerry Bock and Sheldon Harnick. A Pulitzer prize winner.

1961: *How to Succeed in Business without Really Trying*. Frank Loesser's last score and another Pulitzer prize winner.

1962: *A Funny Thing Happened on the Way to the Forum*. Stephen Sondheim's score to a book by Burt Shevelove and Larry

Gelbhart. A rare and successful farce musical based on the plays of Plautus.

1963: *She Loves Me.* A beautiful score by Jerry Bock and Sheldon Harnick based on the film *The Shop around the Corner.*

1964: *Funny Girl.* Jule Styne's and Bob Merrill's perfect score that sang the life of Fanny Brice. It introduced, in the leading role, Barbra Streisand.

1964: *Anyone Can Whistle.* A flawed musical with a grainy but nevertheless memorable score by Stephen Sondheim.

1966: *Cabaret.* John Kander and Fred Ebb scored this musicalization of John Van Druten's *I Am a Camera*, out of Christopher Isherwood's *Berlin Stories.*

1967: *Hair.* Galt MacDermott's fusion of rock and jazz that sat somewhat uncomfortably on an old-fashioned musical comedy book. Evocative of its time, it was the first musical to mirror the commercial music scene.

This list is, of course, arguably incomplete. There have been a host of composers and lyricists who have found favor and success. Among them would have to be listed Vincent Youmans, Arthur Schwartz and Howard Dietz, Sammy Cahn, Burke and Van Heusen, DeSylva, Brown and Henderson, Sammy Fain, Robin and Rainger, John Latouche, Gordon and Revel, Kay Swift, Cy Coleman and Carolyn Leigh, Jerry Herman, Stephen Schwartz, Cryer and Ford, Dubey and Karr, Nancy Hamilton and Morgan Lewis, Hugh Martin and Ralph Blane, Tony Newley and Leslie Bricusse, Charles Strouse and Lee Adams, Udell and Geld, Sherman Edwards, Schmidt and Jones . . . and others I may have inadvertently omitted.

Just as there have been many great song and lyric writers, there have been monster successes in the musical theater I have not included, although not inadvertently: *The King and I, The Sound of Music, Camelot, Hello Dolly, Mame,* and beyond the sixties, *Promises Promises, Applause, Godspell, Jesus Christ Superstar, A Chorus Line, Evita, Dreamgirls, Forty-Second Street, Cats,* and *La Cage aux Folles.* The ever-diminishing number of musicals that each season saw the light of day (and stayed around long enough to bask in it) bore witness to the fact that the handwriting was on the wall: show business was now big business, and big business was what a show had to do to bring in a profit. In such a climate, the conservative musical that takes few chances is a better deal for the investor than one which aims for originality.

Since 1970, only the work of Stephen Sondheim can be described as memorable. Beginning with *Company* and continuing with *Follies, A Little Night Music, Pacific Overtures, Sweeney Todd, Merrily We Roll Along,* and the Pulitzer prize–winning *Sunday in the Park with George,* his musicals have determinedly explored the outer perimeters of subject matter that can be sung. The disquieting fact that rarely are his musicals profitable in no way diminishes his ever-growing reputation as the foremost creative artist working in the musical theater today.

I do not mean to imply that only originality and radical choice of subject matter should define the "memorable musical," but it is clear that we are sadly delinquent in the two crucial elements that illuminated yesterday's musicals—namely, great scores and great performers. So built-in were these components that dedicated enthusiasts asked very little of the book of a show. It was a filler between the songs and the dances. The scores were the thing. When I was a teenager during the thirties, it was considered a mark of sophistication and distinction to know, by heart, Cole Porter's verses and Larry Hart's second and third choruses. Everyone may have attended musicals to be entertained, but we always took the score of a show seriously.

Along with "Words and music by . . ." was the equally significant "Starring. . . ." Great performers—singers, dancers, comedians, clowns, leading ladies, and leading men—paraded before the public season after season but what they *said* was never more than merely serviceable. What was sung, and who sang it, was all. Because the librettos were of little to no importance, their words were not scripted by eminent playwrights, and musicals were often looked down upon by those who considered it low-brow. For over fifty years even the word *theater* was never coupled with *musical*. They label was *musical comedy*, and it was kept apart from *play*. The *theater* was *art*, and plays were *theater*. Dramatic artists were the actors who played them out on the stage. Musicals were always characterized as *entertainment*, and entertainers were (and I still believe them to be) consigned to a place where they earned good money (as good as their more esteemed peers) but never the respect afforded, say, the Lunts.

Audiences for musicals not only did not expect drama or even elevated comedy, but they stayed away if someone tried to force-feed it to them. The word *opera* managed to kill *Porgy and Bess* until its fiftieth birthday, when the Metropolitan Opera presented it. Even then, critics had a hard time dealing with it. Were it not for the unbounded affection in which everyone everywhere held the score, the critics, again, would have critiqued it right out of existence. The same can be said for Kurt Weill's *Street Scene* in 1947 and *Lost in the Stars* in 1949, Marc Blitzstein's *Regina* the same year and, to a lesser extent (for it ran over a year), Frank Loesser's *The Most Happy Fella* in 1956. In this particular case, Mr. Loesser was determined to keep *opera* out of any description of his work, going so far as to call it an "extended musical comedy." I cannot know his private reasons for doing this, but my guess is that his conditioning motivated him to believe that by resorting to the lower-brow descriptive, he had made it more marketable.

Latter-day Sondheim debuts on Broadway, but there is a fight going on, no mistake about it. There are those who would be a good deal more comfortable if his musicals were seen on opera stages; once his work was banished to the world of "art," his detractors could rest easier. Sondheim's daring investigations of what can be sung on the Broadway stage have given other writers the courage to widen the scope of what is permissible and profitable to sing about, and this must be considered a giant step forward.

Even a glance at the evolution of musical theater shows a consistent and ever-developing excellence, ranging from those early simplistic entertainments that were played out in front of and behind drops and 'travelers' down the years to the musical and design complexities we have become accustomed to. Unfortunately, this growth has occurred at the same time that there has been an alarming dip in the caliber of the performers who once were an integral part of the standard of quality by which a musical was measured. In the last fifteen years their position of eminence has been usurped by the director or the director-choreographer who, by creating the new "concept musical," has done considerable damage to the cause of great performing. Is there any real difference between one company of *A Chorus Line* and another? Does anyone care who is appearing in *Cats?* If *Evita* is sung by A or by B or by C, is that musical imperiled or is its effect diminished? Who is in *Forty-Second Street? Nine? Dreamgirls?* And even when putative stars appear, billed above the title of the show, is it not their celebrity that, more often than not, attracts the ticket buyer rather than their ability to hold the stage? And, again, if great performances are so rare, what will define them to new generations of theatergoers and, most important of all, to future actors, dancers, and singers? Not the least of Lily Tomlin's stunning artistry is that today's audiences can witness it, live, on the stage of a theater where the notion of an understudy or a stand-in is inconceivable.

It is supremely difficult to give young performers any idea of the comic genius of Fanny Brice, Bea Lillie, Bert Lahr, Willie Howard, Ed Wynn, Eddie Foy, Jr., Bobby Clark, and other great comics who appeared on the musical stage throughout the first fifty years of this century. We are luckier in the case of performer-singers; their recordings can recall them to us. However, Gertrude Lawrence's most ardent fan would agree that, note for note, the sound of her voice was not where her magic could be found. Noel Coward, on record, is uniquely himself but the sight of him was even more so. Ethel Merman's recordings are an acquired taste. Her voice was the essence of the quality of her style with a song—when you *saw* her sing it. Al Jolson's old 78s, like Caruso's, require understanding and forgiveness when a Dolby'd ear listens to them, for he, too, had to be seen. How fortunate we are to be able to watch Fred Astaire on the screen! To attend all his films is to begin to understand the meaning of excellence and to have some idea of the amount of sheer sweat and labor it must have required to achieve the illusion of such seamless ease. The same can be said of W. C. Fields. His films are a treasure, but how favored I would have been to have seen him on the stage doing battle with his rigged billiard table in the 1915 edition of *The Ziegfeld Follies.*

Performers once worked their lifetimes to impose a personal style on their singing, comedy, and dancing. Having worked in vaudeville, on the Borscht circuit, in burlesque, and in nightclubs, they were masters and mistresses of their craft by the time they stepped onto a Broadway stage. They built their careers throughout all the years they were able to work "unblessed" with a television machine that curses anyone appearing on it with instant maximum celebrity despite possible minimum ability. Similarly, today's concept musicals might well be threatened by too outstanding a performance. They make more lenient demands on the actor, the dancer, and the singer because they are created out of an image the director places over the material—an image that becomes something of a presentational prison in which the cast is held captive. Under such circumstances, the individuality of a performer is subverted, since the whole is deemed to be more important than any of its parts. It is the look of the piece and, in most cases, its splendor that seduces the audience and keeps them in its thrall. *A Chorus Line*, from its inception, concerned itself with the concept of the anonymity of the players on stage. *Evita*, by virtue of its physical design and its costuming is photocopied whenever a new production is mounted. And *Cats* manipulates audiences with its production values and, by masking the cast, utterly denies each performer any recognition.

It is now a thing of bittersweetness to sit around and mourn the past. For a while, nostalgia enjoyed commercial currency, and in some instances, it still does. We have seen revivals of almost everything revivable and, with rare exception, we have seen, too, that the golden age was not always pure gold. And when it was, enough became more than enough. However, the end of the line is in sight. Unless a superstar can be persuaded to tour, audiences have more than had their fill of *My Fair Lady, South Pacific, The Music Man, Gigi, The Sound of Music*, and *Brigadoon*. True, their scores are lovely to hear and rehear, but they have little to say to a generation under the age of thirty conditioned to the world of rock and roll. I do not suggest that we turn our backs on this extraordinary heritage that is so much a part of the American collective unconscious, but it is time to put yesterday's musical treasures on hold.

*T*he Present

In my time, the chronic illness of the "fabulous invalid" was never reported with the degree of relish that today's media lavish on it in general and on the musical theater, in particular. Audiences, with no awareness that the patient was so badly off, were flocking into New York on the eve of the summer of 1985 only to be greeted at every turn with horrific reports of the theater's declining health. On June 6 of that year, NBC took an 8½-by 10½-inch advertisement in *The New York Times*. Superimposed on a photograph of a silk-hatted, white-spatted actor in a deep bow, was the banner:

Is Broadway Taking Its Final Bow?

Beneath the photo, in smaller type, another question, aimed at poignancy, was posed:

Will the Lights Go Out on Broadway?

The public was asked to tune in and hear a motley group of actors and directors "who know the inside story" pass it on to listeners eager to hear the morbid diagnosis.

There has always been concern for the perenially ailing theater, but today the illness is publicized with a new lip-smacking zest reminiscent of a *National Enquirer* headline.

Has the theater become a dinosaur that refuses to recognize it is extinct? Have Broadway musicals evolved into megaspectacles at the expense of good scores and memorable performances? And, worse still, is England beating us at our own game with box office successes like *Jesus Christ Superstar, Evita, Cats, Song and Dance, Les Miserables, Starlight Express,* and *Phantom of the Opera?*

A month earlier, again in *The New York Times*, in May 1985, an article about the end-of-season tally, historically relegated to the "Arts and Leisure" section of that newspaper, was given front-page prominence. Samuel G. Freedman, their "man in the theater," called it "the worst economic season in a decade" and went on to report that the "thirty-three new shows that will have opened by May 31, the official end of the season, represent the fewest in any season this century." The bell was further tolled: "Broadway's slump this year can be largely traced to the lack of a new hit musical to stimulate both income and public excitement. Eight musicals opened this year, four are still running and none can be certain to survive the summer." *One* "new hit musical?" Had Broadway's lifeline narrowed to so insignificant an insignificance?

In the same month, Jack Viertel (at the time the drama critic of the *Los Angeles Herald Examiner*) editorialized that perhaps audiences were deserting the theater because it was offering nothing more than what they could see for free at home on television or by delving into the vast, inexpensive video cassette rental library. He went on to say that "by staying away from conventional kinds of plays, theatergoers are in effect restating that essential audience plea: "Astonish me." He correctly speaks of the musical theater as the one remaining "nonrealistic theater the audience has any familiarity with in this country" but adds the sad comment that "the combination of high price and a dwindling talent pool (or a talent pool that has refused for the most part to catch up with contemporary music)" has made the musical an "expense-account event most of the time."*

Are these men correct? In Mr. Freedman's case, you cannot fault the statistics. And Mr. Viertel justifiably points an accusing finger at the stodgy, old-fashioned musical theater and suggests that it is dying of its own conventionality. Is it the price, then, or the product that is responsible? One has only to look at the concert halls, opera houses, ballet theaters, and dance films for half the answer:

Again, in *The New York Times* in May 1985, John Rockwell reported that, in 1960, there were 42 professional ensembles of which 25 had counted as major orchestras committed to playing 'serious' music." The American Symphony Orchestra League divides orchestras into several categories, the top three comprising what the League calls "professional ensembles." In 1984, there were 166 professional orchestras, 30 of them major. As for opera companies, "in the 1964–65 season there were 27 American opera companies with budgets over $100,000; last season, 1984, there were 154."§ Most spectacular of all are the statistics on the increasing number of people who attend dance events of all kinds. A Harris poll reports that, in 1964, an audience of 1 million had, by 1980, grown to 24 million.

---

*It seems clear to me that the talent pool has more than caught up with contemporary music, for the hills are only too alive with the sound of music from *Jesus Christ Superstar*, *Evita*, *Cats*, *Big River*, and *Chess*. The popularity of "Don't Cry for Me, Argentina" or a "Memories" or even a "What I Did for Love" is due less to the intrinsic worth of these songs than to the mass-marketing techniques employed by the recording studios that release them up to a year before the opening night and, by dunning them on radio and on MTV, manipulate them into sizable 'hits'.

§These statistics are offered by the Central Opera Service, a fact-gathering body sponsored by the Metropolitan Guild.

In 1984 alone, 58 million people went to ballet and modern, folk, and ethnic dance recitals. If there is a plague, the theater alone seems to be suffering from it. Only the movie industry shows signs of a similar pathology. Just as audiences were once enticed to leave the theater for the equally popular-priced popcorn palaces so, too, are today's movie audiences staying home to watch their films on television and VCRs. But since their inception, movies have fashioned a product that was confessedly popular in order to gain the widest appeal. On the other hand, one could still attend the theater—both legit and musical—with the assurance that one would see an entertainment—an art form, if you will—that claimed direct descent from the early Greeks, from Shakespeare and Molière down to Chekhov, Ibsen, and O'Neill. In recent years, as the price of the theater ticket has become more and more elitist, it has become necessary to broaden and popularize what is offered on the Broadway stage. Regional, Off Broadway and West End theaters have begun to address the problem by creating dynamic statements that Broadway often imports. The theatrical genealogy is currently enriched with the likes of Albee, Mamet, Rabe, Shepard, Pinter, Stoppard, and Shaffer. Only the musical theater still struggles to find a voice that talks and sings in a language that television and film cannot adopt as their own.

A vibrant musical theater must learn to regard yesterday's trove of great shows as belonging to a past that rarely informs the present. I am not against yesterday's masterpieces. I am against the need to think of them as today's masterpieces. Much as I love the glorious library of show tunes, as a teacher I find discomforting and disheartening this endless reprising of them; discomforting because they are of the past, and disheartening because, too often, today's composers are either impelled to imitate them, refuse to take them further, or badly rewrite them. For the most part, the songs we hear today have been written before and better. There is something to commend the act of crowding around the piano to sing Cole Porter or for a stiff cover charge, to hear Bobby Short do it his way. But I have a nagging fear that if we remain unmindful of the exotic nature of this kind of activity, we will become more and more fossilized and removed from those who do not give a farthing for yet another chorus of "Let's Do It." Conversely, the passion that young people have for Stephen Sondheim's songs is not difficult to understand. His music is their music and his words sing about the problems that abrade their lives and their loves. When his critics complain of his lack of sentiment, they betray their age. Composers and lyricists who wrote songs that once told us that "Life Is Just a Bowl of Cherries" and "There's a Great Day Coming Manana" and besought us to "Get Happy" never had to read today's and tomorrow's newspapers or turn on this evening's and tomorrow morning's TV news.

I am not making a plea for the serious musical. The label "entertainment" does not appall me. I am even ready to cast a vote for mindless entertainment, recalling well enough the inanity of so many historic musicals whose books, unlike their scores, are happily forgotten. Sequins and lavish settings have been with us at least as far back as the first *Ziegfeld Follies* in 1907, but just as the serious musical can be, at the same time, entertaining, the glitzy musical cannot ignore what Mr. Ziegfeld recognized as an integral part of the formula. Beautiful girls, yes, but also wonderful comics, dancers, and singers—performers who were as much a part of the success of those shows as the pretty girl who was like a melody.

For those singers who aim for careers on opera and concert stages, the question "Where am I going to put it?" is never posed. There are opera and concert stages available around the world and winning out over one's competition is still the open sesame to those stage doors.

Although the life is hard and the pay far too low, ballet companies and dance ensembles continue to proliferate and thereby offer employment and experience to the young "serious" dancer.

Even the "serious" actor can work here, there, and everywhere to perfect his or her craft in front of a paying audience even though there may be little or no pay to do so.

But for the "serious" performer who wants to act, dance, and sing in less classical environments, the picture is grimmer. The show business that produced Rex Harrison, Fred Astaire, and Ethel Merman is nonexistent. Even the marketplace that created Frank Sinatra has long been laid to rest. Big bands, fronted by soloists who were identified as singers as soon as they opened their mouths, are no longer a part of the pop scene. Nightclubs in which an Ella Fitzgerald sang in her own exclusive fashion have been preempted by the large

Las Vegas and Atlantic City rooms where that kind of singer is rarely heard—and not at all if the singer is not a big-name artist. Supper clubs and boîtes, the historic venues where young singers and comedians could be discovered, have all but disappeared. The very few that remain do not allow a singer enough time on the floor to grow, gain a personal public, and become a Mabel Mercer, while comedians in improvisational groups and "comedy stores" have only one dream—television exposure.

The disappearance of live TV variety shows has left the dancer high and dry just as it has future Sid Caesars, Milton Berles, Martha Rayes, and Carol Burnetts. In the last ten years, however, dancers have seen their somewhat exotic world metamorphose into something of an all-American passion. *A Chorus Line* opened in 1975 and still runs on Broadway while record grosses are racked up for films that blatantly advertise dancing as the incentive for seeing the film: *Saturday Night Fever, Fame, Flashdance, Footloose, That's Dancing, Breakin', Breakin' 2, Electric Bugaloo, Beat Street, Fast Forward,* and the film of *A Chorus Line*. MTV offers enough choreography to please the most ardent enthusiast, and all this activity ensures a continuation of the dynastic succession that stretches from Bill Robinson and Fred Astaire and Gene Kelly down to Honeychile Coles, Gregory Hines, Jeffrey Hornaday, and Marine Jahan. An interesting footnote: As the demands of the choreographer create more and more devilishly skillful dancers, the expertise required of the popular singer deteriorates in inverse proportion. The hills may be alive with the sound of music, but to watch and listen to it sung can often be a trial.

Again, I do not ask for a return to the old. Frank Sinatra, still as popular as he was more than forty years ago and with all age groups, is as much a man of his time as Michael Jackson and Prince are of theirs. But can these last two men, gifted as they are, hold a stage by themselves as Ole Blue Eyes most assuredly can, with nothing going for them but the dynamic nature of their voices and the charm of their style? I wonder. Peter Hall, director of the British National Theater, in an entry in his diary dated June 17, 1978, reviewed his reaction to the film *Saturday Night Fever*: " . . . a feeling of manipulation pervades the whole affair and of course it works on the audience. I think that what depresses me is that up to quite recently, I have always believed popular art, in all its manifestations in history, was popular because it had merit. In some sense, it was good. The public's own vitality saw to that. But now this isn't so anymore. Market research provides the right product, the public is manipulated: *1984* has come." I do not know if I am in total accord with Sir Peter, but I do know that flimflamming has become an international sport.

ACT TWO
SCENE ONE

❦

The Twenty Most Often Asked Questions . . . Answered

For the actor, the choice of teacher is a personal one. There is a multiplicity from which selection can be made. Teachers practice in almost every city in the country, and drama departments are commonplace in colleges and universities. One can study with the great, the near great, the old and the wise, and the young and the foolish. There are messiahs and gurus and teachers whose reputations are small but to whom students swear eternal devotion. Pick up *The New York Times, Variety, Back Stage, Dramalogue*, and the *Hollywood Reporter*; even the most cynical member of the show business community will be impressed with the sheer number of advertisers. What determines the students' devotion is their particular needs and how the instructors meet them. With no malice intended, the profusion of teachers is due, I think, to the uncodifiable nature of acting. It is only in this century that efforts were made to get down in writing what had never before been systematized. There are as many systems as there are teachers. How valuable they are is for their students to say. Some study to learn the how-to of acting, some to be coddled and cosseted, some to be validated in their career choice, and some to kill time. Whatever the intention, there is a teacher for every actor possessed of questions that require answers.

When the actor, the dancer, and the novice singer begin to sing, the same multitude of choice is available. Singing teachers, however, enjoy a position in their students' lives that is particular to their field. This is so for several reasons.

First, the subject is so internal in its function that the beginner must surrender to the teacher wholeheartedly with no before-the-fact knowledge of the effect of what he or she is being asked to do: will it work, simply not work, or, worse, be disastrous? More often than not, as the student's perception grows, the techniques learned are a mystical combination gleaned from two, three, or even more tutors and from an increasing personal knowledge of what the voice, in the particular body in which it lives, requires.

Second, although the acoustical production of the human voice is codified, there are many road maps offered to the beginner. The way sound is produced and resonated is scientifically demonstrable. The methodology employed to learn how to make it work for you is still the creation of the singing teacher, and it is inarguable that no single teacher can hope to be all things to all aspiring singers.

Third, at risk of straining some old friendships, I'll acknowledge that singing teachers can be an odd lot. Because what they teach is arcane, many of them foster the impression that personal eccentricity is part of the package. My own history includes some rare memories spent in the bend of a piano. The outrageous Mme. Dilly in the Bernstein-Comden and Green musical *On the Town* is not pure fiction. Not surprisingly, good singing teachers are advertised by their students in only one valid way: their vocal techniques are sure, effortlessly achieved, and increasingly facile. As in the case of a recognized professional acting teacher, all questions asked of a qualified singing teacher are answerable, no matter the degree of the student's ignorance or, of the extent of the damage previously done to the unsuspecting beginner.

And now the actor, the dancer, and the singer, possessed of acting techniques that work for them and newly acquired awareness of how to produce well-resonated and breath-supported vocal sound, are faced with a new, dark place in which to flounder. How does one put it all together?

It is unfortunate that the study of the art of performing in the musical theater is not as easily available as it should be. The reasons for this are many but I imagine that the crossbreeding of the actor-dancer-singer has created a new hunger to plumb the secrets of performing that, until recently in theater history, were organic to the artist—secrets that had never been purchased from instructors.

I have compiled a list of twenty questions that are most often asked of me wherever I teach. They are asked by everyone, everywhere. The amateur, the student, and the professional share a common ignorance on the subject of singing. Degrees of sophistication and experience appear to shed little or no light on bewilderment. The actor, the dancer and the singer arrive together on a platform of confusion. It should be of some comfort to hear that one is, therefore, not alone.

Some of the questions relate to singing in general, some to singing at an audition, and some to singing on the job. There is no significant order to the list. It is of some importance to remember that the answers are mine and, therefore, arguable. Show business is not an exact science whose mathematical equations can be proved. Whatever valuable information one accrues is, at best, empirical. Finally, if a picture is said to be worth a thousand words, the sight of a great performer at work will always be worth more than twenty *thousand* well-answered questions. I recommend watching to reading, but when performers are not readily there to see, perhaps these answers will be of help.

1. Why Am I So Frightened to Get up and Sing in Front of People?

If there were to be an order to these questions, this one, by virtue of its universality, would have had to be the first. For the actor and the dancer who are, after all, singers by choice and not birthright, it may be encouraging to learn that it is not the possession of a gorgeous voice that brings a sense of ease to performing. I know of too many singers who experience the same fear of singing for me to try to placate nonsingers with the assurance that when they sound better, they will feel better.

Next to appearing in public in the nude, singing presents us (or so we believe) at our most naked. We feel it betrays us—in whatever manner we may define that betrayal—and we are unwilling to be our own betrayers. No wonder the remark most often heard in my studio, after the performance of a song, is, "It went so much better at home." Singing in private is a turn-on. We can abandon ourselves to the sheer joy of making our own music, behaving in any way we choose, able to function freely. And all of this is vouchsafed us as long as we are assured we are alone. Let an audience in, even if it be only one in number, and we race to hide whatever we feel needs withholding. It takes crafty coaxing to come out of that closet. What is even more upsetting is the realization that, when you enter the *business* of singing, you yourself must become the coaxer. No one can be expected to do it for you or be expected to care whether you do it at all. Even a teacher is paid to teach, not to cajole.

What is of interest is that we seem to *need* to sing. Singing appears to be a response to impulses the primitive part of the brain feeds into our conscious mind, and, in turn, pleasures us with emotional release. Singing shares with dancing this strange compulsive, yet joyous, inclination. The students I teach may be terrified to sing, but they are determined to do it, to have their say and a song to say it with. It must be pure masochism. The analogy of going to the dentist is apt. We go because we must, knowing that it is good for us, but knowing, too, that it will be unpleasant at best and downright painful at worst.

The fear of singing in public is universal, but the need to deal with it is necessary only when you choose to make singing your business. The majority of the human race leads lives in which there is no need to "come out." Few professions require it, and an occasional chorus of "Happy Birthday," an accompaniment to a shower, or a sing-along with the radio in your car will furnish sufficient musical outlets for most of us.

For those who are impelled to sing for their suppers, there is the usual old-wives' medication: Afraid of the water? Jump in. This system has much to recommend it. Its only drawback is that, for some, it may well turn them away from swimming forever. If you are all too aware of what you are not doing well, advertising your swimming or your singing in public may do you very little good. If, however, one's sensitivity threshold can be raised, hard knocks in the marketplace work to your advantage. This is especially true if you are able to remain objective and study what you do and its effect on an audience, or, even better, have someone there to proctor the results and direct you accordingly. I have always been of the opinion that constant work is the best educator you will ever have. But any advisor who suggests this system as an alleviator of fear ignores a hard fact of show business reality: there is no such thing as constant work. And so we come to study.

In the last fifty years, and with increasing popularity, the theater arts have flourished. Where once there was a small community of professional schools and few universities that offered any kind of valid theater instruction, today the undergraduate actor is an honorable alumnus. But musical theater departments have lagged. Conservatories have always been the venue where musicians and singers come together. Dancers attend dance classes as a matter of course from their early years far into and throughout their careers. But when the actor melds with the dancer and the singer and, in fact, all three are interested in acquiring facility in the others' fields, there are even fewer places in which they can conjoin. Each group is fated to study under different roofs and with teachers who are often in conflict. Nevertheless, the hunger to learn how to fuse all three elements into a stylish whole is patent wherever I go to teach. Study is, at the present time, the best method I know of to dispel the terror endured by young performers, because it introduces them to the incontrovertible: We are frightened because we do not know how to do what we are being asked to do. The nonswimmer thrown into the water has but one goal: not to drown. The positive side of this can hardly be defined as swimming. When you do know how to swim, you swim and you have no reason to think about drowning. When you stand on a stage and demonstrate that you know what you are doing, you busy yourself doing it. Knowledge banishes fear and more knowledge banishes it further.

Nervousness and fear are mutually exclusive words. Fear is always destructive. Nervousness is an indication of a heightened awareness brought about by the significance of the event. Auditions and opening nights find us nervous, but the performance goes on and may even achieve a kind of coruscating exhilaration. When I see someone work who professes never to have known nervousness, the performance somehow evidences it. Admittedly, singing in front of people is never easy because it requires an enormous marshaling of one's pyschic and vocal resources to convey the heightened urgency necessary to support language too elevated to be spoken. But when you know what you are supposed to do and, more, how to achieve it, there is nothing as soul-stirring as standing in the center of a song and, as you create its vocal life, making the power of your performance irresistible to an audience.

Singing makes us feel we are naked because we *are* the songs we sing. There is not the make-believe world of the actor or the classic physical language of the dance to hide behind. But songs are the clothes that, when we choose them wisely, display us as we want to be seen. And if, on the bottom line, we do not *wish* to be seen, why are we up there . . . singing?

2. *Asked by Actors: Why Do I Take Criticism of My Singing More Personally Than I Do Criticism of My Acting?*

If singing can be said to present you in full view, criticism of what you are doing—when you sing—can be misinterpreted as criticism of who you are. Singers and Dancers are more able than actors to disassociate themselves from their work because the *techniques* they must learn, although interactive, are separate and apart from their understanding of what defines a *performance*. This is also true of instrumentalists. To a singer, a scale is not a song; to a dancer, an entrechat is not a dance; to a pianist, a Heller finger exercise is not Mozart. This split road they walk upon is presented to them in their learning years from the day they begin their studies. Actors are less fortunate. They are taught that their personal biography, their appearance, their psychology, their gender, and their very essence all make up their art. Is it any wonder that finding fault with what actors will show you is accepted by them as a judgment of all that they are? No one is more aware of this than I. If I ask a singer to change an E flat to a G in a rideout, she does it. If I recommend to the dancer that the eight-bar soft-shoe in the second chorus shows to better advantage in the 'bridge' than in the 'first eight,' he does it. If I suggest to the actor that his performance choice (how he *sees* the song) does not pay its way, his immediate reaction is: "He doesn't like me."

In the world of drama, a play is written by the playwright and, in the rehearsal period, created by the actors and the director. An accumulation of elements, some so subtle that their seminal beginnings remain a mystery, shapes the play into its final reality. Musicals are far less mysterious. Their genesis is more a construction than an accretion. This is not to say that the formulas employed by the composer, the lyricist, and the librettist together with the director and the choreographer are so defined that the plot-plan—and how to make it work—is known to them from the start. If this were so, every musical would be *My Fair Lady*. But the parts of the whole possess an inherent shape and a complexity that requires everyone on the staff to move quickly and knowledgeably. What works must be made to work better, and what will be seen to be deadweight must be removed surgically with a ruthless knife. And there is never enough time. Dancers rehearse for five weeks, while the book and the score are rehearsed for only four. The lids that are placed on allowable money and time create a climate of intense pressure. A musical can be as expensive as a movie.

Actors who are accustomed to directors who address them softly and in private are astonished to find that nothing is private in this new world of musical theater. A play is allowed to simmer slowly. Dialogue is kept in the wings while motivations and objectives are given free rein to develop. Rehearsals of a musical demand other tempos. Dialogue is often memorized and scripts banned early in the proceedings in order to begin run-throughs—halting but necessary in shaping the appearance of the piece—as early as the second week. Concern for the "look" of things is everything. The external is as important as the internal life of a musical—if not more so. Sets must be given time for construction and painting; dancing must be given its space; choral arrangements must be taught and physically 'staged' within the context of the scenes; key choices and textural sounds must be decided upon to allow sufficient time for the orchestrator and the copyists to do their work; costume fittings can rob the director of cast members for an entire day—and all of these things must be fitted into a rigid rehearsal period, since every one of them is elemental and integral to the final production as it will appear on the stage. If one considers the complexity of the task, it is understandable why "Please . . .," "Would you . . .?" and "I wonder if you could . . .?" are words and phrases rarely employed by those responsible for creating a successful musical.

This is not to say that the director is unconcerned with a true and an internalized life on the stage. But he or she will deal with these parts of the whole when the order of the sequence of things permits and will never give to them the minute attention to detail and lavish expenditure of time given to them by the director of a play.

Actors must learn to accept that an immigration into the country of musical theater means they will have to learn new laws not only because they are the laws of the land but because acceptance of them will ensure emotional survival. Toward that end I would suggest that it is good training for actors to begin to think of their work with some degree of distance and to put distance between themselves and others' perceptions of them. Once an actor is in a musical and experiences rehearsal procedures, he or she will be better able to understand that what is being edited by the director is not the person or the personality but the show itself.

A study experience is an ideal starting point in which to develop this distance. Don't bother to thicken your skin. Learn how to pivot so that you can deflect criticism away from yourself and onto your work. Criticism, after all, is not a moral judgment. It is a recognition that something is not working. Whether, when that something is fixed, the result is good or bad will be for the audience to decide. At that point, you and the creative staff will be together, side by side, on the firing line. What began as the hirer and the hired perceiving themselves on opposite sides always ends in this shared community.

3. *You Tell Me So Often That I "Do" Too Much. What Is Too Much and How Do I Know, in My Work, When I Am Guilty of It?*

This is not an easy one because the answer lies within the context of trust and taste.

Trust

You must remember that much of the success of what you are doing will be attributed to the mere fact that *you* are doing it. If who you are and how you project an ease in the presentation of yourself are combined with an interesting (both to the eye and to the ear) performance, there is no need to resort to busy-ness by pressing on the loud pedal. By *busy-ness*, I mean an insistence that it *is* you who is singing. But *you* are singing and to insist upon what is evident is not only redundant but counterproductive. After all, what is simple is pleasing to the eye. Too much hand- and foot-work can be a distraction away from *you* toward what you are *doing*. There is no denying that when a song is weak in melody or flabby in lyric or both, "keep moving" is an old show business rule of thumb that is as true today as it probably was on ancient Athenian stages. But if what you chose to sing and your performance of it has merit, why "argue" that the merit is there by resorting to over-decoration? You must learn to trust that you, the singer of the song, by virtue of the fact of your humanness, can be interesting. It is not so much a question of 'less is more' but that less may be more stageworthy.

Taste

Taste is a ticklish and dangerous word. It can be defined as an intuitive feeling for what is aesthetically right. But being able to define it does not necessarily imply that one possesses it. Without going into the deep waters into which a discussion of what constitutes good taste may lead, it is safe to say this: Any artist worth the name early on learns to put aside ego, or at the very least, to place it at the service of art. When you sing with imagination and taste, there is a fine and distinct balance between you, the song, and the audience. Each element is, or should be, so balanced that no of one part takes precedence over the whole. This is always made clear to us when we watch great performers like Lena Horne or Fred Astaire or Frank Sinatra at work. So finetuned is the balance of their personalities and the vocalization of the material that one forgets to study how their effects are achieved. Rarely does the song take preeminence over the sight and sound of them. When it is all over and we are back on the street, so plangent and indefinable are the overtones of the experience that the event is recalled only as time spent with the artist rather than the memory of the specific material that filled the time. Unless a signature song recalls a singer, as Garland's "Over the Rainbow" does—adjectives are all we employ to describe and define great performers. Unlike actors, who are remembered for the roles they play, singers are recalled for their tone and their texture. Lena is sexy and mocking, Astaire is urbane and elegant, and Sinatra is easygoing and approachable. How hard-won the battles are that these and all performers must fight to shape their art we only come to know when we ourselves have to fight them.

The balance, in your work, of taste and trust is a delicate one. In the case of taste, there is a distinct advantage in learning its outer limits before putting on display the corrected margins. William Blake once wrote, "You never know what is enough unless you know what is more than enough." To this can be added: When you know what is more than enough, you are able to recognize when enough *is* enough. Taste and trust can be cultivated. The former takes a lifetime of continual editing; the latter, a lot of personal forgiveness.

4. *More Often Asked by Women Than by Men: Why Am I Afraid to Deal with Passion in My Work?*

This is a volatile question in that any answer it invokes has within it the power to injure. It is important, as I try to respond to it, that you keep in mind the context in which the question is posed.

I am not a teacher who thinks of show business as a microcosm of life in general. This confession separates me from those instructors who bring a more worldly and psychological gauge to their work. The state of theater, television, and film is too much of a commercial enterprise manipulated by qualified and even unqualified business executives for me to sustain this delusion. When show business, and particularly musical theater show business, is the subject under discussion, the delusion is even more hallucinatory. Musicals are too expensive to risk being anything more than entertaining, while life, let us face it, is hardly a barrel of laughs. This being so, cans of peas and Pandora's boxes are behavioral containers I prefer not to open. My justification lies in the rationale that what a performer appears to be is finally all that matters. An audience believes what it sees, and it will see, on the stage, people whom other people have selected to be seen. That election has been made from the performer's demonstration of skills and not from medical dossiers. In my studio, very little discussion is concerned with the secrets hidden in the psychological biographies of those who study with me. To my surprise, students are often only too happy to air them. Acting classes may have inured them to discomfort, and perhaps even encouraged the practice. The musical theater, however, has no need for this kind of searching and probing. Casting is to type, and radical choices are rarely, if ever, made. If the script calls for a young soprano, a young soprano will be hired—and a pretty one, at that. Character actors, juveniles, ingenues, leading men, and leading women are chosen for their appearance and their talent to entertain. Since this is something everybody has to live with (with varying degrees of dissatisfaction), my line of sight, in my own case, is focused on the performance I am asked to critique. What I infer as I watch it is, with a great deal of effort, kept within the margins of what the casting people and, inevitably, the audience will see.

Training for musicals is serious business. One must learn to sing, to act, and even to dance (if only a little). These are not, by definition, grim activities, but anyone who undertakes their study learns that the cost of the education, in dollars and cents as well as in the pain endured in having to confront the elements that make each of us what we are, can be high.

I have said elsewhere that, when you sing, you cannot tell a lie. Songs, unlike plays, are essentially performed "in private," through that fourth wall where no one is permitted to hear them except Oscar Hammerstein's "big black giant"—the audience. They are truly soliloquies (*solus*, "alone," *loqui*, "to speak"). Their power to reveal character in all its guises is enormous. If there is truth in Flaubert's comment, "Of all the lies, art is the least untrue," the art of singing, at its most consummate, should present the singer at his or her most truthful.

The word *passion* is defined in a major dictionary as "a commanding, vehement or overpowering feeling of emotion," "abandonment of emotion," "amorous and strong sexual affection or desire."

All of this is known to us. If there are those who have never known passion, there is very little likelihood of meeting up with them in the arts. We deal with emotion because it is a basic tool of our trade. But there is a world of difference between experiencing passion in our private lives and calling it into public display for the purpose of interpreting the works of playwrights, librettists, composers, and lyricists.

Of course, "cool" actors have always been with us. To call them cool is not to judge them deficient. Much of what is comic, for example, gains its effect when the "temperature" on the stage is low. Cool singers, too, have successful careers, but my conviction is that the intellectual statement rises as the thermometer falls. Jazz, in its "cool" sense, profits from what the music is doing and not from what it is saying. The very word *cool* implies "free from excitement." The instrumentalist and the singer, alike, create excitement by "keeping their cool." But singing jazz on record or in a jazz joint is a far cry from singing in a show where the book and the score seek to involve the emotions rather than to keep them at arm's length.

And now to the arguable: Women, in the eighties, have trouble dealing with passion because the fashion of the time impels them to avoid any show of vulnerability, displays of emotion, and even demonstration of overt sexuality. With a stunning example of the collective unconscious at work, they will choose to play what is intellectual rather than risk deeper emotional waters. Unisex is their banner, and even their wardrobes proclaim it. For all our liberation, the end of this century finds us not much further down the path of enlightenment and true sexual freedom than we were before the phrase "raised consciousness" entered the language. Today's woman has paid a subtle but nevertheless pricey tab for the slogan "You've come a long way!" Show business may present us with a window in which sexual excess is offered for our delectation, but I wonder whether all that thrashing about is more clinical and joyless than emotionally stimulating. Garbo's Camille is hotter, by far.

Miss Garbo, Marilyn Monroe, Mae West, and today's Vanessa Redgrave, Jane Fonda, and Kathleen Turner were and are women whose womanliness is never considered a loss of sociopolitical standing but a sharing of what can only be explained as 'vive la différence!' Why is it, then, that when the actor-dancer-singer turns to song and its interpretation, something quite different asserts itself. It can be maintained that rock and roll lets it all hang out, but the gender blur is disconcerting. What we do not need now are evasive tactics. What we do need is an affirmation of who we are without embarrassment or risk of contempt from those who prefer to sidestep rather than leap into the fires of passionate abandon.

American men are no less guilty of dissembling. Threatened by Victorian labels that still continue to abuse them, the heterosexual male galumphs or freezes in order to affirm his "right-stuffness," while the homosexual male remains closeted in a low-risk shell. In Salonika, a city in northern Greece, I once saw two truck drivers come into a cafe where I had stopped for a coffee. They ordered lunch and, while they waited for their food, dropped a coin in the jukebox, threw their arms around each other and unselfconsciously began to dance. To add to my sense of dislocation, I was the only one who found it of interest. Watch Montand or Aznavour and you will see that men, when they sing, can use their physical and emotional equipment to their fullest. Their sexual tastes are their own business and, more to the point, not germane. They don't even come to mind as you watch them.

Why can't we open ourselves to passion? We can, but first we must be willing to plumb it. The best starting point I know is to be willing to place it at the service of song. The American poet and critic Paul Goodman once wrote, "whatever is a human passion may be expressed in music and whatever is music is in the human throat to imitate it." To deny the simple truth of this we need only stand in our own way. To suppress what is the essential heating agent in which music "cooks" is a denial of its essentiality. Passion and the song you sing, together, manifest the yin and the yang of great performing.

5. Why, if I Am "Feeling" a Song as I Sing It, Am I Surprised to Learn That the Listener Felt Nothing at All?

Most performers resist any attack against "feelings" and would reject the notion that, under certain circumstances, their private emotional responses might even be considered enemies. Many actors, dancers, and singers speak of their feelings as the mysterious source of their ability to move people. I have always been wary of turned-on feelings that turn off my mind and leave me in the thrall of their insidious power to dominate. Peter De Vries has said, "The purpose of art is to keep the guts tucked in—not to spill them." I believe great singing (performing) is an art.

Songs, and in particular popular and theater songs, deal in cheap currencies. One would have to have a heart of stone not to be touched by the sentiment, at best, and the bathos, at worst, of most of the music we hear today. Leaving aside the work of Stephen Sondheim, who alone writes with his mind as well as his heart, most songs are created to manipulate emotional responses, and if the song—and the singer singing it—cannot accomplish that, the arranger will make certain the accompaniment will. My distrust of feelings is justified, for when singers busy themselves exclusively with their feelings, I watch in fascination as they become the reactor to the song and, by so doing, join the audience in dangerous partnership. It is the business of the performer to *conduct* the emotional responses of the audience and that cannot be accomplished when the job is surrendered up to the artist's own response to his or her singing.

Further, feelings can be self-destructive. They can close throats, make eyes water, shorten breath, and, before performers realize it, cause them to become the victims of their songs—done in by the very weapons that were intended for others. Feelings can lead you into a subjective place where you do not even *require* an audience. Since all things that live on a stage take place, as Ring Lardner once said, in the "land of jeopardy"—namely, the audience's old complaint of "who cares?"—a heavy dose of subjective emotional excess can be a great jeopardizer.

I am not making a plea for intellectual performing, although I wish more performers would consider employing even a fraction of intellectualism in their work. However, it is important always to keep in mind that when you are working, whether it be on a stage, in a club on a floor, on record, or on the screen, it is *for* an audience. You are not singing for yourself alone—you can accomplish that in the bath—but *for* someone, *to* someone, and because that someone is *there.* Your ability to create the illusion that it is their very presence that produced the need to have a song to sing (and even more, the particular song you choose to sing) is what makes the bond between the audience and you a strong one. Great performing has its own physical laws. You get back what you give. It is like an electric circuit through which the current flows without a chance of shorting.

I said I am wary of feelings because they can short-circuit when they are not put to the task of offering themselves up to the listener as a heating agent in which the song can, so to speak, cook. They must not be kept to oneself. They must be shared. It is in the specific methods performers employ that feelings work *for* rather than *against* them. When you find yourself surprised that, although you have felt deeply what you sang, no one else felt anything at all, it is a sure bet you have just lived through thirty-two bars of your musical life unconnected and alone. Back, then, to the bath, where there is no jeopardy, except the possibility of slipping in the tub and doing harm to yourself. But isn't that peril a metaphor for what we have been describing?

---

6. *How Do I Learn to Choose Material I Know Will Be Right When No One Is There to Tell Me Which Song Is Good for Me and Which One Is Not?*

None of us are capable of total objectivity when we try to assess ourselves, but it is an impossible goal that has much to say for itself. As Federico Fellini once said, "Art is the most subtle mathematical operation." Figuring out, even in a fractional sense, what image we project in the marketplace is a valuable exercise, for we can then learn how best to shape that image and, most important of all, what tools we must use to enhance it. We all agree that what we wear is a packaging of sorts. What we sing is no less a one. It is my opinion, and I doubt whether anyone who casts musicals would argue it, that the failure of at least 85 percent of all auditions can be traced to the song(s) the performer chose to sing. Unless the hirer is sensitive enough to suggest a suitable substitution, you are "out" before you can even hope to be "in."

The distance you learn to put between who you think you are and how others perceive you is elementary to good personal merchandizing. Most of us spend years attempting to disentangle the confusion we experience as we try to match how others describe us to our own vision of ourselves. Muddles within muddles further confound this. Not only are we who we think we are but we are forever trying to improve the image. And not only are we seen by others as we are but also as they wish us to be or, worse, as they wish we were not. All of this can drive you up the wall. In any social encounter there is always the possibility that B will *not* find favor with A. An audition, though admittedly not social, nevertheless is an encounter in which B has more to lose than a new friend. In affairs of the heart one can rely on the operatives "love is blind" and "smoke gets in your eyes" not so much to clear up the muddles as to make them irrelevant. Unfortunately, unless parents, lovers, mates, and friends are casting the show, muddles are going to be the glass through which you are perceived darkly.

At the top of the list of those things that blind you at the moment of choice is your emotional response to a song. I do not mean that liking a song, by definition, is a good or a bad thing. It is only that it is of little or no consequence. What *is* important is whether the song carries its weight by performing its function: Does it show you off as you wish to be seen in the required circumstances of the audition? Does it advertise or betray your vocal ability to sing it? Is it a cliché standard that may be heard by those who are running the audition more times than someone could be expected to tolerate any song? These are the questions to ask yourself. If the song you then choose to sing is one you like to sing, consider yourself ahead. If it is not, but it fills the requirements that audition material must furnish you and then gets you the job, consider yourself truly ahead. (See "The Audition Process.") I have always felt that there is something to be said for singing songs you do not particularly care for. It can be good training for the songs you may be asked to sing in the musicals in which you find yourself.

A valuable set of songs that you will need for a general audition should include the following:

1. At the very least, two ballads that demonstrate vocal range. Ballads permit the listener to measure in a matter of minutes how much voice will be made available to the composer and the music director. They are, therefore, more difficult for the actor and the dancer—as set apart from the trained singer—to carry

off with conviction. Failings are immediately and glaringly obvious. Be sure not to give yourself the benefit of the doubt: stay away from songs that demonstrate that you cannot sing them. Remember: Auditions before musicians are auditions before knowledgeable judges. They may not know how to gauge a performance, but they can be relied upon to sift what they hear through educated ears and to measure its sufficiency against a good deal of know-how. Fancy footwork will not upstage vocal inadequacy.

2. You will need more than two rhythm songs because while songs in this category can all be defined as up-tempo, they can be disparate in sound. Why rhythm songs? Because, unlike the ballads you will choose, they offer you material in which you can present your "way" with a song. I suggest your personal selection include:

(*a*) A show tune that is not only theater-oriented but able to display you at your most comfortable. (See question number 8.)

(*b*) A contemporary song that will demonstrate that rock, country-western, and their derivatives and variations are part of the cultural sound of your generation and speak (sing) in a musical language you know. If it is not a language you know, *do not sing it.* Imitation of the real thing can be painful to behold. Can this kind of song be learned in a thirteenth-hour race against the clock? Only your performance can answer that.

(*c*) A Savoy-type song. You will only need one of these in your repertoire. With the success of Joseph Papp's production of *The Pirates of Penzance*, a rash of productions have been cloned and the Gilbert and Sullivan patter song has influenced young composers and lyricists because the form presents a glittering opportunity to flaunt the lyricist's ability to rhyme. All that is required here is a heightened sense of the power of words, what rhymes are about, and how well they can be articulated. Since the lyric is all, the vocal line and its range can swing from the simple to the simplistic. Need your choice come from nineteenth-century England? Not at all. Riffle through the complete published works of Cole Porter and Noel Coward and through some of Sondheim's songs, and you will have a fair selection of what the best of patter is all about.

3. One or even two "heavy" songs that will give you an opportunity to show your ability to deal with drama. Here, too, the lyric will be important, since it will furnish you with script. However, much of the value of this kind of song lies in the composer's contribution. Do not forget that music has extraordinary power to move the listener with its own language. For example, if you are able to sing and perform songs like Rodgers's "Soliloquy" from *Carousel,* Weill's "Lonely House" from *Street Scene,* or Sondheim's "I'm Still Here" from *Follies,* the chances are you are as good a singer as you are an actor. (*Note:* I do not offer these titles as suggestions for audition material. One is too long and oversung, one is an aria of sorts and difficult to sing, and one is long and too self-serving.) As your abilities tilt the scale in favor of one at the expense of the other, be sure your choice of song mirrors the gain or the loss.

4. Miscellany: This group of songs will always be dependent on your special talent to amuse. If you tell a good story, have a narrative song that shows that to be so. There is no need to learn one if you are not, by nature, a storyteller. A miss here is a mile. Narrative songs live in the doing and not in the telling of them. See Danny Kaye at his singular best to measure yourself against a master. If you are a dancer who sings, you should have a song in which you can stage some choreographed work. A vocal, followed by two or three "eights" danced, and a possible reprise of the last "eight" sung are sufficient not only to proclaim your proficiency but to ensure that you do not overstay your welcome. If you are demonstrably a singer, one or two songs that display some vocal fireworks would be valuable.

5. The cry for comedy material has echoed down the halls of time since the first job giver said to the first job seeker, "Have you got a funny song?" From the dourest to the drollest, every actor, dancer, and singer searches for three minutes of published comedy that they can sing even if they do not possess a grain of humor. Let it now be said: There is no such thing as three minutes of published comedy material that everyone has not heard so often that boredom, rather than amusement, would be engendered with yet another rendering. This may not be true if the creative staff is under thirty and not conversant with yesterday's howlers. Circumstances will then have granted you the reprise. But I stand by my guns with the following advice:

There are those among us who, possessed of a gift from the gods, are funny, and there are those who, deprived of the gift, are not. The idea that a funny song is funny no matter who sings it is as absurd as the thought that every old actor is Lear. What is implied, when you are asked for a funny song, is not a number but evidence that you can be amusing. That quality may well be within the range of many actors, dancers, and singers who may not be relied upon to tell a joke but can be trusted not to kill one. There are many songs that can be used to demonstrate that you are one of those without proclaiming yourself a comic, comedian, or clown. Often an oblique approach to a straight song can do it for you. An extreme example of this would be Mel Brooks's and Anne Bancroft's duet in *To Be or Not to Be* of "Sweet Georgia Brown" in Polish. A characterization placed over a standard can reveal a sense of humor. I recall an audition by a well-known actor who gave a tipsy, but nevertheless lovesick, reading of Gershwin's "S'Wonderful" that scored admirably. Noel Coward's "Chase Me Charlie" works if the lady singing the song becomes the amorous cat aching for Charlie to jump over the wall. The point is that, if you are someone with a comic imagination, the possibilities are as many as you are able to invent. If, however, you are not, by nature, a funny soul, no published or unpublished song I know of will provide what the gods have denied you. Robertson Davies, the Canadian novelist, in describing one of his characters in *The Rebel Angels* writes: "What he has is wit, not humor, and wit turns inward. Wit is something you possess, but humor is something that possesses you." You can buy the wit of Noel Coward and Cole Porter, both of whose collected works are now available in print, but much of what may be considered by many as serious can be transmuted into comedy by those who are possessed by humor.

When all your material is chosen, learned and rehearsed, it is a good idea to purchase two copies of each song. One copy will be treated much as an actor notates a script. Write on it all pertinent information concerning phrasing, subtext, staging—all these, having been recorded, will recall your performance whenever you pick up the song. A second copy should be reserved for your accompanist or any pianist who will have to play it. It should be clean and clear, and you should follow these guidelines:

1. Note, at the top of the sheet music, the key in which the song is to be played. You should not mark a key with six or seven sharps or flats unless you will always have your own pianist on call. No pianist should be expected to sight-read, for example, into the key of F sharp major when F major and/or G major are easier keys to play in under pressure.

2. Notate all cuts and additions, special "vamps" and extended "rideouts"—any and all information essential to the accompaniment you expect to receive. These changes, additions, and corrections must be inserted in legible print.

3. If you use an arrangement of the song that is too complicated to record on the sheet music, have it written out by a qualified copyist.

4. If you are using a photocopy of the sheet music, tape the pages together in the proper order to facilitate rapid and manageable page turning.

5. Finally, do not mar, fold, bend, or stain the copies that pianists will have to read and play.

As in the case of the clothes you choose to wear to an audition, the songs you choose to sing should present your assets and cannily dissemble your liabilities. Don't forget: you are packaging a product—yourself. The best and the worst of products still require only the best packaging. As in the merchandizing of anything, shrewd presentation can make a product attractive to the purchaser even when it may be less than what it claims to be. In the show business world of auditioning for work, the purchaser is the hirer. The cautionary warning can be rewritten to read: Let the seller beware.

7. *What Are the Problems Inherent in Singing a Ballad?*

Ballads are slow scripts. Unlike spoken soliloquies, they are not delivered at your tempo but in the time signature decreed by the composer. As they spin themselves out, they emerge in a stately and noble rhythm. It is all too easy, when you first hear yourself sing one, to define ballads (from the actor's point of view) as plodding and even leaden.

All songs are sung with a constantly moving subtext that sustains the consistency of the song's flow. It should be clear that a ballad, necessarily flowing slowly, requires a more intricate subtext to support it and to keep it interesting. It is important to remember an old show business truism: Speed—that which is fast or slow—in the theater is achieved by sustaining interest and not, as at a racetrack, by maintaining motion. We have all experienced situations such as watching a farce that, although it is played at a breakneck pace, still leaves us yawning, and we have all sat, riveted in our seats, as we witness the slow, but enthralling progression of a space-shuttle countdown. Ballads gain speed to that degree that you can keep your "thinking" interesting.

From a vocal standpoint, all ballads are slow, but they do not need a heavy overlay of body language. In point of fact, they can get by, and often do, with almost none, although I do not recommend its total absence. What a ballad requires is that it "sit" on the singer with a specific sense of place and of focus and a reason to sing it. When these are all set into motion, there is a distinct sense of physical comfort experienced by the singer. Subtract these elements and replace them with only the lyric itself, and you have made "mono" what should have been stereophonic. The body immediately tightens and becomes self-conscious. Deprived of sensible motor responses, it can only perform mindlessly, or worse, in a charade of the lyric. For the listener, there is a sliding scale of forgiveness: the better the voice, the more willing we are to settle for less to look at. You can sometimes see this taken to its final absurdity at the opera, although, even there, vocal splendor and dramatic tension can, and in rare instances, do co-exist.

Just as the actor has much to learn from the craft of the singer, the singer must learn that language lives on many significant levels. The verbal statement of the song is only the tip of the iceberg. The language sung in a ballad, to keep the metaphor going, is more beneath than above water level. Beyond a good articulation of the lyric, you should deal with what the song is about and not with what it says. When you do this, a ballad can, figuratively, pick up tempo because it literally picks up interest as it goes. Irwin Edman, in his preface to *The Works of Plato*, has written, "It is a question among psychologists whether thought is not simply mute speech, words without the music of the voice." When you sing, thought is given speech, because the words are given music. Each is bound together to achieve . . . a stately, noble language.

8. *What Are the Problems Inherent in Singing a Rhythm Song?*

In your repertoire, rhythm, or upbeat, songs are essential baggage. For the actor and the dancer, they seem to promise a safe place in which to take up residence. The classic assumption is that speed of delivery will conceal any vocal inadequacy. As for the singer, a rhythm song either will sit well or not, depending not so much on voice as on a native coziness with jazz. When the singer has moved far away from his or her beginnings and is identified as "classical," the performance of a rhythm song looks and sounds as if it were picked up in a Berlitz beginner course. Let's take a look at each group separately:

For the Actor

1. Most actors, at the start of their singing studies, do not experience anything near joy; rhythm songs, as a genre, tend to deal with that emotion—and often in an unmodified way. The appearance of an actor imitating what is clearly not felt can work extreme damage to the sight and sound of the person.

2. If the actor's knowledge of how to "work" a song is primitive, a rhythm number will betray this lack of skill. Speed of delivery calls for a facile and polished technique. Without this, what you see may border on the manic. The most practical and effective way I have found to teach elementary technical exercises is to place them on ballads. Their very slowness allows the performer more time to co-ordinate focus changes, body language, and good phrasing. A ballad, after all, is nothing more than a slow rhythm number. As technical facility increases, the performer begins to understand that a rhythm number is nothing more than a fast ballad.

For the Dancer

1. Dancers err in thinking that rhythm, when vocalized, will afford them the same sensation they experience when all they have to do is move to it. The truth is that, just as actors who sing tend to forget everything that defines them *as* actors, dancers may go rigid when they, who were once mute, become possessed of a voice.

2. You cannot dance and sing at the same time. You can dance and then you can sing and/or you can sing and then dance, but you cannot do them both simultaneously. Of course one can, but doing them in a rhythm song can be self-annihilating. Watch Astaire and see how simple he keeps his physical life when he is singing an "up" tune. Even though film permits dubbing (as a weapon against breathlessness) one never sees him tapping around the floor when the song is first stated. True, a dancer's "fills" may be more sophisticated than an actor's and a singer's, but the actual dancing only begins with the end of the vocal.

3. Sooner or later, a dancer's audition must include rhythm material, because it can be danced to after it is sung. Therefore, a rhythm number gives the dancer some degree of exclusivity. This is not to say that Ella Fitzgerald and Mel Tormé do not "swing," but they do not "sway." Astaire and Kelly do both.

For the Singer

1. If, in your singing life, you worship before the throne of sheer sound, rhythm songs, with very few exceptions, do not afford an opportunity to practice your religion. True, a rideout can get an audience to its feet when it is effulgently belted out for eight, ten or twelve bars. I have even seen the lie put to the old chestnut that a "rideout does not a song make," but we can all agree that there has to be more to a song than its finish.

2. Good rhythm songs may possess good words, but if they don't, they are better sung in clubs or in concert than at auditions. Singers sing vowels with more splendor than actors and dancers do, but vowels need consonants before and aft, which, in turn, make words. Often a beautifully sung "up" tune is not as valuable as a well-articulated one. This is especially true of the songs of Cole Porter and Noel Coward. It is no accident that their rhythm songs were not introduced by legit singers but by performers who could sell as well as sing.

3. Rhythm songs delight in a swinging performance. Purity of tone and a slavish attention to the score are inimical to a successful presentation of the material. Without attempting to define *square* to the uninitiated, it will appear that allegiance to tone and nothing more will make heavy what is meant to be light, and render earthbound that which should fly.

And so actors, dancers, and singers, each in their own way, share different manifestations of the same disease. Remember, then:

1. If ballads, because they are slow, require a complex thought process to sustain a script that threatens always to sag, rhythm songs need very little. One objective, one attitude, even one point to be made can see you through an eight-bar phrase.

2. Locate any physical tension; isolate and rid yourself of it. Pay particular attention to unlocking your fists and monitoring the rising and tightening of your shoulders. Tension in both these locations are dead giveaways of resistance somewhere along the line.

3. Stop the tapping foot and the snapping fingers. The orchestra will take care of establishing and maintaining tempos.

4. Keep your breath moving and remember to re-inspire what you have expired.

5. Resist the claim that, because you are a square, rhythm songs will never be well sung by you. I do not mean to imply that each of us can hope to hear what Mel Tormé or Ella Fitzgerald hears, but jazz of one kind or another is an American birthright. It bombards our ears every hour of our waking lives on radios, turntables, Muzak, and soundtracks beyond the tolerance of even the most passionate chauvinist. Recognize that if you are uncomfortable with this kind of song, you are, to some degree, suppressing a legacy that is the essence of what rhythm is all about. So, relax, and . . .

6. Go with the song, and . . .

7. Enjoy.

9. *What Do I Do with My Hands and My Feet?*

This question is the great tormentor that perplexes almost everyone who stands up and sings—and many others who just stand up.

Hands and feet have lives that are led and dictated by what we are thinking. When you stop telling them what to do, or worse, fail to deal with the significance of the lyric (which is what creates organic body language) they will go up, go down, go out, then up and down and out again in an endless semaphoric ballet of nonsensical gesture. They can be as destructive as a two-year-old reaching for a crystal ashtray on the coffee table. Like two-year-olds, they want to be told; to be given the margins of permissible behavior. When those margins are not defined, hands, feet, and children, will test you in order to find out how far they may go before you yell, "Stop!"

When I teach, I tend to yell "Stop!" early in the game, because I ask a "good nothing" from the performer before a "good something" can be trusted. Also, when the quality of the body language is of little to no value, nothing is to be preferred. What people do not see, they cannot fault. The performer's intention may well have been to stand there and sing. "Do" something, and that something is immediately vulnerable to criticism.

There are some people—rarer than unicorns—who have never thought about their hands when they sing. They move them and define shapes that flow from one beau gesture to another with the grace of a Makarova. "Pretty" hands are not, in themselves, without virtue. But they are, finally, decoration. How long can decoration remain pleasing to the eye? Not long enough. We may like what we see, but a law of diminishing returns is soon operative. Since decoration is less than skin-deep, emotional response to it is cut off by the very prettiness of what the eye sees.

There is only one way I know of to erase physical self-consciousness: You must not busy yourself thinking only what the audience hears you singing. Think only of the words, and you will paralyze or, worse, pictorialize. Mindless gesture and shameless indicating (in the actor's meaning of the word) will be what you get for the price you pay.

But hands have a disturbing habit of wanting to get into the act. As a rule, they are always too high and too wide when they have little or nothing to say. It is good training to teach them their place. If they can perform their task lower, teach them to do so. Remember that it is not the doing of something that is valuable but how *well* you do it. How well you do it will be advertised by how well you get in and out of what you are doing. Wide and high may have their moment in the sun but then what? Where do they go next? Too wide and too high? And how do they get there without betraying a manifest lack of style?

Only when you are free of the script (lyric) of the song, will you find your hands and your feet and, for that matter of fact, all of you, behaving in a sane and human manner. But this requires more than learning the song. Your imagination, your sense of *why* you are singing it, your skill at creating conflict (drama), your attention to the significance of what you are saying (singing)—all of these, supported by a sane focus directed through the fourth wall, will introduce you to what singing and, in fact, life is all about. We speak because an idea occurs to us and we feel the need to communicate it. We sing because the idea is more important, more urgent, more needful of the language of music to make itself understood. Music gives speech a greater dynamic. You have only to watch great singers (performers) at work to realize the tyranny they hold over your attention.

As you increase your power to work *through* the song as well as to *sing* it, you may find no need to move. The script may be too dense to permit it. But when what you sing is insufficient to the task of explicating your thought process, move you will by virtue of the fact that . . . you are thinking.

What do you do with your hands and your feet? Leave them where they are. Allow them to execute their contribution to your performance when they must. Just as they function when you speak, they will do what they have to do to complete the "picture" of what you have to sing.

10. *What Is the Simplest Method for Picking up a Song and Knowing What to Do with It* (Other Than Merely *Singing* It?)

In a sense, all songs tell you what to do with them. What the lyric says and the weight of how it says it provide a clear message of its inherent strength. When a lyric is not so much weak as it is simplistic ("I'm Gonna Wash That Man Right out of My Hair" from *South Pacific*), I would not lean too heavily on it. But when the words are profound ("Pretty Women" from *Sweeney Todd*), or deeply personal ("Time Heals Everything" from *Mack and Mabel*), or complicated in their poetic structure ("Pretty Little Picture" from *A Funny Thing Happened on the Way to the Forum*), or busy in the speed in which they have to be delivered ("Another Hundred People" from *Company*), or witty ("You're the Top" from *Anything Goes*), these qualities allow you not only to lean on the song but to trust that it will support you. Remember:

1. Body language and well-executed focus are the tools you work with to make the meaning of the song readily understandable. See questions 3 and 14.)

2. I have said that you cannot lie when you sing. Each song you perform is *your* song. Therefore, you cannot moralize or be wiser than it is. The listener may opt to take sides, but all that is denied *you*.

3. Just as you cannot be wiser than what you sing, you cannot be less wise. One demand among many that the work of Porter, Coward, and Sondheim places on the performer is that, since the song is yours (they may have written it but you are singing it), you have been recast into a person of wit and urbanity and—in the case of Sondheim— someone possessed of an ironic knowledge of behavior under stress and a unique personal understanding of the human condition.

4. You must never seem to be commenting on what you sing, in the sense that your performance choices appear to belie the lyric. If you disagree with what the song says, either dissemble the disagreement or do not sing it at all.

5. The degree of busy-ness you place on a song should be measured by the importance of what you are saying. If you want them to listen, don't give them too much to look at. If there is very little to listen to, don't bring that to their attention by giving them nothing to look at. In the theater, you can trust a cardinal principle: an audience will always look *before* they listen or, worse, look *instead* of listen. It is not even a question of choice. You can take their attention away from anything being said with just the slightest movement, for even that will catch their eye and close their ear.

A further sad but true point of order: Audiences ain't what they used to be. In the first half of this century, ticket prices ranged from 50 cents to $5. But, while the box office may have been populist, what was seen on stage ranged from low- to high-brow. To go to the theater was a natural and unexclusive act—the culmination of hundreds of years when it was the only available entertainment. Since the fifties, with the cost of tickets as high as $50, the box office has priced itself out of affordability. A large fraction of the audience has turned to the movies, to public and cable television, and, in extremis, to conversation and reading. With a new, financially elitist box office, what is offered on the stage has had to accommodate itself to a different, more innocent audience whose ability to pay is the prime essential. Their limited attention span and their contempt for silence during the proceedings are responses conditioned by the hold television exerts on the listener. I know these are incendiary words, and there are rare exceptions that put the lie to them, but today's musical theater relies on spectacle, sequins, and sets as much as, if not more than, on what is being said and sung. And if it doesn't, at those prices, it had better do so if it wants to attract the kind of people who can afford to pay.

What has all this to do with the topic under discussion? Where once an audience could be trusted to understand and be amused by

> Where is the old-fashioned boy?
> The kind who thought Freud
> Was German for joy?*

*From *The Garrick Gaieties of 1926*.

today it probably would be cut, if it was written at all. And if it did survive the scissors, the performer, obeying the rule of, "If you want them to listen, don't move," wouldn't dare to raise an eyebrow, let alone a hand, if he wanted to be heard—and even then I doubt if the couplet would get a snicker.

Songs also tell you how dense a subtext you need. Some songs, again in the case of Sondheim, live in tension and sing in a language ripe with overtone. Their subtexts are more complicated because the "heard" speech is vivid, metaphoric, and often allusive. This is not to say that they call for the kind of thinking that creates body language, but elevated speech is not well-served by an empty mind. Other songs, perhaps as good, speak more directly and say exactly what they mean.

The more you sing and perform well, the more the question of "What do I *do* with a song?" ceases to plague you, because a growing sense of personal style, in all your singularity, appears on whatever you sing. You will become more aware of how and why you move. Things do get easier as you become more skillful. This last sentence is a perfect example of speech that is not elevated. Were you to sing it, I would suggest a great deal of movement.

11. *When I Have Auditioned, Why Do I Feel, in Fact, Know, That I Could Have Performed Better if I Had Had the Chance to Sing the Song Twice—or Better Still, Three Times?*

This question is less revealing of the nature of an audition than it is of the nature of the performer. In the classes I teach, it is cousin to: "It went so much better at home." (See question 1.) Both the question and the claim are blood relatives because they share the same answer.

When you use a song to excite you into singing it, you are reversing the process of what singing is about. It is *your* energy and passion that give the song its life. Music on paper is a matter of print, not fuel. It is you who are moved to sing a song and not the reverse. When a song is asked to energize the singer, anything can affect the performance. The menace of an audition or even a class will weigh you down with distraction, and only repetition can neutralize its power to destroy—or so you believe.

It is something of an insanity to ask that a song fuel and move you. Yes, it has the capability to excite you and your audience. But that force, very much like its atomic counterpart, packs a lot of destructive energy. It can do you in if you fail to manipulate it to your advantage.

When you create the *need* to sing, you create a song to sing. At least, that is the impression a great performer leaves—that there never was that song until he, she or you chose, at that instant, to sing it. When need births song, its implicit power can be "read" on the audience to the extent that *they* appear to be moved.

We have only the word of the actor-dancer-singer when he or she reports on the excellence of work at home. I have often wished I had been there to see it, hidden behind a drape; perhaps then a more objective assessment could have been made. We will never know. Even if we grant the performer's ability to hold the scales as well as sing them, what he or she is experiencing is the freedom to sing out without any outside judgment placed on the act. Work that went so much better at home went so much better because it took place there. Unless audiences can, throughout your career, be crowded in and seated behind that drape, you will have to go public. Then the joy of singing will be found less in the freedom to sing than in doing it well. Creating a song from moment to moment from the vamp through the rideout will assure you a first performance not in need of a second or a third.

A great teacher once said, "Don't come out thinking, 'I've got a great song to sing,' but 'I've got a great song to sing for you!'" Replace your need for approval with a sense of your right to sing whatever you choose to sing. There is no law I know of that forbids anyone that right. There is only one law in show business: Do it well.

12. *How Do I Get Past Technique and Begin to Surrender to Music?*

This is not a universal question. There are many singers who surrender to music with wholehearted abandon. Unhindered by anything on their minds, they experience a kind of primitive pleasure in "singing out." Unbounded energy has its virtues. Its single drawback is known to us all—and if you have not learned it yet, wait. As one grows older, *energy* may remain in our virtue column but *unbounded* is retired from our vocabulary. The question becomes operative when the actor, the dancer, and the more sophisticated singer of songs learn the importance of knowledgeable underpinning to support their work and upon which they can rely:

Let us agree that education is painful. There is a kind of comfort in ignorance. As the old chestnut goes, it is bliss. Take one step out of empty-headedness and you are on the road to a life in which what you know you don't know can be a constant cause of torment. The quest for knowledge is like climbing an endless series of hills. Each time we accrue whatever we think we need to make us wiser, the horizon presents still another hill to climb. When you scan the topography of singing, there are many hills (thought processes) to scale. For example:

1. The song itself has a melody and a rhythmic clothing that must be delivered as the composer, the lyricist, and the arranger designed them.

2. Phrasing, or the strategy of when and where to breathe (or merely remembering to breathe at all), is, at the very least, a matter of survival and ideally allows the audience to hear a sane rendering of the lyric.

3. Proper vocal production is paramount since it ensures audibility and the singer's continued good health.

4. Subtext, or that which defines the song and sustains its interest, is another important consideration. Songs, like words, are born of idea, and a consistent flow of ideas permits the audience not only to *hear* but to *comprehend* the lyric.

5. Body language is the result of motor responses to impulses that originate in the brain. When the mind signs off, hands and feet indicate their mindlessness.

6. Focus, the "to whom are you singing?" element of your performance is an indicator of sanity. Rolling eyeballs do not advertise a sound mind.

When all these technical demands are met, the audience hears and sees what appears to be an easy performance. They are singularly unaware of how it is achieved. And so they should be. Technique is not their business and, although it is the business of the performer, no one can estimate how long its study takes before it is computerized into habit. Some of us are slow and some are fast. The tortoise and the hare have taught us that achievement is measured only at the finish line.

There does come the time when habit makes it easier to surrender to the sheer act of making music, but I wonder if any of us ever indulges in *total* surrender. A small voice is always there to alert us when necessary. I cannot believe that we would have it otherwise.

13. *How Does a Planned Audition for the Stage Change When I Discover It Must Be Performed in a Room—Large or Small?*

This problem has become so commonplace today that I have begun to think that a musical that will inevitably be played on a stage may very well be cast with performers who have never stood on one. Is there a difference? Yes. Singing in a room and singing on a stage are two quite different exercises. Casting directors appear to have no problem with this but I know the performer is not as untroubled. (See "The Audition Process.") I wonder, too, how affectionate casting directors would have been toward the young Ethel Merman had she auditioned 4 feet away from them? I know of many established singers who cannot work under such intimate conditions. There are singers who have no trouble with the loss of space but who might not have the size to fill a major musical theater house. And are the casting director and the creative staff able to tell the difference?

But the reality must be faced. Economics may have forbidden the rental of a theater. Major musicals may be cast in large rooms and small musicals in small rooms and, in both cases, adjustments will have to be made when what you planned to do was conditioned by the demands of a stage. Two factors are important:

1.　If you are singing a ballad where simplicity is all, you will have to alter nothing. If you were prepared to show more because the song required more, things will have to be scaled down.

2. How much you will have to scale things down will be decreed by the space between you and those before whom you will be auditioning. When that space gains distance, you can afford to cut less. If they are "on top" of you, what might have looked stylish on a stage will look too large, too busy, and too much. Another adjustment: if you had played wider to the left and right, less wide will be more beneficial.

There will be other obstacles. The room you are in may double as a dance studio, and you will find yourself facing a wall of mirrors: resist the urge to watch yourself at work. Those auditioning you may be sitting in front of a row of windows: ignore the irritating glare. There will be small comfort in thinking, "Better me than they," but it is true that if *they* are blinded, they will be unable to see your work. Not being able to be see *them* can even be reckoned a blessing.

Let us face it: auditions for musicals range from ideal to downright hell. Adjustments will have to be made each time you enter a room. Particular circumstances may make them more or less murderous. The trick is not to be the murdered victim. Fight to keep up your personal fourth wall no matter how difficult it is to construct. Even cellophane-thin, it is your shield.

14. *Should I Work Directly to Those Who Are Auditioning Me; Should I Make Eye Contact?*

No.

Considered from Their Line of Sight

You are robbing them of their task. They are there to watch and assess what you are doing and how well you sing and to place all this within the allowable givens of their requirements. If, by working eye-to-eye with them, you force them to forsake these functions, the confrontation is a waste of time. When someone sings to and at you, you feel impelled to react. If you are a decent sort, an insipid smile settles on your face as you try your best to look receptive and approving. The whole affair becomes ironically depressing. The smile doesn't fool anyone, least of all the person who is singing to you.

Considered from Your Line of Sight

The songs you sing do not concern the person(s) auditioning you. *How* you sing them does. To be told that, "Someday he'll come along, the man I love," presumes that the auditioner is interested in hearing about it. When a woman sings the song to a man (or men), he (or they) may feel discomforted but the damage will not be great, even though he is not the man who will be coming along. But consider a man singing to a man, "I love you, hums the April breeze." What was an audition is now an absurdity. The actor may justify the choice of eye-to-eye focus with the rationale that a song seems more important when a human being, and not the figment of one, is receiving the information. To him, the gender of this person is not integral—not even under consideration. He is probably not even aware of it. It is the reality of someone *being there* that he is using and nothing more, or personal, is meant. All this may be so, but in no way does it erase the discomfort of those who are on the receiving end of the song.

The simple fact is that eye-to-eye contact is denied you. The denial is evident. When you are on a stage, it is difficult to see anyone out front, and even if you could, the restrictions set up by the presence of the fourth wall forbid it. Of course, if you are addressed by a "voice" from out of that source (your new reality, namely: being drawn into a conversation with someone), you will then have to make an effort to see the someone who is talking to you. Apropos of that, I offer a small warning: Answer whatever is asked of you but resist small talk, banter, and any effort at ingratiation. Remember, you are there to perform. You are, after all, on a stage and not in a cabaret. Putting your stage performance into a room may place a strain on that fourth wall, but it must not and should not eradicate it entirely.

Working in a room creates new imperatives. If you are close to those auditioning you (up to 12 feet is a good gauge of distance), work to a spot that is eye level to you. Another method of judging that height would be to imagine that you are singing to someone as tall and no taller than you are. Since you will be singing to people who are sitting in front of you, you will not be singing *to* them but just over their heads. As the distance between you increases, this level of focus will seem more comfortable. As it decreases, your ability to invest that focus with a "life" to which you can react is arguably taxed. Nevertheless, the odd thing about focus is that it appears to be true when it is experienced truly.

Just as eye-to-eye contact is senseless, working *too high* in a room that does not possess a mezzanine and balconies can be equally maddening to the beholder. It is interesting to note that when you are working on a stage, focus height does not rise as much as you would imagine. Again, eye level will be high enough with an occasional reference that may take in the now existing mezzanine and balcony.

Focus choices for a "house number" (any song that does *not* have an explicit "you" or where the "you" stated means "you all") liberate you and allow you to sing not to one but to one and all. Where to work to can be answered by asking yourself these two questions:

1. Is it a "power line"? This can be defined as the first time you sing the title of the song, a joke, the very top of the song, the top of the bridge or release, or the last line or moments of the rideout. All of these lines in a lyric have innate importance and should be spotted center (in front of you). Any major points (power lines) you make are squandered if they were thrown to the sides of the house.

2. Is the line of interest to everybody? Is it a repeat of the title? A setup *for* the joke? The line(s) preceding the release and the rideout line? These can be focused anywhere *but* center. They can be spotted generally around the room or the theater, or you may elect to direct them to the left or the right of a center spot.

Are focus choices pretty much frozen once you have made them? I would have to say yes. Until you know instinctively what you are doing, better safe than sorry. Nothing I know demonstrates sanity more than eyes that behave intelligently, and nothing I know betrays the amateur more than eyes that have no clear notion of the rule of "to whom am I singing?"

Two further rules of thumb:

1. Always sing in the place in which you are singing. If it is a room, do not fantasize it into a theater. If it is a theater, increase the intensity of your performance so that it can be seen to reach the back wall. Another way of defining this would be to know the size of the space in which you are working and deal with it accordingly.

2. When you feel comfortable with the level of your focus, it is probably (from the point of view of the spectator) too high and too wide. You will appear to be singing to walls (or boxes) or to the ceiling (balcony). Lower and narrow your targets.

Your choice of where and to whom you choose to sing must never be provocative. Attention to your work must generate interest and not confusion. If those who are casting the show are thinking, "Why is she singing to me?", "Why is he singing to that door?", "Why is she singing to the sky?", "Why is he *doing* that?"—whatever is good about your work will be lost in the distraction occasioned by these questions.

A good performance is seen and described in its entirety. When any one thing takes precedence over the whole, be assured that your lack of skill has been confirmed. "If it can be seen, it isn't any good" was a piece of advice given to me by an eminent teacher as she struggled to explain the essence of bad acting. It is also a definition of bad performing.

15. *What Do I Do When the Pianist at an Audition Refuses to Play the Music I Hand Him or Her?*

Don't argue.

Although I stress the dangers inherent in singing with a pianist who has never seen your music, the sorry truth is that lack of money or thirteenth-hour battle conditions may force you to rely on the kindness of strangers.

At an audition, strange pianists (ones you do not know) can be strange bedfellows. *You* require them but *management* employs them. Thus, they appear to have a foot on both sides of the fence, but don't you believe it. Their allegiance belongs to the boss. I do not want to imply that they are the enemy, but even the most benign among them must never be treated lightly.

To make matters worse, musicians have a powerful union that is protective and supportive. No matter how draconian the measures taken may be to support a failing show, musicians never feel the pinch. The cast is asked to take cuts, and they often do; the writers (composer, lyricist, and librettist) may be asked to forfeit royalty payments, and they often do; the producer(s) may be forced to surrender fractional pieces of the action—but the salaries of musicians are as fixed as the sun. This gives them a sense of importance and explains why other artists perceive them as secure and free of care when a musical is in trouble. It has always been my belief that this immunity has a reassuring effect on pianists and allows them to feel somehow superior to the performers who pass through a day of audition playing. A low threshold of tolerance is also traceable to the lines of singers who hand over barely legible copies of music and undernotated arrangements in keys no one can be expected to master at sight.

I have known excellent pianists who can play anything (leaving aside a Sondheim song in C sharp major) after a moment's scrutiny. I have known others (who, by the way, receive the same wages as the more able ones) who can barely play "Chopsticks." What is even more alarming is that no one out front can tell the difference between the two . . . or so it seems. It is a roulette game, and you will never know if you will be safe and secure or dead and buried.

But whether a particular pianist is or is not competent, certain truths about pianists in general must be acknowledged:

1. Because they are employed by management, they can be expected to know what, in particular, the staff is looking for. Anyway, more than you do.

2. Even if they are motivated by boredom rather than Good Samaritanism, they can deter you from singing what is certain not to score—if they are of a mind to.

3. You may define as obduracy their refusal to play what you have placed before them, when it is only an attempt to discover if you brought with you something more fitting for the occasion. And you should have brought enough variety of material for just this kind of emergency.

Therefore, if the pianist refuses to play, take heed to his or her alternative suggestions. If you are advised to sing sixteen bars of anything other than what you were prepared to perform, do it. If the pianist proposes "Happy Birthday" because you have nothing more suitable and "Happy Birthday" is, at least better than what you brought—do it. The thing is: don't argue. Good gamblers recognize when the odds are stacked against them. (See "The Audition Process for a more detailed definition of how to keep the odds in your favor.)

16. *Is a Knowledge of Music an Essential Requirement for Getting into a Musical?*

I assume this means you cannot play an instrument or read music at all. Rest easy. The answer is a resounding *no!*

A musical is a construction. It employs the talents of dozens of artists and artisans. With the exception of an opera production, nothing as complicated exists in the theater. A list of the highest to the lowliest of people without whom a show could not be created, or be maintained, is awesome.

It must be clear that no one element of the machine could hope to know all there is to know about each component part. It is true that there are conductors who are instrumentalists. There are actors and singers who can dance, and singers and dancers who can act, and even that rare bird who can do all three. There are choreographers who can direct, and directors who can do the lighting for a show. I have known composers and/or lyricists who can sing as well, if not better, than the cast the audience will hear sing the score. But all this prolifigacy is finite. No one can do it all.

Music is the most arcane ingredient of a musical. How songs are created, written down, scored, and arranged is, more than likely, outside the scope of what most of us know. It is an exalted and noble art that, unless years are given to its study, remains outside the comprehension of the average person. Therefore, there is a staff of musicians to deal with the average person during the rehearsal stage of a show. Actors who have signed a "white contract"* will be taught what they have to sing by the composer or one and sometimes two pianists who will be on call for just that purpose. Constant repetition of the score during the weeks of rehearsal will enable the performer,

---

*In the musical theater there are white and pink contracts. A white contract signifies that the performer is listed in the cast of characters, in a plot line, and therefore will be speaking and singing on stage. Pink contracts are signed by members of the singing and dancing ensembles.

even if he or she cannot read or play a note of music, to be letter-perfect by the time the show plays its first full run-throughs. Suggestions for both the phrasing of the material and the nuances of its vocalism more often originate with the composer. Yesterday's tune-smiths have, in recent years, been superseded by educated musicians who not only know how they want their sungs to be sung but can be relied upon to bring to the attention of the performers whatever nuances may not have been apparent when the songs were first learned.

As the career of a performer develops, a considerable amount of information is picked up along the way and the performer's musical sophistication will increase. Or, if the singer is a well-trained musician, he or she, with the composer, will choose the best rendering of the music. One way or the other, the cast is in good hands. I make no plea for musical ignorance, but it is not a deterrent for securing work.

This ignorance is less likely to occur among members of the swing ensemble. If the vocal arrangements are demanding, chances are that those who have been chosen for the choral work will have had to demonstrate their abilities in audition. The task of this group will be to make luscious sound. Sopranos, contraltos, mezzos, tenors, baritones, and basses all can be expected to have more advanced musical training. They know what singing (or vocalization) is all about. They will be able to sight-read and will not need tutorial help. However, if you are a member of this group, there is little likelihood that you would have asked this question.

17. (a) *From the Actor: How Important Is Singing Correctly and Well?* (b) *From the Singer: How Important Is a Knowledge of Acting?* (c) *From the Dancer: How Important Are Both?*

(a) For the Actor

Very. When actors refer to *muscle*, they means brain power. To singers and dancers, and to the world at large, it is not a euphemism: muscle means muscle. Even granting that, without instruction, an actor speaks correctly, knows how to support and control breath and to resonate sound (and this would be granting a fiction), we speak within a range of no more than an octave (if that much) and this is far too limited for the demands of the musical stage. Baritones, naturally born or trained, must be able to sing a good F at the top, and tenors higher still. Sopranos must have an A flat below high C and probably more and "belters" should be able to belt out a C sharp or even a D. There are scores that call for them to go as high as an F! But this requires a mix of head and chest tones (*Evita* comes to mind). There is no way any of these ranges can be produced without study, and if there are those who can do so in all innocence, they must be considered uniquely blessed.

Eight performances a week can work surprising damage to vocal cords. Unless the acoustical production of the voice is there to sustain you, you can very well come to grief. I have sometimes heard it suggested that the new equipment employed to magnify sound in the theater should obviate the need for the actor and the dancer to acquire good vocal technique. But Vega mikes do not make sound better, only bigger. If you sing impurely and inaudibly, what will be heard is the impurity, and it will be heard by everyone in the theater.

Even if an actor never sings a note, learning a proper vocal technique should be a cornerstone of early training. There are too few actors who consider their voices to be integral elements of their art. As part of that early training I would add a time step, a waltz clog, and a soft-shoe.

(*b*) For the Singer

The new, young American singer is not necessarily the pillar of concrete singers were once thought to be. There is an increasing awareness that music is not only something to be sung with tonal beauty but that some service, and more than the lip variety, must be given to the interpretation of the material. There is still a long way to go. The actor should not be expected to sing—even with extensive study—as elegantly as Leontyne Price. Nor should the singer be expected to have, at call, the emotional range of Olivier or the grace of Kelly; however, often the singers I meet have none of neither. Still, listening to the sounds they make, they lose all understanding of what they are singing about and how to make it understandable to others.

Just as the actor who tries out for a role in a musical will have to endure a singing audition, so will the singer be asked to read. If I had my way, the first day a singer sings a scale, he or she would have an acting class scheduled. Add to that, a time step, a waltz clog, and a soft-shoe.

(c) For the Dancer

There was a time when the answer to the dancer's question would have been: Not very. But today, dancers, mute by the very definition of their art, have emerged into the world in which actors and singers live. *A Chorus Line* has introduced to millions not only what dancers do but what they are thinking while they do it. And they can sing about it, too. You can find them in acting classes, and singing teachers point with pride to those students who sing almost as well as they pirouette. I know of one renowned dancer who sings even better than he spins. Dancers and singers are the original settlers in the musical theater. Actors are immigrants, and although they can often pass as the real thing, Fred Astaire and Lena Horne have nothing to worry about. Dancers have gained their voices and there is no turning back. Add to that, no need to learn a time step, a waltz clog, and a soft-shoe. *Da* da da *da* da, *da da*!

18. *Agents?*

This question and the next two are not about performing but are ancillary to it because, like the weather, everyone inquires about it and can do very little except live with it.

There are three windows in which professional performers are seen: In work for which they are paid, in work for which they receive no pay, and at auditions. The middlemen or -women who see to it that these avenues are open to commerce of all kinds are agents. Even if actors could find and obtain employment without these intermediaries (as they often find they do), they could not do so all the time, and negotiating for themselves would be an added task they are seldom, if ever, able to perform.

Agents are said to be good or bad. This is not a reference to their characters. An agent may be considered good by one performer and bad by another, depending on whether the agent finds work for you. Actors, dancers, and singers change agents for this reason alone: work is or is not forthcoming. I know of very few performers who have had a lifetime relationship with one agent. The revolving-door principle is standard. Agents take on performers because they admire, and believe they can sell, their work. Performers take on agents because they hope this will be so. Each may profess affection for the other, but this affection is not germane to the action. My personal feeling is that it can pollute the partnership. The warmth of the relationship can make leave-taking painful when the time comes to go through the revolving door. Better to quit while you are ahead and keep it strictly business.

How to Get an Agent

How *not* to get one is by badgering. Since work and the payment therefrom make for a continuing association, it will be work (and its quality) that first attracts the one to the other. Dunning, on the part of the actor, is a worthless occupation. Agents, like lovers, are aroused by a gentler approach. One time-honored method: When you find employment and you feel your work advertises you advantageously, contact agents and casting personnel. Importuning invitations to see you perform should be made, followed up, and followed up again. Many agents make it their business to attend as much theater as they can either in person or through proxy assistants. A combination of notification and the possibility that they will have seen you without suggestion will result in both of you coming together. Some agents hold interviews and/or auditions at specified times and on their own premises. Some attend group auditions either arranged by union decree once or twice a year or set up in mutuality by a group of performers. This latter-day arrangement is relatively new and has become commonplace in Los Angeles.

Without an agent, you will have to stay informed. Show business publications become your help-wanted bibles. Announcements of auditions (on both coasts) are to be found within the pages of one or more of these dailies or weeklies. In other cities, you can find out available work by the simple expedient of asking someone who has been in the business a minute longer than you.

The established artist needs the agent not so much to find work but to negotiate the best contract for it. In this case, being agentless is bad business practice, although I know of some actors who prefer lawyers to work out their deals. The more celebrated you are, the more this is allowable. In general, every successful performer needs a third party to obtain optimum terms to be paid by the party of the first part to the party of the second part.

The tie that binds performers and agents is, at best, a silver-plated cord. It is a love-hate, push-pull, on-again-off-again marriage. There is justification for this on both sides, and I make no brief for the guilt or innocence of either partner. I remember an actress who came into class one day in a high state of elation. She had just signed with a prestigious agent. As she announced her triumph, from the rear of the studio, another actress—like the voice of doom—could be heard above the noise of congratulations: "When you see him next, thank him for the most miserable unemployed year and a half of my life."

Another member of the performer's team may be a manager. Like agents, managers have their good points, for which you will pay handsomely. They receive 15 percent of any and all money that comes to their performers, whether or not the work is obtained through their auspices. Since a manager, by law, cannot contract for your services, you will still require an agent. The agent's fee is always 10 percent of your earnings, which means that one quarter out of every dollar you earn will be subtracted from your wages before the government takes its bite. Are managers requisite baggage? That depends on how much value you place on their function. Successful agents have many clients and cannot be expected to perform duties that, to them, are not considered crucial. Managers purchase plane tickets, make hotel reservations, and perform all the trifling but vital services because, unlike agents, they have relatively few people to service. With a small list of clients, a manager's primary function is to push a performer's career by any and all means, limited only by his or her expertise. In the case of celebrated managers, that expertise can be impressive.

For the more well-known performer, a manager can be a good investment. Agents, with artists to sell now and in the future, prefer not to alienate those who have jobs to give out. Managers are spared this concern. They dare more. Employers and management do not intimidate them. They have leverage with a client who is salable, and they will use their power position to make often outrageous salary demands that an agent might be loathe to push for. As the oft-heard cliché goes, "75 percent of a good salary is worth more than 90 percent of none."

For the beginner, there are different factors to consider. You can get lost in an agency where there are many people to be serviced. A manager can keep you in the forefront of the crowd. You will have to gamble that the gain will be worth the cost.

Most performers prefer the sense of comfort afforded by having an agent with whom they have signed. There may be contrary evidence for the beginner. Playing the field—that is, allowing more than one agent to work for you without signing with any one of them—allows for wider coverage, since one agent may be unaware of something another agent knows. It is quite likely that, in the final tally of your career, you will have found more employment for yourself than any agent(s) will have obtained for you. One hustles with or without representation. I know of no agents who, if you bring them employment, would not be thrilled to take you on, draw up contracts, and happily deduct their commission from your wages.

To sign or not to sign is not the question. Individual strengths and weaknesses determine the road you choose to take. If you are not afraid to play the field, by all means play it. If you have no gift for personal advertisement or for the long shot and you feel safer in the knowledge that someone is looking out for you (or so you believe), go after and sign with the agent for whom you have set your cap. The thing to remember is, as the saying, in another context, goes—a good one is hard to find.

19. What Is a Workshop Production and Why Is It Needed?

For as long as anyone can remember, the theater has been called the "fabulous invalid." For a while, the musical theater seemed to be one part of the whole that somehow stood outside the sickroom. Good plays may perish for want of an audience, but good musicals, banished as they are into the world of entertainment (if not art), have always been relied upon to attract an audience willing to pay to see them. And pay they do. As production costs have soared, so have the prices for tickets. What you could see for a $1.10 in the twenties and thirties, now entertains you for $50. But one need not have been clairvoyant to recognize that musicals were slowly inching their way into that sickroom, in dire need of immediate medical attention. The medicine developed to stave off the demise of the patient has turned out to be effective—the workshop. Under more covert circumstances, writers, directors, and choreographers can now see what they have and do it with the blessing of the Actors Equity Association (AEA). Determined by contract, the script is cast and rehearsed for six to eight weeks and then played before invited audiences of no more than 100 and for no more than six to eight dress rehearsals. From this experience, the writers may then retire to their corners to rewrite or overhaul the work and, again, with the permission of the AEA, call the cast together for another workshop production. In both instances, the performers are paid according to contract agreement, and they are further protected by established union safeguards that reimburse them for their financial sacrifices if and when a full production of the piece in question moves on to Broadway. All contracts are ad hoc, but the general profile remains the same in all instances.

Workshop productions are applauded by everyone concerned. The patient's inevitable death—its life having been contingent on $5 million or more to sustain it—has been averted for the moment. The creative staff can see their work off the page and on to a makeshift stage. What is then discerned as wrong can be made right without the hysteria and the expense of overt out-of-town fixing. The producers are happier still. They can see what they are buying without an enormous outlay of money and, more important, before they ask the general public to buy it. When a workshop production betrays a fatal malignancy, it becomes an act of compassion and good business to put it away there and then, but if there is strong evidence that the disease is curable, subsequent workshop fixing can result in a musical that can live out a long, rich life.

There are some negatives to all this: Performers, being the trusting souls they are, work long and hard for minimum wages in workshop and can be dropped for what may appear to be arbitrary reasons.

Workshops can be reprised and even go so far as to announce their transfer dates uptown only to have the whole thing called off by an act of what seems a last-minute caprice of the management. The protections afforded actors do not soften the blow. But, then again, the same would be true had they been fired out of town (an infinitely more painful circumstance). And what may seem capricious to the cast may be nothing more than wiser heads recognizing out front what the performer, working on the inside, can never hope to see.

Are workshops needed? Anyone concerned with the musical theater and its survival would have to answer with a resounding yes. A look at the list of musicals that have matured in workshop and moved on to Broadway corroborates the benefits of this new practice to make perfect—e.g., *A Chorus Line, Ballroom, Nine, Dreamgirls, The Rink, Sunday in the Park with George,* and *Baby*. It is reasonable to assume that none of these musicals would have survived a Broadway opening without the polishing and shaping that a workshop production first afforded them. The titles of these shows confirm that the musical theater is slipping away from the old standard descriptive, "tired businessman's show," and is beginning to reach toward new and more daring horizons. *A Chorus Line* concerns a group of young dancers caught in the drama of a casting call for a musical we never see. Although audiences everywhere have related to its theme, there is no gainsaying that the subject matter, before the fact, is both parochial (to people in the theater) and exotic (to people not in the theater). *Sunday in the Park with George,* a masterpiece about a masterpiece, examines the struggle of the artist to survive in a world where commerce and art conjoin. *Nine* is a musical treatment of Fellini's biographical film *8½*, in which the artist, at a career crossroads, is forced to confront his life by confronting the women who peopled it. *Dreamgirls* is a fictional recounting of the rise of a trio of singers modeled after the Supremes. *Baby* sings of birth and how three couples cope with pregnancy. *The Rink* dealt with the metaphor of a dying Coney Island amusement concession, and *Ballroom* with menopausal life changes. None of these is the stuff of standard musical theater. Workshop productions made their lives possible. There is room for the *Forty-Second Street* type of entertainment, but too much nostalgia is, in itself, a proclamation of stasis.

Workshop productions of musicals afford composers, lyricists, and librettists an opportunity to see their work without the terrible

Damoclean sword of an opening night hanging above their heads. Similarly, in the case of the legitimate theater, blood loss was stanched by the creation of Off Broadway and Off-Off-Broadway. In those smaller theaters and, further away, in regional theaters across the country, and on and off London's West End, plays could be produced and attended without the intolerable dynamic that sinks a play after its christening and before it can slip down the track into the Broadway sea. Now that musicals cost as much as ships, workshop productions ensure us of new product without the fear that failure will further inhibit producers and backers from trying again.

20. *How Can I Get an Equity Card if I Haven't Worked and the Only Way I Can Work Is if I Have an Equity Card?*

This question betrays the beginner's ignorance of union policy and marketplace practice. You do not need membership in the Actors Equity Association (AEA) to get work. Employment is the sole requirement for eligibility. Equity is a *union* and not a *hiring agent*. The producer of a play or a musical who contracts for a performer's services simultaneously creates a union member. The only exceptions to the procedure are to be found in stock, dinner, and certain LORT (League of Resident Theaters) theaters. Equity, by permitting these theaters to function under contracts that allow a ration of union to nonunion members, considerably aids in their survival.

In a first-class production, every member of the cast is a union member whether he or she was one before being hired or became one upon entry. As such they are guaranteed benefits and minimum wage scales that have been hammered out and incrementally augmented through confrontation and strikes since the birth of the union on May 26, 1913.*

You do not automatically become a union member when you secure employment in stock, dinner, or small regional theaters. This is because of nonprofessional ration allowances. However, you can

---

*Maximum salaries are not discussed here because a star's value and a featured player's worth are negotiable.

achieve automatic eligibility upon accrual of fifty weeks of employment in an Equity theater that offers the Membership Candidate Program. (Information on this program and a list of the theaters that offer it can be had on request from the AEA).

The charge that the producer will go for the cheaper of the two when he must choose between the professional and the non- is pure cynicism. We must believe that the hirer will favor whoever most enhances the production. He may very well choose the nonprofessional but he does not consciously do so to make the production worse—only less expensive. Mistakes will be made, but it is also a faulty rationale to suggest that the union member, by virtue of the designation, would have been a better choice.

At this point, we must try to define the undefinable. Talent, ability, and an aptitude for demonstrating them under pressure are not absolutes that can be accurately measured. No one will argue (least of all the Equity membership) that there isn't an appalling amount of third-rateism in the union. But no one (most of all the Equity membership) who yearns for higher standards would care to sit in judgment of others in order to maintain those standards. For what *are* the criteria and for whom are they intended? In the classic words of George Kaufman, "One man's Mede is another man's Persian." Actors Equity cannot presume to be a casting agent. It is to be hoped that those with little or no ability will not work for long whether or not they hold union cards. And even if television celebrity should have come their way, it is an ephemera that goes as quickly as it comes, for it rests on ratings and not on guaranteed evidence of quality. As the ratings go, so goes the celebrity.

Just as a professional with an Equity card can be inadequate at his or her craft, so might the amateur or the nonprofessional be more able than his or her Equity-validated counterpart. It is important to remember that the lack of a card has never kept gifted young performers off a stage. Too many prized careers began from just such humble beginnings. The talented newcomer's arrival on the scene will always keep Actors Equity from being a truly restricted, closed-shop union. Such a union would be counterproductive to a profession that must continually renew itself or perish.

Judgments are made more difficult when the production and the performer are given labels. A professional production competes in the marketplace and live or dies by the rules that apply to all games of profit and loss. A nonprofessional production makes no pretense at being anything but that. School productions and camp shows are essentially intramural affairs and exemplify *amateur* in every sense of the word. Actors Equity is only concerned with the professional production of a play or a musical, since it is a labor union that encompasses professional performers in the legitimate theater. Since this is so, critical evaluations that judge a professional production to be *amateur* (in the editorial meaning of the word) and an amateur production to exhibit a distinct *professional* (again, in the editorial meaning of the word) sheen are irrelevant.

The same equivocal fuzziness defines performers. Professionals can be so described because they are not dabblers but serious, full-time paid workers in the marketplace. These descriptives only define integrity of purpose and an availability to work if work can be found. How *good* their work is considered to be is not at issue. The word *amateur*, on the other hand, implies the nonprofessional, but, again, it is often employed as a pejorative that suggests the dilettante.

To compound the confusion: As we have seen, the nonprofessional may perform in a play or a musical and receive payment for services rendered while the professional can appear in a "waiver theater" and receive no pay at all. Just as Actors Equity has given certain theaters the right to employ nonunion members, it has permitted its membership to work in theaters of no more than ninety-nine seats and to waive their salaries. Performers agree to this unprofessional (if not nonprofessional) arrangement out of a conviction that they will be seen to more advantage on a stage than at an audition. These muddles within muddles are not introduced to debate whether management may be taking advantage of the performer's complaisance or even to question a system that may in fact work to the actor's possible profit. The young beginner who works in a dinner-theater production of a musical may gain valuable experience, but the wages, while lower than union minimum, are nevertheless wages. The actor in a waiver-theater production may entice an agent who may not have been interested until the actor's work was seen, and this assuages the performer's conscience for giving work away for free. But the theory that work is the best teacher may be contestable today. The young actor-dancer-singer in a long run of dinner-theater musicals may very well have learned nothing but bad habits that result in the third-rateism Equity members deplore in their union. And working for no salary in waiver productions can do terrible damage to the professional performer's self-respect.

To sum it up: With or without membership, you can get work or remain unemployed; you can be paid or unpaid; you can be talented in the extreme or not at all. In all cases, an Equity card remains a prestigious possession that performers at the beginning of their careers often perceive as a status symbol. The $500 price tag in no way diminishes it both as a desideratum and as a mark that you are on your way—a professional, at last.

SCENE TWO

The Interviews: How They Did It and Do It

---

*R*obert Preston

*I*n 1952, when he appeared on the Broadway stage in *The Male Animal*, Robert Preston reintroduced that style of actor-performer that, until then, was associated only with the light-footed elegance of the theater's William Gaxton and the cinema's James Cagney. This quality of physical grace and virility is particularly American, for although it has its counterpart in the work of Noel Coward, Jack Buchanan, and Rex Harrison, the very Englishness of these men separates the two styles. When Bob Preston acted, sang, and danced Harold Hill in *The Music Man*, it was evident that the musical theater had found a preeminent representative of a remarkable and rare breed of artist. Although he was not to do that musical until 1958, his performances in the plays he had appeared in previously had that nimble refinement one associates with the musical theater performer. Only the songs and dances were missing. The role so captured his essence that for us he is forever the Music Man. Other men have played and will play the part, but his image alone is what we conjure up when we think of "Seventy-six Trombones," "Trouble," "Marian, the Librarian," and "The Sadder But Wiser Girl."

Astaire and Kelly can outdance him, of course, but they are dancers. Domingo and Pavarotti can outsing him, but they are singers. Olivier and Gielgud can outact him, but they are actors. He holds residence in all three neighborhoods. For confirmation of this sweeping statement, see *Victor-Victoria*. If you have already seen the film, see it again.

DC

Before your performance in *The Music Man*, people would not have thought of you as a song and dance man, but your biography in *Who's Who* claims that one of the many plays you did in the thirties, in California, was Robert Sherwood's *Idiot's Delight*. Doesn't the role of Harry Van call for some singing and dancing?

RP

Yes, but it was at the Pasadena Playhouse, and so there was no professional choreographer or music director. The dance numbers just sort of staged themselves. It was supposed to be this crummy sextet working their way through the Balkan circuit. A couple of the girls could dance, so we worked out our routines. I was an athletic kid and it was easy to pick up a step quickly. And I've always taught myself to be ambidextrous—and that works out with the feet, too.

DC

Athletic talent, then, can be an advantage for the actor?

RP

Well, my gym training became the roles I was doing. They were always athletic, you know—everything I did. Even pageants at the Hollywood Bowl when I was a kid. The thing that amazes me, as I look back on it, is that I had not seen Alfred Lunt.* They had played the Biltmore Theater here in Los Angeles, and although I had seen

*Mr. Lunt and his wife, Lynn Fontanne, appeared in the original play.

everything they had done, I never got to see *Idiot's Delight*, for which I am glad. I never mentioned to Alfred that I had played it as a kid. But I was awfully good in it for an eighteen-year-old who wasn't supposed to know what he was doing. As I look back on him now, there were instincts there that were so right. The first time I heard Jack Carter in a club, he had this little gimmick: when he told his joke, he punctuated it with "Heh heh! Heh heh!" And that is what I did with Harry Van. Whenever he said something that was supposed to be a joke—not with the audience, but in conversation like this— he'd say the snap line and go "Heh heh." It was cornball and it was "right on." If they hadn't known what he was doing, it would have been annoying to an audience, but they caught on to it quickly. Harry Van couldn't sing and he couldn't dance but he was the carrier of a great deal of the play's philosophy.

DC

At the time, did you you realize the play's political significance?

RP

I didn't until later, when I was working in the movies. In those days I was so far removed from ideologies. I went scot-free through all the terrible period of blacklisting because I'm about thirteen years younger than that whole [*Pasadena Playhouse*] gang and I never went to university. And then, too, our subscription audience was gathered from Flintridge, La Cañada, and Altadena, and we had to be careful what we gave them. But every once in a while we'd feed them something.

DC

The Pasadena Playhouse must have been an extraordinary theater. How do you account for its success in a movie-oriented community?

RP

Gilmore Brown. That's why it never caught on again. He died and the whole philosophy died with him. Thank God for men like him because it rubs off on you. God help the kid in a play that I'm rehearsing who sits in a corner doing a crossword puzzle. Because that is where the fun is. That's where the work is going on. That's when you're back to school again. I never had a coach, but I had a lot of directors, and every time you have a director you respect, you're going to school with him.

DC

May we talk about singing? It was twenty years before you sang and danced on a stage again?

RP

Well, I'd done two Gilbert and Sullivans in high school. I played the judge in *Trial by Jury* and Sir Joseph Porter, KCB. Now, there you get into patter song. I got interested in them, and I can do every patter song they ever wrote. But I did them for my own amusement. Consequently, when you're given the number "Trouble" to audition for Meredith* . . . well, it's the greatest thing for an actor, because you can't fall off that rhythm without breaking your leg. But you know what Meredith did? You'll get a kick out of this. That was the first really professional musical I had to do. I would get into a sweat suit and tennis shoes the first thing in the morning and—we were in the Broadway Central Plaza rehearsing—and I was running up and down three floors between the book and the music and the dancing all day long. At one point in the show, as written, I had to jump up on stage—the platform in the gymnasium—and grab their attention by bursting into "Seventy-six Trombones." And that was the only thing at this point that was giving me trouble. Getting down "in one" was no problem because I used the simple gimmick of making the audience the other half of River City—because they [*the cast*] could only be staged around me in a semicircle, so I just completed the circle with the audience. And it worked for me and it worked for them. But I said to Meredith: "I can't just go into this number. I need a handle." And he said to me, "Like what?" I said: "I don't know. Something like . . . working them up . . . something like the "Trouble" number does." Well, he went into the ladies room and, in about fifteen minutes, he came out and gave me an envelope. I have it framed now. He had written, in pencil. [*He, Harold Hill, is on his feet.*]: "May I have your attention, please! Attention, please! I can deal with your trouble, friends, with a wave of my hand, this very hand. Please

*Meredith Willson, the Composer-Lyricist-Librettist of *The Music Man*.

. . ." and he had written the whole recitative! And I said: "Jesus! I could sing "The Star Spangled Banner" after that one!"

I'll tell you how it works, David. Now, I don't have absolute or relative pitch. I have actor's pitch. Some years after I'd stopped doing the show, a musician friend of mine—ten years later—saw the libretto on my piano and he said, "How close to the pitch can you come with any of these songs?" And I said, "Within a quarter-tone." And he said: "This late? Do you have perfect pitch?" And I said, "No, actor's pitch," and then I went into the song, a cappella, and then he would hit the note on the piano and I was never more than a quarter-tone off.

DC

But that's a gift, of course.

RP

I don't think so. I think it's a trick.

DC

Perhaps, but singing must not be a terrifying thing for you to do.

RP

I won't allow that to happen to me.

DC .

But there is a split in the road where actors and actor-singers separate, don't you think?

RP

You know, Larry Douglas had to go on for me. I missed one performance in *The Music Man*, and when I came back from the long weekend, I said to Barbara Cook, "How did it go Saturday night?" And she said: "Well, I'll tell you how it went. You know where you say, 'Oh, think, my friends, how can any pool table hope to compete with a gold trombone? [*He is Harold Hill again Imitating the Sound of a Slide Trombone*] rah rah rah de dah dah dah'? Well, Larry said, 'Well, think, my friends, how could any pool table ever hope to compete with a gold trombone? [*This time, in a deep, "serious" basso*] . . . rah rah rah de dah dah dah'." He was a singer.

DC

That's what I mean. That split in the road doesn't seem to exist for you. By the way, if you'd never sung before, how did anyone come to think of you for the role?

RP

It's an interesting story. I had finished the run in *Janus** in April. Marty Ritt[§] had not come out to California yet. He called me and said: "Don't do anything this summer. Sam Handelsman's given me carte blanche to do four shows of my own choice at the Theater in the Park in Philadelphia." Then he tells me he's never worked 'in the round' and that he's going to get a hell of an acting company together. He asked me if I wanted to do *The Front Page* and *Boy Meets Girl*. I had never done either of them and, well, I love Marty. He staged it like a carousel. I was in the Hall of the Mountain King. I played Hildy and, as you know, he gets progressively drunker in the show. I played him so high before he came on that, as he got drunker, it was really the roll around. I don't remember a thing about the show except that it was a ball. And the same was true for *Boy Meets Girl*. The other writer was played by Leon Janney, and we did a double. We set them up for each other just the way I'd seen writers feed each other in writers' conferences. Well, Da Costa[†] saw it because he was following us with his production of *The Little Hut*. Kermit[‡] saw it because, well, he saw everything, but he especially saw everything that Marty did. So, when they stopped looking around for a musical comedy performer to do it . . . They'd asked Ray Bolger and he'd said, "Sure, but give me fifteen minutes in the second act where I do my . . ." and they wondered what the devil happened to the Music Man while "Once In Love with Amy"—or whatever—came out. Danny Kaye, too, had the same sort of . . . Well, I guess that they just got tired of this and said: "What about an actor? What about Preston? That looked like a musical he was in in Philadelphia. And if he can

---

Janus, the play, by Carolyn Green, was produced in November 1955.
[§]Eminent stage and film director.
[†]Morton Da Costa, the director of the original production of *The Music Man*, affectionately known as "Tec."
[‡]Kermit Bloomgarten, the producer of *The Music Man*.

just carry a tune, we know he can play the part." Well, as I say, they gave me "Trouble" to audition with. I worked on it for about a week and, except for the arrangement here and there, what I did for that audition didn't change a hell of a lot right up to the performance.

DC

Had you ever studied singing before this?

RP

It's in the script. "Here he sings." "Here he plays the trombone." So, you learn it. Putting on that sweat suit and those tennis shoes helped a lot, because in the second week of rehearsals Tec said, "We've got to be careful we don't put shoes on you and inhibit the way the character's starting to move." Well, what fed what, I don't know. I was dazzling them with my footwork, but I was also Harold Hill, always ready to hop the next freight out of town. I also found I could point the action when it wasn't Harold—when something else was going on, I could throw the audience to it. And I could grab them back when I had to. And it was a thing of . . . feet. A thing you just fell into doing.

DC

I saw you play Oscar in *Twentieth Century* and Joe Ferguson in *The Male Animal* and I remember, even then, thinking, "He'd be wonderful in a musical. Why hasn't anyone ever thought to ask this guy to do a musical?" I particularly remember the football monologue in *The Male Animal*. It was like a ballet.

RP

I helped a little on the football stuff because Thurber* didn't know much about it. Do you remember how funny the picture was? Bob Benchley stayed overnight at Rosalind Russell's house in the movie. I think Bob Montgomery was the leading man. One of those "no sense of humor," light comedians who were so great because they didn't have any personal humor. *That's* what you do with Joe Ferguson to make him funny. Absolutely wash his sense of humor away. Well, I

*James Thurber, with Elliot Nugent, the co-author of the play.

remember Bob [*Benchley*] drank all night long while the domestic argument was going on. He was their lawyer. And we find him next morning—Bob Montgomery comes down in his dressing gown and Benchley's asleep in the chair—right where they left him. And Bob walks up behind him and puts his hand on his shoulder—touches him just like that—and Benchley [*He jumps up from his chair convulsively and lopes across the lawn.*] wound up by the fireplace. I never forgot it. The number of steps and the rhythm of the way he got there could not be improved upon, couldn't be changed.

DC
Not every actor is able to do that.

RP
A play is a musical, you know. A lot of people don't realize that.

DC
You mean that the actor-dancer-singer should approach both similarly?

RP
Absolutely.

DC
How did this theory inform *Ben Franklin in Paris*, for instance?

RP
Ben was a robust old man. Sidney* knew the age of the Ben he was writing, and he didn't let that inhibit him in what he was going to require of him. And Michael Kidd, the director-choreographer, knew it, too. Ben had to be forceful, winning, and all-consuming in his opening number. Well, I invented myself. And one night, Shelley Winters came back and she said, "Pres, how old is Ben Franklin at the time of this show?" And I said, "Eighty-seven." And she said, "Well, you're sure as hell not playing an eighty-seven-year-old man." And I said, "Neither was Ben."

*Sidney Michaels was the librettist.

DC

Then, the performer must recognize no difference in the playing of a musical, a play, or an opera?

RP

That's right. That's why Pinza* could cross over. That's why he was the big star he was in opera. He was the best actor they had in that company. And George London, God rest him, he would have followed in that same path. Or take Bob Hope. He brings his stand-up comic's delivery with him wherever he goes. He can absolutely trick an audience into laughing. He'll get this tremendous laugh, and two seconds later, you say: "What the hell did I laugh at? That wasn't funny." But his delivery makes you laugh. He *tells* you that you have heard a joke.

DC

Doesn't the word *style* define what you're talking about, and do you think, as I do, that the word is somewhat out of style?

RP

It's a conscious thing. If you were to tell Pacino or DeNiro that they had style, unless they were doing something they considered required style, they would be very angry with you because style is not what they are after. You know, people talk about the Method, but I will never talk about how I work. There are certain things I do that I can talk about that I'm doing mechanically for a reason, but I will never talk about *how* I work because if I put it into words, then it is on a conscious level and it won't work for me anymore. Have I worked in the Method? Of course I have. Every time I've worked with a director who espouses it. On the other hand, do you know Henry Hathaway? Now, there's a director who cannot direct an actor at all. But Henry has a magic thing. He has an ear that will not accept a false note. He can hear "phony."

DC

I once assisted George Kaufman, and he directed very much like that. He'd stage the show in three or four days, and for the rest of

*Ezio Pinza in *South Pacific*.

rehearsal he'd pace in the rear of the theater with his hand cupped behind his ear and never look at the stage again. He'd give me dozens of notes to give to the cast: "Tell him to cut that word out of the line" or "Tell her to cut that." And the line would always be better and even get a laugh where there hadn't been one before.

RP

That's marvelous!

DC

I once heard Rex Harrison try to define his particular style. He recalled that, as a young man, he'd been fortunate to work in certain kinds of plays—those hermetically sealed English drawing-room comedies that always had a well-known English star in them who was celebrated for the kind of acting style they required. Harrison described how he'd stand in the wings and watch their feet. It was their feet that fascinated him. He'd go home each night and try to imitate what they had done.

RP

Dancers have an expression for that. They say, "He has 'neat' feet." Very early on, when I was a child actor, I'd try to approximate the shoes I was going to be wearing in the show. And I never wore a jacket rehearsing a scene if I wasn't going to have a jacket on in the show. You got rid of all those crutches. Actors who smoke when they aren't going to be smoking in the play—that's a crutch they haven't let go of yet. It's the same thing as saying, "It'll be there." When I got to the point where I could say it, I'd tell young actors before rehearsals started: "Laugh all you want today, fellas. I'm trying something new." And you would have at something, and it was absolutely wrong, but you had to get it out of your system. It would stay in the back of your head if you didn't get it out. And you had to fall on your ass. That's what rehearsals are for. Rehearsal is not to be perfect from the first day on. It's where you make your mistakes.

DC

Do you think that the Method, in its effort to achieve reality on the stage, has tended to murder style?

RP

No, because good directors like Bobby Lewis and Mike Gordon both were camp counselors in the early Group Theater days, and they are great stylists but they are great realists, too. The one thing that does bother me about some actors is their speech. Now, I love Danny Aiello, but I wish he'd done something so that . . . He never . . . Well, for instance, I don't hear Michael Caine's cockney anymore, even though it's still there. But *he* has style.

DC

Yes, but he's an Englishman whose heritage is not only removed from the training associated with the Method but has its own theatrical and historical imperatives. Don't you agree?

RP

That's right. They are born to it. But in a wholly different style, there's Bob Hoskins, who's an actor who has never risen above it, even though he's been hitting the classics lately. But this man has real power!

DC

Yet again, another Englishman.

RP

That's why I deliberately chose them. Danny [Aiello], I'm always going to know the number and the block he was born on. That's where he's going to be. Every character he's going to play will be from there.

DC

Do you think this is an inadequacy in a young actor's training?

RP

Of course it is! How can he play a man from California? How can he play a man from River City, Iowa? DeNiro, for instance, had to do absolutely no preparation, in his speech, to play *Raging Bull*. That's who he was. That's how he's going to be. But, *The Deerhunter* sounded the same way. I'll always be grateful that I'm California-raised. If there had been a standard of speech in the United States, it would have come from California in those days. As a grammar-school kid you had a teacher from Iowa, you had a teacher from Indiana, you had one from Massachusetts, you had one from the deep south. And this all became a blend. You never heard the hard *a* or the soft *a* or the terrible *r*'s. You had a California *r*. My folks had Massachusetts in their speech. My father still does. I have none. It's very simple to "do" him. I'm very good at accents. That's important, too. I was doing *The Old Lady Shows Her Medals* for Lux Video, and Fielder Cook, I think, was directing. He said to me, "Do you have a Scots burr?" And I said: "No, but I'm working with Maggie Wycherly. She's playing the old lady. I'll just pick it up from her." And we had two of the best burrs you ever heard on live television. And I found out, when it was through, that Maggie had never done one before. She was listening to me! Isn't that funny? We both must have had some idea of what a burr sounded like.

DC

Do you mean that the absence of any dialect in his childhood allows an actor to hear and learn dialects in his adult years?

RP

When you're young and first hearing language. When I was a kid, there were four of us who were given carte blanche at the Pasadena Playhouse. We were the kids that Gilmore Brown thought were going to make it. We weren't part of the school. We were just working. So, he gave us the chance to take whatever classes we wanted. Well, I brushed up on French and German again, just for kicks. And I went to eurythmic classes when I wasn't working on a play because it was good exercise. And fencing, too. I'm a natural left-handed actor but I always knew it was wrong to fence left-handed. To do anything left-handed on a stage disturbs an audience, and they don't know why, so you must learn to do things in the orthodox way instead of sinistrally. But, "Thank you, Daddy." Me and my kid brother, down on the Santa Monica beach, would walk along with my dad, who was an experienced ball player, and he'd have us [*He is on his feet, bending and picking up imaginary stones first with his right and then with his left hand while he chants*] "pick up a stone, pick up a stone, throw the stone, throw the stone. Pick up a stone, pick up a stone, throw the stone, throw the stone." That balances both sides of you—even your brain. It's always better to be a switch-hitter.

DC

Were rehearsals for *The Music Man* a nightmare? After all, it was your first Broadway musical?

RP

Having done many of them in my life since then, I know they can be just that. It's so bloody busy; so much is going on. We had an understanding in *The Music Man*. Since they were taking a chance on someone who had never done a musical, our understanding was that, if after one and a half to two weeks of rehearsal, it looked as though it wasn't going to work out, we would part company and no one would be upset. But it started to work from the first day, and we all knew it. The songs I had to do were perfect for the kind of voice I had at the time.

DC

Learning songs and being choreographed was not distressing?

RP

Not for a moment. And I'll tell you why. This is a mechanical kind of thing I do in the theater that I *will* talk about because I don't specify anything. You do what you can in rehearsal. There's only so much you can do. You tell yourself: "That's it. I'm ready now for the first audience." Well, after that first audience, you go back to your hotel room and you're in bed with the only person you cannot lie to—yourself. And, if you're an honest actor, this is what you do. You say, "I'm uncomfortable here. . . ." You don't say anything more than that because let's find out the reasons later. "I'm uncomfortable here . . . and here . . . and here. Why? Is the line wrong? Do I need some help from the director? From the author? Something I haven't come to grips with?" I'm talking about actor's discomfort, not character discomfort. Because if there is one moment in the play—be it in the third act—of personal discomfort, it is going to color the whole show. More than that, it's going to color your drive from Connecticut to the theater. Because until that moment is through, you're going to be unhappy. So you get rid of it. You get rid of all those moments of discomfort right up to the point where there's nothing you want to do on opening night except go to the theater and do the show. And, sometimes moments evolve into something comfortable and right. I remember in *Nobody Loves an Albatross*, Ronnie Alexander, Gene Saks and I were the only three who thought it was funny. Even the rest of the cast wasn't sure. Well, in Boston, we got lukewarm reviews, and Elliot Norton* came back and tried to help as much as he could. He said: "That's not funny. It's mean." So, one night I said to Gene: "I think this is mean. I'm going to play it mean." Well, the cast didn't know what the hell I was doing. I played the meanest son of a bitch. If Nat Bentley, the character, hadn't been such a charming guy, that was how mean he would have been anyway, because he was doing lousy things. So, I played the meanness. And the audience was like this—up against the back wall. Well, the next night it all lightened up again and we knew it was working, but for some reason or other, the audience just wasn't buying it. Now we get to the opening night in New York and I'm on stage just walking around—I like to listen to the audience coming in, hear that noise, because they tell you something before the curtain goes up. And Gene comes running out on stage and says: "You know why they're not buying this? We're not telling them what they're in for!" And I said, "What do you mean?" He said: "Play the whole show as it is. I'm just going to change the opening curtain." I said, "What?!" Well, you see, the curtain opened on a bare stage and then the action started. He said: "You're a writer. But they don't know you're a half-assed writer yet. You're just a writer." Now [*He is on his feet, setting the stage*] . . . that's my bedroom over there. And here was a coffee table. And he says: "We'll put a script on it. The curtain goes up . . . let them wait . . . then you come on . . . you're going to get a hand. You don't acknowledge the audience. You walk over, you pick up the script, then you go out the door and you slam the door behind you. Now . . . let them wait! You'll know when to come back." And I let them wait. All of a sudden, I heard a titter and then, it broke! And as the laugh broke, I came back on. I threw the script back on the table, and we went

---

*Alexander was the Playwright, Saks the Director, and Norton the dean of Boston drama critics.

on with the show. But we had done that to them. And they bought it! And Walter Kerr's* line was, "God bless its crooked little heart!"

DC

By the way, do you get along with choreographers?

RP

All of them. I've loved every choreographer I've had. Onna§ rented a studio and we—she and her assistant and a pianist—worked there at the very beginning. She had the pianist do some rippy-tippy-tippy, and she took me by the hand and we started to walk [*He is on his feet, moving*] . . . and we walked, walked, walked and then, she went [*He does a nifty hitch kick*] . . . just to see if I was going to follow, and we were in perfect sync. Well, we were there about a half an hour and she says: "The hell with this. I was only trying to see how much I could bring you into the choreography. I'm going to bring you right in—in the "center" in the ballet."

DC

I've asked this question of each performer I've talked to: How do you deal with eight shows a week and two on Wednesdays and Saturdays when you have to play them through rugged winter weather? Are you bothered by colds, sore throats, the flu . . . ?

RP

They're all in your mind. You cannot have that. For about a half an hour on Thursday nights [*during the run of* The Music Man], I would have what the cast called my "Thursday voice." But, then, as it warmed up, it came back again. This was just a reaction to the two Wednesday performances. But it was two performances of *that* guy —Harold Hill—who was at fever pitch through the entire show. I could have done ten performances of *I Do, I Do*, even though there were only two of us. Mary [*Martin*] could only do six. Well, it was fun to just do six.

---

*The then *New York Times* drama critic.
§Onna White, the Choreographer of *The Music Man*.

DC

But you never had medical problems that affected your singing?

RP

No. I went to a throat doctor every Thursday, and he put two drops of gentian on my vocal cords just to shrink them back down again. That's all. He knew I smoked. He told me I was stupid. I said, "I don't smoke while I'm in rehearsal." But that's the wonderful thing about rehearsing a musical. You look forward so to opening night . . . opening night in New York not out of town, because that's still work time. All of a sudden comes opening night in New York, and you only have to do the show eight times a week! It's like a vacation!

DC

Was making the film of *The Music Man* difficult? I mean, in the sense of duplicating what had worked so well on the stage?

RP

No, because Onna was the choreographer and, even though she was going to enlarge things, she was going to do it on its own small scale. It was still going to be the tiny thing we did. The library, even though it was a big library, still had a small feeling. I could broaden out when I led the band and the parades and we went from building to building out on the street where I could take long strides. And I never think I'm working in a different medium. Something automatically tells you that you don't have to be that loud here and that you ought to do "that" there. It always depends on where you are. At the Playhouse, we would work on the Main Stage, which was slightly bigger than the Booth.* And then we would work in the Lab Theater upstairs, which had about 200 seats, or we'd work in the Playbox, where if you took a note out of your pocket, it damn well better *be* the note because someone's going to lean over your shoulder and read it with you. You fill whatever space you're in. But there is still a proscenium, and as a performer, you still have to "wear" it. It has to swivel with you. Mike Gordon used to say, "Maurice Schwartz, I hated the son of a bitch, but he had a wonderful line." When Schwartz came on—he didn't care whether it was the City Center or downtown

---

*A theatre in New York that is considered small.

at Sixth and Houston—he would always say, "I reach up; I take the proscenium and I bring it down over my shoulders." He also said, "The first thing you say—you don't actually say it—but you say it: 'Here *I* am!' "

DC

You have done two unsuccessful musicals, *Ben Franklin in Paris* and *We Take the Town.* Is there anything one can learn to predict a possible bad choice?

RP

Well, *Ben* worked for me because I actually got an eleven-month run out of it. *We Take the Town* closed in Philadelphia. I have heard so many smart prople say that you don't go into rehearsal with a show until you're sure that it's 85 percent right. Well, I say you don't go into rehearsal with a show unless it's 100 percent right. Then, if you find it's not, you fix whatever it is—the 15 percent. But, don't ever expect that kind of work to be done out of town by the people who did it the first time.

DC

How does that account for shows that get fixed out of town?

RP

Somebody else finds out what's happening. We had a run-through of *The Music Man* for an audience of about 750 people before we went out of town. It worked like a charm because we were in rehearsal clothes and had just two rehearsal pianos. The good thing about that was that the director, being the smart man that he is, had something to go on the minute something didn't work. It had worked on a bare stage in rehearsal clothes. For instance, "Pick a Little, Talk a Little" didn't work because of the goddamn hats. He said, "Take those hats off the ladies so we can see their faces!" So, the costume designer said, "But they're those wonderful chicken hats!" And he said: "I don't give a damn! They've got those wonderful chicken faces so let's see the chicken faces!" The opening number wasn't working and he said: "Hell! It worked with two pianos! Meredith, you've written the greatest train music in the world here, but it's covering up my scene. This is the train . . . you can put in as much [*He makes soft train*

noises] beep bedeedle beep beep, whatever you want, but thin out
that arrangement!" And that's how it gets done.

DC

But, on a second guess, would you have elected to do *Ben Franklin
in Paris* and *We Take the Town?*

RP

Sure. I had a ball with *Ben* and I made a pot of money out of him,
too. I was the only one who did. As for *We Take the Town*, it was
the best thing I've ever done in my career. It didn't work because
there was no way they could finish it. Pancho's* got to die. We know
that he's dead, so everything in the second act just pointed toward
that, and there was no one who could work out the book. The music
was great. Barbra Streisand has recorded a lot of it. It was a wonderful
score. I called Goddard Lieberson§ in the middle of our second week
in Philadelphia and I said, "Come on down and see the show, Goddard." Because, you see, Columbia Records was the sole backer of
the show. I said: "We have to close it and save it. It's not going to
make it this way." Well, he came down and saw a matinee and he
came into my dressing room and he said, "We'll close it for repairs
because this is the best lousy show I've ever seen!" And that's exactly
what it was—the best lousy show!

DC

Can you play an instrument?

RP

I play the trumpet and the guitar and I can play the piano so I can
read music.

DC

What memories does *I Do, I Do* recall?

---

*The musical's leading character was the Mexican revolutionary Pancho Villa.
§The late director of Columbia Records.

RP

Now, there's a show that works because of the performance of the songs. I'll tell you what I mean. We had Johnny Lesko as our Music Director but he was also rehearsal pianist. He knew, from the very first day of rehearsal, that Gower* was not going to allow the band to be in the pit. He'd said: "I cannot have wall-to-wall musicians in the bedroom. They'll be behind the scrim, out of sight." So Johnny pushed the piano to the back wall, turned his back on us and just listened to us breathe. From then on, throughout the run, our intake of breath was his upbeat!

DC

It was yours and Mary Martin's input, then, that resulted in the show's success?

RP

We had known each other for many years. I gave her her first screen kiss, you know. We just locked the door—we had the Forty-sixth Street theater, and the bed was already built and it could turn. We had our lunch on the bed. The assistant director was a dancer—Lucia Victor—and her assistant was Bob Avian, a dancer, also. So when it came to the choreography, Mary and I would sit in the front row with Harvey and Tom§, who were there at every rehearsal in case they were called upon for something—which they were, many times. Gower would choreograph it with Lucia and Bob, and then Mary would get up and do it with Bob, and then I'd get up and do it with Lucia—and then Mary and I would do it together. It was as easy as falling off a log. Before we were even ready, we would have a run-through—books just out of our hands—so Gower could get a picture of the flow. When he was choreographing "Love Isn't Every-thing," he called the prop man, who came on and said, "What do you want here?" and Gower said, "Bring me every kind of toy you can think of. Bring me all kinds of clothes. Bring me clotheslines." And we just worked everything right into the scene. Now, both of us

---

*Gower Champion, the late Director-Choreographer of *I Do, I Do*.
§Tom Jones and Harvey Schmidt, the Composer and Librettist-Lyricist.

are not stymied by props. It's very simple for us to tie the action into the word, and so we broke the back of that number and we moved on. Then, Gower said: "There's a little sameness here. I need a little 'up' tune. See what's happening in the story. Ah! The kids have grown. She's looking forward to them being out of the house." He turned to Tom and Harvey and said, "Write me something like 'when the kids get married,' and they left and, next day, they came back with "When the Kids Get Married" and they played it for us. Gower said: "That's lovely, that's lovely. Just what I mean. Now, we need a topper. Mary, do you play an instrument?" And she said: "Well, I played a little fiddle when I was a child. I could learn to make sounds on it again." And he said to me, "How about you, Pres?" I said, "If Mary's going to have a fiddle, I want a C melody saxophone." Johnny Lesko goes, "Whoops!" I said, "What the hell made you say that?" And he said: "I love the sound it makes. I know because I used to make my living with it." I said: "Great! You'll be able to help me!" So, the next day the prop man came in with a fiddle and a C melody saxophone, and we ad-libbed the song around until we got to the part where I say, "Mary, here's your fiddle", and she says, "Michael, here's your sax [*He is doing the "business"*] . . . da da da dum pah pah . . . and off we'd go. It stopped the show every night! And then, of course, they could write the final verse: "When the kids get married, I'm gonna be in vaudeville. . . ." It just capped it right off.

DC

Is a two-character musical harder to do than a larger, more dazzling show?

RP

Well, of course, someone has to be onstage at all times. I made three of my costume changes right onstage and incorporated them into the number. [*He is up, singing in mock rage and standing on one leg.*] "My daughter is marrying an idiot!" A perfect song for putting on your pants and shoes, and it fills the stage and gives Mary a chance to get into her nice gown. Everything was choreographed. My dresser said: "My God! We've even got fly-buttoning music!"

DC

In that bio in *Who's Who,* you are quoted as claiming Harold Hill in *The Music Man* as your favorite role. I can't resist asking if you created the archetypal image of Harold Hill or if Harold Hill is really no one but you—and, in fact, if he colors much or all of your subsequent work? And is this a question I should have refrained from asking?

RP

No, and I'll tell you why it isn't. A lot of Harold Hill's movement gave the music director the tempo of a song. "Seventy-six Trombones," when I had jumped up those gym steps, began with this gesture. . . . [*He performs the gesture.*] It was my gesture. "May I have your attention?" Upbeat, downbeat. [*The movement of the arm is just that: a conductor's cue.*] And so he's right there with it, you see. Now, while we're playing, they're getting the road company together. Forrest Tucker was going to play it. He was an old friend, and a great athlete. People don't know that, but he had letters in five sports at Georgetown University. I went to see a rehearsal, and he was playing the scenes and doing the songs just fine, the way Tucker would say them—and he was perfect for it—and then he would do . . . [*Again, he is on his feet, to execute a dance step peculiar to him.*] They had put him in my footsteps! Every step I was doing, they gave to Tuck. I said, "Tuck, you look like a big, blonde faggot!" And he said, "Well, it's what *you're* doing." And I said, "But you don't know *why* you're doing it." Then I explained to him: "You're ready to escape. You're going to hop that train." And he said: "Oh! Nobody ever told me that!" And his movements started to become fluid again as befits a six-foot-five guy instead of a six-foot fellow.

DC

So Bob Preston created Harold Hill, and Harold Hill didn't create Bob Preston?

RP

Right. I've never used anything of Harold's since then. A lot of people will say, "There's a lot of Harold Hill in that" and the reason is because it is coming out of my body and my voice. But it is not the same movement, ever. Never, ever again on a conscious level. It might be an occasional flinch or something but I'm thinking so completely away from that guy. I've never wanted to do him again.

DC

There is surely no sign of him in *Victor-Victoria*. Was that lovely creation your own or based on men you've known?

DC

Many men I've known.

DC

Did you consciously borrow their behaviorisms?

RP

Not so much behavior as attitude. I have never known a truly unhappy gay person because I've never known someone in any business in which it was imperative that he remain in the closet because his life would have been ruined if it had been known that he was gay. So I was able to play a perfectly adjusted guy. Blake* and I had an understanding, right from the beginning, that he was not going to be a "limp-wrist." But, when the moment came, he could do the outrageous thing a gay man will do—and especially with a woman. When he says to Julie [*Andrews*], "I want shoulders! Shoulders! [*He is on his feet, arms and hands illustrating, with relish, lavish parabolas to describe the lady's gown.*] . . . Tons and tons of shoulders!"

DC

What is the difference between behavior and attitude?

RP

Noel Coward said to me, backstage at *The Music Man*, "Who does your costumes, and why does he dress your young leading lady like that!?" And I said, "Well, Noel, he's not especially fond of young ladies." And he said, "Well, none of us is, dear boy, but we don't dress them that way!" [*He laughs.*] When you think of an attitude for Toddy§ this was perfect.

---

*Blake Edwards, the Writer-Director of the film.
§The character's name in the film.

DC

And Toddy's behavior? Was that something you consciously mapped out for yourself?

RP

In general, I *knew* what I was going to *do*. Julie and I were good friends, but not this close. We had four weeks of rehearsals—just the two of us, in London, before the picture started. There was one number, the little duet, that Blake would never let us rehearse, because that was going to be off the cuff, ad lib. And it was, by God! It had happened to me once before with Mickey Rooney. I was playing his older brother, and I was protecting him from the director. And he turned to me, on camera, with a look that was just what the role required. And this happened with Julie. She was helpless in my arms and she needed this guy's help. It was just perfect! We shot for five or six weeks before the rest of the cast came to London. We did it in sequence so the relationship could build. And it was there. It was built into the shooting schedule. We were there because we had to do some prerecording, learn the numbers and the dance routines. We were the only picture filming on the lot, so all the sets were built and ready for us and we could shoot in sequence because of that. Nothing had to be torn down.

DC

There was a time when playing a homosexual had something of a stigma attached to it. That's pretty much a thing of the past?

RP

Of course. Nothing has ever engendered anything like the mail I received for *Victor-Victoria*. And strangely enough, from women. The Gay Alliance out here, at one of their functions, gave me an award. I didn't know what I was going to say until I saw the show that they were putting on for themselves beforehand. It was so breakaway that I thought, "Oh hell, anything goes." So, what I said to them when I was given the award—I was going to say that I was tickled pink, but decided not to—was, "The wonderful thing that made this work was that I knew I wasn't going to play a limp-wrist. I wanted the straight audience to accept the man, and they did. The gay audience knew how gently I was treating them, and the straight audience said, 'We know he's not playing gay because Robert Preston isn't gay [*He takes a beat.*] . . . or is he?' " And that works!

DC

How do you feel about young people who want to go into show business today, now that it has dwindled down from a viable to a stringent career choice?

RP

I've heard kids say, "I want to be a superstar" and so many of them are learning their business on television in front of 10, 12, and 18 million people. But then, too, there are the regional theaters that we have now that we never had before.

DC

And yet, with all the changes, young people everywhere have an astonishing enthusiasm for the music we grew up hearing.

RP

Well, all of it is lasting, and it doesn't belong to their parents' generation any longer. Those show tunes are two generations removed. When it is that far away, it's like Shakespeare. Now it has its own intrinsic worth, no matter what mom and dad say. Linda Ronstadt comes out with a beautiful album, and the kids buy it just as they would buy one of the top fifty. Let me take it one step further. Let's take you to King's Road in London, where the real punkers started. I'm there and I find out, accidentally, that the big cult album with the kids is *Mack and Mabel!* And how did it start? Their championship skating team did an ice dance to my "I Won't Send Roses"—I mean, my vocal. And everybody said, "What's that from?" And they found out and, all of a sudden, that album hit the charts and sold more than it ever sold here. The whole damn thing—rock and roll—is its own rebellion to begin with. It would have had its Chubby Checkers and then a fast death if so many parents hadn't objected to it and made it the thing to do. The minute you say, "My God! Turn that thing down!" the volume has to go up. [*He shrugs with amusement.*] Now I understand they're hurting their eardrums!

Lena Horne

Lena Horne can be considered our most prestigious chanteuse. She has made occasional appearances in films and musical theater as far back as the forties and as late as the eighties. But it is as a singer of songs that she is celebrated.

Today, black vocalists are recognized as integral members of the entertainment community, and racial origin does not banish the artist to nightclubs, Harlem vaudeville, and fringe record labels. But it is not so long ago that "black" and "white" show business were two distinct entities. From the beginning, Lena Horne has been a part of that long journey into the light.

Unlike her peer sisters Ella Fitzgerald, Sarah Vaughan, and Aretha Franklin, she is not and has never been available to us through strings of ravishing recordings. Even her work in nightclubs—rooms in which those other ladies may have also appeared—was marked by a visual dramatic presentation and an urban sophistication that was hers alone. Beyond her sense of the drama and comedy inherent in whatever she sings, is her beauty. The sight of her is as much a part of experiencing Lena Horne as the sound of her voice. Time must be her closest friend, for it seems determined never to work any visible damage to her enduring loveliness.

In recent years she has appeared in her one-woman show, *Lena Horne: The Lady and Her Music* on Broadway and on tour to an acclaim and a rediscovery of her artistry that affirmed what never needed reaffirmation. Onstage she holds the audience in a breathless silence as she moves across the stage with the knowledge at all times of where she is going and how best to get there. Each song is a small life lived within the linear time slot rounded by a vamp and a rideout. Between these poles, when she travels that distance, is what singing is all about.

DC

When I first saw your show, I was surprised to hear you say that you had begun your career in the Cotton Club as a dancer. I had always thought that you were, right from the very beginning, a singer.

LH

No. I started out dancing. My mother outgypsied Gypsy's mother. She should have been the performer. And she was. She was an actress with a black stock company: the Lafayette Players in New York.

DC

Doing black plays?

LH

No, there were no black plays—no black writing—then. Except minstrel shows. I remember she did *Madame X*, and when I was very small, almost four years old, I played the baby in that play. We were in Philadelphia at the Earle Theater and the original baby got sick and my mother put me in the crib. And I was all right. I had been listening to her. When she played in *Way Down East*, I'd be with a bunch of kids that belonged to the cast, watching the show from behind the fake fireplace. I was five when they put me onstage. When the curtain opened and I suddenly saw this tier of faces, I started to cry. The next time I was in show business was when I was sixteen. My mother was hungry and I was hungry. She had married a new stepfather. She had friends that had been in the Lafayette company and she heard from them that they were auditioning for someone to be in the chorus line of the Cotton Club. She took me down there— I was almost sixteen—hiding from the truant officers, and they took me in because I was cute. I didn't know how to do a damn thing. I had had dance classes with my girlfriends in Brooklyn when I was a teenager, but I was not a good dancer. But, because the Cotton Club worked that way, they took me on. They did brilliant shows. I was in a line of twelve chorines and I was the youngest one, aside from one other girl in the chorus. Since my mother couldn't be, she was determined that I should be in show business.

DC

Did you offer any resistance?

LH

Oh, yes. I missed Brooklyn and my friends that I had grown up with. I had come from a very middle-class Brooklyn family. My grandmother was a social-service worker, a teacher, who was an ardent fighter to get young teenagers educated and off the streets. My mother came from a middle-class family. Her father was a "polite drunk" and her mother taught in the school system and her grandmother had raised her. She was Senegalese and spoke French, and she despised black people. So, my mother was raised to be a lady, to do nothing with her hands and to be beautiful for a rich man or a husband.

DC

How was she lured into show business?

LH

She was a dreamer. She married my father, who was a beautiful man. They divorced when I was three years old because he was a renegade and didn't want to shine shoes for the bosses, and so my mother left me with my grandmother and went on the stage. She was beautiful! And she could act and she could sing like a bird!

DC

And the audiences? Were they all black?

LH

Yes, that's right. They never played to white people. A lot of great actors came from that Lafayette stock group . . . Rose McClendon and Andrew Bishop . . . and Georgette Harvey. They worked as long as they had money. They worked at the Lafayette Theater in New York, at the Earle in Philadelphia, and at the Howard Theater in Washington and then they went south. There was no place else for them to work. Historically speaking, it's a marvelous story. There was Charles Gilpin, but he worked in Europe with mixed casts. This was in the early twenties. My mother's only motivation for living was the stage and because she couldn't marry and have the life my grandmother talked about, the theater was her fairyland. She could not understand that I was dreaming about being a little girl who grew up in Brooklyn, went to school, and finally married one of my chums. I had no thought of theater at all.

DC

How did the dancer change into a singer?

LH

That came after two babies and a divorce. I ran away from the club. My mother got me out, and I was put on with Noble Sissle's Orchestra. I didn't sing, I tap-danced in front of the orchestra, and the guys sang. I'd do one little song, sort of half speaking and half singing. I had no vocal ability.

DC

You didn't think of yourself as a singer?

LH

Oh, no! I could carry a tune only because I have a good ear and I was fairly intelligent about a lyric. But, after two days, I would have no voice because, you see, I have a postnasal drip and I had no way of knowing, then, how to deal with it. I've met so many singers who have the same problem, and this disability held me back for a long time. Even through the days I was singing at the Copacabana I would have to go to the doctor every day. Until I learned how to lick it. Paul Robeson told me how years back because he had the same problem. First, you close up all the vents the air-conditioning comes out of and make everybody miserable. That stuff they use in them is what I'm allergic to. Then, you use a lot of warm salt water and baking soda and you rinse your nose out. I had to learn how to do that.

DC

When did you begin to take yourself seriously as a singer?

LH

I'll tell you when I really began to sing for my *life*. When I had been with Sissle, I went through years of looking attractive but singing lousy, which of course, I didn't like. So when I got married—we were hungry then—there was a woman in Pittsburgh who was a pianist, and she had connections with wealthy white people. She would play at their parties for money. She said to me, "Come and sing at some of these parties with me and make $5 or $10." And that was the first time I realized I had something that gained attention. I didn't dance, but I sang some of the Rodgers and Hart and Cole Porter songs they were doing at the new Cotton Club on Broadway.

And people began to listen. Not so much because of the tone that was coming out but because of some belief I had in what I was saying. And I was getting accustomed to singing in front of people . . . not somebody way around somewhere whom I didn't know and who was smoking and eating and didn't give a damn anyway. That was in '38. Then the separation came, and I really had to make some loot to feed my two kids. I went back to New York to Sissle and I asked for a job. He couldn't do anything for me . . . we were still in the Depression. That's when I had this agent I'd met while I was with Sissle. He took me around to the clubs downtown and that was the first time I began to get into this horrible thing about, "You don't look black, but we would hire you in a minute if you were Latin." But I couldn't sing the blues when they wanted black singers.

DC
Was that because you couldn't or were you just uninterested in that kind of music?

LH
My grandfather and my mother listened to Bert Williams and Caruso. Also, we were a Catholic family, and so I never heard gospel singing in the Baptist church. Even when I was in the south, I wasn't allowed to associate with . . . I was taught I was not a field hand. I was not a slave. And slaves had invented gospel and blues. I had all this wrong, rigid background that has a lot to do with the way I am. Also, I was taught by my grandmother never to show emotion. My mother would leave me with strangers, and I learned to hide my feelings. I never came out of my emotional shell even when I was singing.

DC
Which, for most people, singing allows.

LH
That's right! But I realized it was a job, and so I developed a sort of "attitude" in my singing in those early days at the Waldorf and the Copa. I was aloof. Stylized. And it was also the thing that made the money for me. And, then, they were trying to make other black girls sing like me and not be "free" as Aretha Franklin is now. When Diana Ross first started, Berry Gordy brought her to me—I was in

England—and he said, "Now, this is the lady that we want you to be like." Dozens of girls went through this thing of having to be another Lena Horne because that was what was accepted in those years.

DC

Did you look the scene over, then, and measure it intellectually?

LH

No, I didn't. But, as I was going along, I recognized my prejudices against the system and against white people. And, I also knew I had this power—this cold, outwardly composed, glamorous image from MGM. They certainly didn't know what to do with me. What I resent about the early beginnings, too, was that they impeded me. I didn't know how joyful I could be after I finally really did it. But that took a long, long time. That took marriage and a family. But I had one great teacher, the first one that really had an impact on me physically and made me produce more: Kay Thompson.* Thank God I met her! She was an old friend of Lennie's.§ She's meshed in my whole beginning with him at MGM. I was at all the parties and someone would say "Oh, would you sing a song for us?" . . . I was going through all that. Well, I sang all the right things. Cole Porter—who was out there—Gershwin. All the great music. And then Lennie began to construct a musical background for me. He made arrangements for me. Each new arrangement, it would be a higher note or a deeper note. I think he knew that I was an intellectual singer, so he would construct these architectural things to stretch me. And Kay had begun the "power" thing—the strength and where it came from. Most of mine comes from my belt which it pushes up. I found I had more physical comfort in standing a certain way, with my knees out, you know . . . and my face . . . [*She makes the classic facial expression that is one of her trademarks.*] Yes, Kay began to teach me, and Lennie began to write for me. And I was always more comfortable if

---

*Kay Thompson was an eminent coach in New York and at MGM in the early forties. She subsequently appeared with the Williams Brothers in a brilliantly successful nightclub act. She retired to write the famous series of children's books about Eloise at the Plaza Hotel.

§Lena Horne's husband, Lennie Hayton, now deceased.

it was a rhythmic number. It interested me, especially if the rhythms were intricate, and it helped me develop an interesting style, because I would get bored with an ordinary, unchallenging vocalization of a song. And, of course, there were other things. My kids were growing up, and we still had no place to live. Lennie and I decided to get married, and we had to marry in Europe because, even in that year, there was still a law in California against mixed marriages. So, all this nonsensical crap was going on along with the career.

DC

But "all this nonsensical crap" and everything else you've been speaking about was going into the furnace where it was annealed into your . . . does it embarrass you if I say . . . art? I think that must be the one good thing to take out of such a shabby history.

LH

It's true. But it's too bad you don't know it when it's happening, because then you'd go about living it differently. . . . Well, after a while, after a very long while—almost twenty years—of our working together and singing everywhere—and I mean we sang to all the chic audiences—the next thing that happened was Adlai Stevenson, who was running for President. Herbie Baker wrote a song for me, "I Love the 'Guv' " that I sang at a money-raising benefit. And that was the first time in my life that I got a laugh, because the song was very clever. I had never gone into "special material" and, of course, a laugh—as unaware as I was that it would come . . . and I guess it came because I *was* unaware—did something marvelous for my ego. Then he changed it to "I Love to Love," so that I could use it in cafés, and people began to laugh. I got this great surge of power, you know, that only a laugh can give you. When Kay and I used to clown around, she'd say, "You're the best living room comic we ever had." But I had never dared do it in public. Nevertheless, *they* thought I was funny. I didn't. I was only able to be that way with people I was close to because all these vicissitudes had left me rather tongue-tied. So they could see that side of me that nobody else ever saw.

DC

It seems as though you kept picking up pieces of yourself along the way all through the years.

LH

Exactly! Early in my career I had a black band leader tell me: "Listen, girl, there are 20,000 more beautiful black women can outsing you any day of the week. You just got to be the one to be chosen." So all the labor I've had was to stop feeling somebody was doing me a favor. I hate that. I had to learn how to sing, to teach myself how to be human, be a woman—and that's good because what the people get now is the sum total of all of that.

DC

You and Lenny came to some kind of crossroads, I believe.

LH

Well, there came a time when I began to see that Lennie and I had begun to eat off each other. We were really tranquilizing ourselves. I suddenly had reached the point where you say, "I've had the best of this and now I have to . . ." But, you see, I had never worked with anyone but him. Toward the end, we would have to scurry when we knew we were going to have another engagement. We'd have to come together, and the new ideas weren't coming, and so I said I would have to have someone else. And Lennie, you understand, had given up years of writing for other people. He'd settled into a kind of rut—a comfortable one—but he was not working and spreading that great talent that he had. So, I stayed in New York, and he went back out west. I worked with two or three other arrangers, and, without knowing me, they began to try to stretch me and then I made a dreadful record. But when I listened to it, there were one or two things I could hear. They were new and strange. And I had discovered the Beatles, and I loved what they had to say musically. I loved their choice of music, and the way they wrote it was very tasty. I don't think anybody since has matched them. They had such beautifully thought out chord sequences and changes. And I knew they didn't settle for the cheap, easy thing. Lennie and I had a big fight about it. I said: "You know, music will never be the same. It won't be like the 'behind-the-scenes' music in the movies. It won't be the way we had been. Something's got to give."

DC

Were you still seeing each other?

LH

Oh, yes. We went to see *Hair* together. That was just before he died.
And we had many discussions about this. He wasn't happy, because
he heard bad things, too, as well as good. Of course, the trap he fell
into was that he didn't know that, by then, Hollywood and TV had
turned the good into the bad. When he'd gone back to do his scores,
he'd had to write "boom boom boom boom." It broke his heart. I was
feeling my way along, with jazz arrangers, with gospel and, of course,
protest music, which was in. This was in the early sixties. And protest
music was what I felt, deep inside, was what I hadn't said. Bob Dylan
and those people were coming along, with the Beatles, and they wrote
with literacy—with a poem under, a story under. And then I went
south for the first time since I was grown. I was more or less an
orphan. I didn't know "Lena" and I didn't know anybody who had
known me until I went back there. And I found people I had lived
with who knew me when I was a little girl in Brooklyn. You see, my
mother would bring me down there every year. Well, I was hearing
young black singers, and I would speak in the schools. Then, I went
to Jackson, Mississippi, and I was with Medgar Evers three days
before they murdered him. I sang in a Baptist church one night, two
nights before he died. I was with Billy Strayhorn, Dick Gregory, and
my son. I had always been an activist, not because I was political
but because I was frightened; you know all the crap that was going
on. So when they killed him, and I saw young black people—a whole
new generation—doing these things, I had this kindred feeling. It
brought me to my senses because, you see, I'd never belonged to any
set. But now I began to think, "If I can sing in that church . . ."
And I hadn't even sung anything that they liked; I was just doing my
same old stuff, and they listened! And that was the most different
audience I'd ever sung in front of. "How wonderful! I haven't fallen
through the floor. I'm not dead!" I was crying; I began to cry a lot.
I'd never cried before!

DC

You had passed through a kind of semiretirement, hadn't you, Lena?

LH

It was almost five years, and I was desperately in need of cash. But
now, as I began to sing, I was able to hear the sound I made and I

would think about it. And then when they killed [*Robert*] Kennedy
and Martin Luther King, it seemed like a floodgate had opened. There
had been a lot of deaths in my own family. Lenny died and . . . well,
I thought I couldn't survive. It was Alan King who dragged me back
on the stage, and when I sang, I was different. I began to "listen"
to what I was doing and thinking. I listened to the audience. Even
to the quiet. I had never listened to it before. It had just been quiet,
but now I listened to what they were thinking and I began to sing. I
was different because I was letting something in. The tone was developing differently. I could do what I wanted with it. I could soften
it. I wasn't afraid to show the emotion. I went straight for what I
thought the songwriter had felt at a particular moment because he
must have felt what I'd been feeling or else I couldn't have read that
lyric, I couldn't have understood what he was saying. And I used my
regretfulness and my cynicism. But even my cynicism had become
not so much that as . . . logic. Yes, life *is* shit. Yes, people listen
in different ways. Some nights they're unhappy at something that has
happened to them. OK. I can feel that knot of resistance. OK. That's
where I'm going to work to. That's where I'm going to soften it up.
And the second "eight" would be different than the first because the
first was feeling it out and the second would change because I could
come in "to my mood." And sometimes I said: "OK. I'm going to hit
that note," and I'd never hit it before and I know I can't . . . and
I'd hit it! And it would be . . . Ah! We'd all be happy! And I sensed
their relaxation because I used to notice a kind of tenseness on the
part of the audience. It developed out of this relaxation . . . a tone
that was softer, more liquid. And you know, I found people not talking
about "style" any more. They were talking about "We heard Lena
and she said . . ." It was a whole different feeling! And it also
develops an "ego." I can't wait to have it happen to me. It's so
marvelous and useful. I used to tell the audience if only they understood how much a part of the performance they are!

DC

You spoke about that in your show.

LH

But, I do think that, a long time back, if I had had more and more
of that urge to be a star and be on the stage, I would have suffered

and not eaten and gone and scrubbed floors, and then gone and had my lessons, and then been on the stage and then waited all that time between, maybe taken dope, maybe done this and that—the intellectual side of me saved me but it also kept me too protected. It kept me at a distance in my performing. What I enjoy so much, now, is the freedom to sing. Some nights when I sing "Stormy Weather," I'm out of my mind with anger—not *at* people but at what we go through in our lives, you and me—and it has a whole different sound from three nights before when I was feeling kind of happy and "Stormy" was . . . Aaaah! But then, on another night, it would be fierce, because now I'm "going to fight it!"

DC

I was going to ask you whether, when you pick up a song after a while, you find that you are singing it differently, but you seem to have answered that. Now, I'm tempted to ask if you reject repeating the way you may have done it in the past.

LH

Thank you! Thank you! Because I do!

DC

Do you have a personal system you use to choose the songs you will sing or is it purely a question of, "I like that song"?

LH

It's usually "I like that song." But I find it very difficult now. I found it difficult when I was fifty. I always thought young music wasn't suitable, but I'm having second thoughts about that because now and then you find a writer like Stevie Wonder who writes a kind of universal music. Thank God! It's ageless. And some of the women singer-writers are writing the same way—songs that a woman who is sixty-seven, as I am, can sing and not sound . . . But, you know, even at the beginning, I was always shy to sing a song like . . . Well, I don't mean to compare myself to Eartha Kitt. I only use her as an example, but Eartha was always a girl and a woman who was completely at ease as she extolled herself. It wasn't that I was shy, but I never believed I was a sexpot. I was a sensuous person and a feminine person, but I never dreamed that the audience—that the men sitting out there—were perceiving me in that "Oh, she's a hot number!" way. And I said to myself, "If they ever realized that all I was thinking about was what I was going to eat after the show or maybe I'll have a drink . . ." Never getting away from the song, but in between the numbers, I was thinking, "Let's get through." And they're saying, "This sexy broad!" It's more difficult for me now, but I find that if the writer has humor, then the whole damn thing's funny, anyway. What is unfortunate, I guess, is that I like all music. But, I think most of us do.

DC

But I'm sure that, by now, when you hear a song, you know more or less if it is a good or a bad song, in the sense that it will or will not work for you.

LH

Yes. I do know that. And I know about routining and the scheduling of it. Because it doesn't work in certain places.

DC

How important is a song to a singer? I have heard you sing songs that are wonderful pieces of music, but I've also heard you sing some that were trivial and even silly, and they worked equally well for you.

LH

I sang a song this year in England that was not terribly well received. It was an odd song, but it taxed me vocally and kept me from getting lazy. I sometimes make a mistake and choose a number that does not interest the audience, but I'll sing a couple up front that do interest them in order to soften them up. Then I do that song. I don't think an actress can do that, but a singer, if she's got enough guts, can get away with doing a song that's set with her vocally and physically and yet is not a crowd pleaser.

DC

How about the opposite: the crowd pleaser that you don't like to sing?

LH

That's where old-fashioned show business comes in. I was working once at Bill Miller's Riviera . . . a wonderful place that used to be across the George Washington Bridge. I did a couple of shows each night, and one night, when I came off after the second show, Sophie Tucker came backstage and said, "How dare you not sing 'Stormy Weather'?" And I said: "I didn't sing it because, first of all, it is not my song." That was still in the early years after the picture.* So I told her: "It was Ethel Waters's song. I never thought people would associate it with me, and I've fought many years against 'Stormy Weather'." And she said: "I don't give a damn about what you went through with 'Stormy Weather.' Whether you like it or not, it has become your signature, and if you are ever so stupid as to do a performance and not do it, you are losing 50 percent of your audience." It took me a few years to come to the conclusion that she was absolutely right. The second bit of advice I got one night was when I opened at The Talk of the Town in London. I had just finished working in *Jamaica*.§ Yip wrote very clever, political lyrics. But it is different on Broadway. They're there and they're sitting and listening. But cabaret is different. I sang one of the songs from the show, "Napoleon," and even had some extra lyric. It was all very clever, but I noticed when I sang it that the audience was restive. That was the first time that had ever happened to me, because the audiences in London are usually very polite. They were not listening. Noel Coward came back and he said to me: "Darling, I'd be the first one to deny the fact, but it's quite true that you must never let the audience know that you are brighter than they are. When people are drinking in a cabaret, not intimidated by a proscenium, they don't want to have to think about what the lyric is saying. And you are actually asking us to listen to rhyme and meter and to the ideas behind the lines! And some of us were too drunk to bother!" And I knew he was right. After all, we're entertainers. I don't mean we should just make them laugh. We should make them laugh, cry, do anything, but we are being paid. We're not doing it for nothing.

DC

Lena, would you tell me about Harold Arlen? I heard him on the radio this week. It was his birthday and, although I had heard he was very, very ill, he sounded like the Harold Arlen I remembered

*Miss Horne had made a film, *Stormy Weather*, in which she had sung the song.
§The Harold Arlen–Yip Harburg musical.

when I met him in the early fifties.* He was asked if he had a favorite
singer who represented the ideal voice for his music and just as fast
as you could say "Stormy Weather," he said, "Lena Horne." Do you
think that he is a composer whose music offered you a particular
sound that made it easier to communicate what you were feeling at
the time when a musical language was the only one that could do
that for you?

LH

I was always aware that he was a superior writer and I was always
proud to go with the best because I knew that they were on top of
everything that we know about life—that they can write musically a
grander attitude than life really has. And he had written the first song
I ever sang in public, at the Cotton Club . . . "Lady with a Fan."
And I was bad in it. Two nights and . . . forget it! And I knew him
in California. We'd be at certain parties and I'd get up and we'd sing.
His range was incredible! I guess I never really thought about it until
lately, but I did do a lot of his things.

DC

When Frank Sinatra sings a concert, he invariably gives verbal credit
to the men who arranged his music. Do you feel strongly about the
quality of your arrangements?

LH

Well, Lenny was the best I ever had. I don't have a favorite one now.
And, mostly what we've worked out for the stage are things in which
I've had some input. Naturally, it just comes out now. I open my
mouth and say, "Well, no, I'd rather do this this way." And so it's
a joint effort, and I find that young musicians go along with it. And
they put their thing in, which is useful, so it is a kind of blending.

DC

Here's a question that may sound a little as though it was dragged
in out of left field, but could we talk a little about clothes and their
importance? I don't think I have ever seen you perform in a dress
that wasn't eye-filling. Are your clothes designed less as gowns than
as costumes that must function in a particular way?

*Harold Arlen died in 1986.

LH

They used to be very high style . . . breathtaking, always expensive but, at the same time, constricting. I couldn't walk. I was like a geisha. And they also constricted my movement. As the years went on, I began to chafe at that sort of thing. I remember the first time I went back, after Lenny died, and I had nothing to wear. I had met Georgio Sant'Angelo and I wore the first of those gypsy dresses he made. It was very open and free—no bones—and I felt comfortable. Also, I was beginning to . . . I had always turned to all sides of the audience to be looked at by the people, but now I began to turn to people so I could get something from them. And I was able to move in these new things. Now I can only work in a gown that flows.

DC

How pressuring were the demands of a one-woman show like yours?

LH

None of it was pressuring onstage. Offstage it drove me crazy. There were the niceties with the press. And the audience—it was as if I belonged to them. I suppose anybody who has been in the theater a long time has this happen, but it was very new to me. They take over and possess you completely, and their troubles become yours. Sometimes I had to stop reading my mail because it would influence what was going on on the stage. But you don't know what to say when you've had such a ball with them and they come back and say: "God! I was going to kill myself last week. But now I'm not afraid." It begins to give you a feeling of responsibility that you do not want. They get familiar with me. Now, I'm very familiar with them on the stage, but when they come back, they've invaded that. Even in cabaret, I never mingled with the audience. This is a wholly new thing.

DC

Was the show a difficult one to do night after night? The energy level seemed as though it would exhaust a marine.

LH

It's discipline. I'm sure that's an old-fashioned but, nevertheless, important thing that I hold on to. I don't want to be a sloppy performer. And when I know I'm just on the verge of becoming self-indulgent,

I say, "Now, quit it!" Part of that familiarity gets to you. The garbage truck goes by, and one of the guys says, "Hey, Lena, whatcha doin'?" And you have to remember not to fall into that trap with the audience. It's very dangerous.

DC

Tell me, Lena, are you one of the lucky few who never had to study singing? Ethel Merman once said she didn't believe in vocal study. She just opened her mouth and out it came.

LH

No, I believe in good study, but there are a lot of bad vocal coaches. Even an opera singer, one I'm very fond of, told me her voice had been ruined, and she needed two years to get it back together. If they don't know Kay Thompson and they don't know you, they're in trouble.

DC

Do you have your own way to warm up before a show?

LH

First of all, when I get up, I'm full of that . . . that stuff . . . and I have to go through all that medical work on my own self. But I find that you've got to talk to somebody first. You've got to say hello, even though I hate everybody in the morning. You have to speak to get it up. I got this from Eileen Farrell. We do the same thing. She says: "When I get up in the morning, after I've had my coffee and said hello, I try to hit my top note. If I have trouble and don't hit it, then I start humming and doing breathing exercises." And she says that it's very seldom she can hit that top note. She says, too, that she doesn't start there, but slowly works her way up to it.

DC

And this system works for you, also?

LH

Yes, it does. And I get in tune. My big problem is that I say I'm going to take it easy, but I get caught up and, if I'm not careful, I'm singing full out, and that's terrible. If I don't like the song, I'm easy, but if I like it, look out! I'm in it!

DC

Can you read music?

LH

No, I can't. But I can read the design, sometimes. I know that that's a middle note there and this is a low one; some parts of it go up and then suddenly, they come back down again. I have some trouble with intervals, halftones, and rest marks, but I always have a pianist there who teaches me the song.

DC

Lena, may we talk about young people and some of the problems they face breaking into our business? Wherever I teach, I am asked the same questions, but I'm never sure of the best and the most honest way to answer them. Questions such as: How do you get a record? Should I put an "act" together? How do I get into the musical theater?

LH

I think it is wonderful that actors know about you, because you are a refuge and they get work. But I don't know what to say to the young people just coming along. There is no training ground for them and no apprenticeship. They've got to get a few dollars together the hard way to keep themselves going. It's very hard.

DC

When I was watching your show, I was thrilled that there were so many young people in the audience. I always thought of you as "mine," and I felt as though my generation was giving your show to them as a kind of a present.

LH

It was a shock to me. I never expected any but my contemporaries to enjoy it, and all the young people were so wonderful. They'd come back, and they kept me so excited because I was getting something.

DC

So were they. In an interview you gave to *The New York Times*, you said that if you couldn't have been a singer, you would have liked to have been a teacher. What did you mean by that?

LH

I wanted to be a teacher all my life. First all, all my people, except my mother and my father, were teachers and principals of schools. My grandmother graduated when she was sixteen years old, and my mother's mother taught in the public schools for thirty-four years. That was what I was supposed to be. And I have always had this great admiration for teachers. If we could have had a black Oppenheimer, I would have killed myself for him. I would have been a teacher because if I had been there in that family, and everybody around me had a book, and I lived with books, and . . . well, there would have been nothing else for me to be, except married. And I get along rather well with young people . . . fourteen, fifteen . . . that age group. I don't know why, but they come to me—everybody's grandchildren except my own. And they say to my grandchildren: "Oh, your grandma's so easy to talk to. She understands what I'm saying." A lot of them think that people die when they're twenty-five. The older folks—the fifties, forty-fives, and even the forties—they're saying, "Now we're not afraid to be sixty." And I say: "Jesus Christ! You're so young!" And I get very angry because it took me until I was fifty to enjoy what I was doing!

DC

It was the nature of our generation. We worked so hard running away from what we then worked so hard to run back to.

LH

Oh, yes. And nobody does anything to reinforce our real selves. It was all done to undo us. And we're very cruel to each other.

DC

You are one of the really great singers who has also done "book" shows and films. So many singers have never done that. They're either banished to, or prefer to remain in, cabarets. Did you plan your career that way?

LH

In the beginning I was in those films because of a fluke. Later, all I ever wanted was to be on the stage. That was when I finally said I was a "working woman." And when I did *Jamaica*, I thought I'd made it, but nothing happened for another ten years. You know, we're very slow in the theater. The good thing is that it makes us strong.

DC

How do you feel about singers like yourself and, perhaps, Judy Garland who . . .

LH

[*Guessing what is on my mind*] We're not recording artists.

DC

Not before the fact maybe, but, after the fact—once you have been seen—one treasures the record.

LH

Yes. The best ones I've ever made were when I was recorded singing to people—to audiences. Like the one at the Waldorf.

DC

Do you think that your ability to dramatize a song and to make it something of a theatrical happening makes your recordings less valuable as a total statement of your work?

LH

Yes. I would have liked to have been like Natalie Cole, but then I would have been manipulated by the morals and the taste of the moment. Now Nat Cole's daughter, when she came out that first year, was hot as a pistol. Then the second year and the next year, there was a different style because they chew up the towel and get rid of it. They have the material there and people who know how to bend their voices to a mechanical sound. Let's face it, everything is going to be electronic—our singing, our whole show business, I'm sorry to say—unless we do something about saving the theater. That's why it's important to train your voice. At least you will have the power to survive to do it in the theater. Voices are made to sound through different electrical instruments, synthesizers, track on top of track. And it's pictorial phrasing now, where you don't need a trained voice and you don't need talent. In fact, if you have it, it's a handicap. Now, take Stevie [*Wonder*]. He has a voice that's clear and true and good. Michael [*Jackson*] was born into this kind of thing. The times have a lot to do with one's singing sound. Just like the books you read and the clothes you wear. He [*Michael Jackson*] is of this new generation. He'll last longer because he's genuinely talented. I think he has more sticking power than Prince, but now the media are building up Prince.

DC

And the point is that they may very well, after a time, dump him?

LH

Yes. Because there are so many more coming, and they can create the new sound that will be desired. They feed it to you over that box and you find yourself saying, "Gee, I like this year's girl."

DC

What I find so sad is that each new generation—and now they are only ten years apart—wants its own heroes and refuses to relate to those who went before it.

LH

Even young blacks. The one thing that they neglect is that being black is a good thing. Because, if you're black, there's a difference. It sets you apart.

DC

I recently read this letter in the "Calendar" section of the *Los Angeles Times:* "Who is Sarah Vaughan?" The editor's answer, and I quote, was, "Jazz singer Sarah Vaughan is Linda Rondstadt to the twenty-fifth power." How would you have answered the letter?

LH

I don't think I could have topped that. You know, if I sang "I've Got a Crush on You" now, they'd say I stole it from Linda Rondstadt.

DC

Lillian Hellman once said: "You always like best the last thing you did. You like to think you get better with time but, you know, it isn't always true."

LH

That's so right! Honey, I've heard myself do some things I knew were not at my best. I think most performers feel that. I do. I'm always nervous before I go onstage. I say, "Uh oh, this may be the night." And I enter with all my antennae out to test the audience, like a fly testing everything. I never take it for granted. I never believe it's going to happen until I get to them. And sometimes when I think it was good, I'll talk to a few people, and they'll say, "You were off tonight." And I say, "I was?" Then, I turn that thing [*a recording device*] back on and I say: "Where did I go wrong? Ah, yes, I hear it." And then, on another night, when I know I'm lousy, they'll say, "Jesus, you were wonderful tonight!"

DC

Do you believe that?

LH

No, I never do. Because we always believe bad reviews. Most performers do, anyway. And I always think I could do better. It's an impossible thing because I want to sound like Aretha Franklin. Of all the ones I know, I know that Sarah doesn't want to. She is like a great, fine Stradivarius. And I know Ella doesn't, but she's so . . . [*She is at a loss for words.*] And the young kids want to sound like Prince or Michael—all models of themselves.

DC

Lena, here's a final question for you. I don't know if you're an opera buff, as I am, but why is the opera so far ahead of Broadway? We see integrated casts all the time, and the public shows no resistance whatever to the sight and sound of what is going on on the stage.

LH

It's a question I've often asked myself. It could be the producers. First of all, it's a money-making thing. Like *Dreamgirls* or three, four years ago, when anything that was black was hot and selling like *Ain't Misbehavin'*. Then, too, we still don't have a roster of fine black writers or even white ones who write for black people. They haven't got used to us being part of the tapestry. A long time back when they did *Subways Are for Sleeping*, I thought they'd integrate the show. But they didn't. And it hasn't happened yet. The producers of the world don't see the necessity for it. They want a fast buck.

DC

But the opera houses are making a fast buck. And a few years ago, *Beverly Hills Cop* was the highest grossing picture of the year, so even film producers are making a fast buck.

LH

You know, I once asked Rodgers and Hammerstein if I could be in *The King and I*. I wanted to play the first wife. I was young when it first came out. They said, "No, your name is too big, and it would throw the thing out of kilter." Now, I wasn't that big. But there it was, even then. I'm afraid we're going to have to leave this one blank. And, Oh God! I'm sitting here wondering what I'm going to do next. I feel awful, and not because I'm full of energy. Now I begin to ache in the morning, and I go through hell just to get so I can go and wash my teeth. . . . [*She laughs, but the laugh soon freezes into deadly seriousness*.] I feel guilty not working. I have this work ethic going, you know. Like . . . like I don't deserve it.

*T*ony Roberts

Tony Roberts is an actor whose career takes place on the playing fields where, for purposes of survival, all present-day performers should be able to contend. At the time of this interview, he had just completed a successful Broadway run in a straight play, had appeared earlier in the year on a weekly television series with Lucie Arnaz, and, as a senior member of the Woody Allen stock company, currently could be seen in that master's latest film.* His resumé further includes

---

*At the time of this book's publication, he was appearing on Broadway in *Arsenic and Old Lace*.

references to his leading roles in three major musicals: *How Now Dow Jones, Promises, Promises,* and *They're Playing Our Song.* It would be difficult to find another actor who can do so much—and so ably.

When we met as teacher and student, it was not only his talent that distinguished him but an ability to keep in perfect balance his comic sense and his intolerance of foolishness of any kind where show business was concerned. Now, many years later, he seems to have found a continual flow of employment—he is on a roll. I think of him as one of a vanishing breed of light comedians, an actor in the tradition of William Powell, Melvin Douglas, Robert Montgomery, and the young Cooper and Gable. And, more than those giants, he can sing.

DC

Your career began in 1962, and as I studied the line of its progression, it struck me how much it illustrates the need today for actors to present their work in a multiple of windows. You've played comedy on stage, on television in series, and on the screen; you've done repertory in regional theaters, played *Hamlet* in a university theater, Petruchio in Atlanta; you've played on and off Broadway; and, to get closer to our reason for talking today, you've sung in musicals in New York, on the coast, on tour, and in England. Was all this a pattern you planned for yourself from the beginning, or does it indicate a survival script for all actors?

TR

I was luckier than most in that my family overlapped the theater and show business. My father had been an actor in his twenties and later became an announcer. My cousin was Everett Sloane, who was a member of the Mercury Theater Players with Orson Welles, and my father's best friend was the actor-director Paul Stewart. I was always surrounded by people who made me realize what a difficult business I was getting into. As a teenager, when I demonstrated an earnestness about being an actor, my father impressed upon me that I had to be prepared to do lots of different things . . . that I had to study singing, movement, to familiarize myself with the classics, that I ought to go to college and learn how to be a good actor, because, one day, I might be called upon to be and do everything.

DC

In a way, he guessed what the business would ask of your generation. Certainly, in his time, *specialization* was not a dirty word?

TR

But he had seen what too much specialization could mean. All his friends were always broke, and he didn't want me to die in poverty. He felt that if I confined myself to being only a stage actor or only a screen actor who had to depend upon a film at any moment, in order to pay my rent, that I would end up like all his friends. It was he who encouraged me to be a working actor instead of a star. That meant being able to do commercials and voice-overs and to sing— if I had to in a play—because he was afraid that if I was not able to do all that, I wouldn't be able to make a living. My father's theory was that stardom is too small a target. He thought it was better to spread yourself across the three media and work towards being a working actor, because an actor who isn't working isn't an actor.

DC

Your career corroborates his advice.

TR

I was blessed.

DC

Would this be your advice to young performers today?

TR

Absolutely. It is a realistic approach to things because there just isn't that much work available. My father also felt I would make it on the stage and that it was a bad idea to go to Los Angeles on spec and be available. His theory was that an actor should make his mark in the theater and then go when you're sent for.

DC

Is that theory a valid one?

TR

I think nothing gets results faster in Los Angeles than saying no to people. To be able to say "I can't" or "I won't" makes them want you all the more. They can't believe that you are not there waiting by your phone. And so I have have tried to maintain the idea that I am a New York actor working on the stage there who is, occasionally, willing to come west if the part and the money are right. Now, nothing could be farther from the truth at times, but that's the image I try to project.

DC

To come a little closer to what you and I are about . . . you are an actor who sings. Could you try to explore how the actor's disciplines alter in order for him to be able to get up on a stage and sing? How different are the methodologies?

TR

The root of the problem is to find the passion that makes someone start to sing. You can speak to another actor on stage without passion because there is a natural one-on-one communication going on. To speak to no one—which, in a sense, is what one does when you sing—and make the, what you have called, "vertical statement,"* requires more motivation than the average "prosaic" play. And then to turn front and pretend that you are expressing yourself to the gods or to someone who is not there calls for shifting that other person to whom you are talking to an imaginary person somewhere on the balcony rail. That person can be a part of yourself you are singing to, but that requires a lot of churning and passion to make sense. After all, we don't talk out loud to ourselves when we're alone in a room. One's inner monologue may be going on, but you don't vocalize it, you don't externalize it. And so, it has to be very strong inside

---

*If dialogue can be imagined as a horizontal line, since one of its characteristics is to move the play forward, a soliloquy can be seen as a vertical statement in that the play comes to a halt while the speaker unburdens him/or herself, informs the audience of where he or she stands at that moment in the play's progress, or speaks of things the other characters in the play may not hear. Since all songs are sung as soliloquies, they, too, can be described as "vertical" statements.

you before you can turn front and face the blankness of nothing and have the need to sing.

DC

Is that learnable?

TR

Yes, in the same way that learning a soliloquy in a play by Shakespeare is learnable. But you must create the world in your head very vividly so that you don't reveal the nakedness of an act which is, after all, kind of silly. So what carries you from being in profile with another actor behind the fourth wall and takes you front into nowhere has to be the conviction of your own imagery, your own imagination, to demonstrate the *need* to have to do it . . . to *have* to sing.

DC

You and I worked together almost twenty years ago. Had you sung before we met?

TR

I had studied singing at the High School for Performing Arts, and I had sung in college musicals, but I was uncomfortable with it because I didn't know how to involve my body physically or, for that matter, any *part* of my body . . . even my face. I was focused on the sound of my voice and the meaning of the song, and I was busy responding to the song instead of creating it. I guess the most important thing I ever learned about acting was your revelation that the verbalization of something was always behind its physicalization if the idea was born out of truth. You taught me how to work, to feel the image strongly enough in myself, and only then could it be verbalized. And that the "life" that was born underneath the song had to continue throughout the song because otherwise the song would die, and when it died, at that moment, you wouldn't know what to do with your hands.

DC

It's not so much that *you* wouldn't know what to do with your hands as that your *hands* wouldn't know what to do because they wouldn't be receiving any messages from that inner voicing.

TR

Exactly. Once I learned how to do that, it totally eliminated my problem, and it still does. I find I use it even in a straight play—which is very recent for me—to resist the temptation to speak and to allow something to happen "on" me which will be far more eloquent and propelling for the words that follow.

DC

Are you musical?

TR

I respond very emotionally to music. It has always meant uncommunicable but very specific kinds of things to me. Particularly, Ravel, Prokofiev, and Shostakovich. I have this feeling that only the composer and I know exactly what he meant.

DC

Then I imagine you have no trouble learning music?

TR

Not a bit. I've studied musical theory, the piano, the guitar, and in the last four years, I've taken up the study of the piano very seriously. I practice a couple of hours each day and . . . [*This is delivered with a good deal of amusement*] someday I'll be able to play and sing at the same time.

DC

Getting into the mechanics of rehearsing, how different are the rehearsals of a play from those of a musical?

TR

I think that when one is in a musical, one depends more on a "third eye" to tell you when you are in your own world—one that no one will go to with you—or what you need to do to take the audience with you to that level of experience. You know somehow, innately, what an audience will buy when you are talking to another actor on stage, because you know whether the other *actor* is buying it. You can see it in their eyes . . . if they're listening to you, looking at you. You know when you say something whether it did or didn't land,

and if it didn't, you try to say it a different way and, if they still don't get it, then you say to the director, "He's got to do something in reaction to what I just did, because if I do it any bigger it's not going to make any sense for me." But, on the bottom line, you know whether it's getting home or not. When you're out front with a song, "in one," you're totally at the mercy of someone saying: "Wait a minute! You can't move that quickly over to stage right on the first verse because they're not with you yet." Someone who will give you specific anchors through the song, which will do the same thing for you that you would have found had you been playing in a scene with another actor. Gradually, through that direction, the song is broken down into units just as a scene is broken down into units. I'm told that when musicians play a piece, they break everything down into three note groups: How do those three notes work together? Which is the loudest? The softest? Are they attached to each other? Or are they staccato? When you are singing a song, you need someone to help you break the song down into those units because you are flying free out there. It goes back to the need to have to be wound up and motivated in order to sing and, to be free to do it, you cannot watch yourself closely at the same time. And so you need that third eye.

DC

You are one of a large number of American actors who went to Northwestern University and studied with the late Alvina Krause. Did you choose the school because she was there, or did you come by the experience by accident?

TR

I was fortunate, when I was seventeen, to be a friend of Lee Strasberg's son, and I had an "audience" with Mr. Strasberg to ask him about my future, since I aspired to be an actor. His advice to me was that it was better to go to college because I would act more and get the feeling of "the boards" under my feet, whereas if I stayed in New York, I'd end up being a waiter. And then he asked me what college I was thinking of and I mentioned Northwestern and Alvina Krause, and he said, "She's the best teacher in America." And that was the best advice I ever got.

DC

Was she all you had hoped she would be?

TR

And more. She's the only other teacher I've ever known, other than yourself, who had a passion about what she was teaching, and the truth of that changed the lives of anyone who ever studied with her. She changed my life, as you did. She died at the age of eighty-six, but right up until her death, she was very vital and involved. She had the gift of showing actors how to intensify their performances and make them important so that the audience didn't leave the theater unenlightened or unchanged by what was going on, no matter whether the play was Oscar Wilde's or Shakespeare's. There had to be communication, some change, some revelation that had to happen, and for her it was a religion. She devoted her life to it. She had no family of her own, and so her students became her family. I was fortunate to be shown the way by her.

DC

I once had a certain resistance to an undergraduate study of acting. It seemed to me that teachers in universities were less able to do it than to teach it and that it would be far more valuable to learn the art of it from the artist himself—from an Adler, a Strasberg, a Meisner, or a Lewis. I have had a change of heart in recent years, and now I am not at all certain my position is as tenable as it seemed many years ago, although I still believe that the "craft" of performing is better learned within the reality of the marketplace, where the young student learns not only how to "do it" but how to get it "done" within the often impossible conditions that the business places on the artist.

TR

All my life I assumed that everyone knew the experience one is capable of having in the theater when one sees a great play, a great show, or a great performance. The assumption, I guess, was due to my arrogance of having been brought up in New York City and having been taken to good theater by my parents. I felt I had a measuring stick for judging whether a piece of theater was good or not. Now I know that everybody doesn't have that experience. They don't know what's possible. Last year, for example, I went to see a play in Los Angeles that people I respect told me was the "greatest"—and I didn't think it was good at all. I thought it was a television movie taking place on stage. But I realized that the people who liked it— and the audience did seem to like it—only knew the experience of a television movie—which is what this play was. It didn't have commercials, so they thought it was *really* good. It also didn't have the involvement, or even the meaning, a great piece of theater must have. What Alvina did with her students was to show them the possibilities, to give them a glimpse of the extremities that could be put forth from a printed play. You *could* make people lean forward in their seats, *could* create an unpredictability in each moment of a play, and you could drive home a moment so that no one could miss it. I don't think her skills went much further than that. She didn't teach a 'technique' for creating these things yourself.

DC

That would then be followed by a second stage of study after the actor left the academic environment and came to New York to study?

TR

Yes. With, for example, you. I didn't understand this when I was younger. In my first play in New York, *Something about a Soldier*, I said to one of the stars who had been a Krause student before me, "Isn't Alvina Krause the greatest teacher in the world!?" And he said to me, "I think she's very good when you're beginning." And I was astonished by this apostasy and thought I would never come to see it that way. Well, I can see it that way now, but, at the time, what she showed me was worth everything and I still believe it is the basis of the best kind of education you can have if you want to be an actor. You know, someone once said that acting is something that can't be taught but that there is a great deal to learn about it.

DC

And so, therefore, it has a place in an academic community where "learning" is an organic part of the environment?

TR

Yes. Where the atmosphere is about learning and not, necessarily, about teaching. You see, when I studied with you, you created the bridge between the academic world, which gives you the opportunity to explore and find out how you can do it and the commercial world, which says, "I don't care how you *do* it or arrive at it"—nor should they—"I want to *see* it." For a young actor, the startling fact is that they don't want to help you find it and that they don't care. All they want you to do is to present it and have it there. You gave talented people a way of going from that indulgent creative atmosphere to one in which the man is waving his baton and you better be there.

DC

May we switch to comedy? If there is such a thing as a Woody Allen stock company, you are surely an honored member of that group. Do you go along with the idea, as I do, that some people are just *not* funny and the element that makes those who *are* funny remains mysteriously elusive and impossible to calibrate?

TR

It requires, I think, some kind of distance on yourself. A stepping away from yourself, in some way, to be able to see the opposites in the moment that make one laugh—to see the inconsistencies—and to be able to package that so that there is the element of surprise accompanied with what Alvina Krause used to call a "comic attitude." That's true, of course, but it is equally true that if you underline the comedy, you can forget the laughs. You have to play it as seriously, if not more so. But if you don't have the ability, I can't see how it can be taught. Someone who can tell a good story, it seems to me, can be an actor. But there are actors who can tell a good story but can't tell a funny story.

DC

Did you know, early on, that you could play comedy to good effect?

TR

I'll tell you a story. I was a kid in camp, I was fat, I was about eleven years old, and I was told I could be a hero if I could go three rounds in the ring with this guy named Edelman, who was three times my size. Looking for valor and glory, I accepted the challenge. I fought him in front of the entire camp. I never landed a punch, never raised my head, and I was pummeled and pounded from beginning to end.

At one point, I looked up and was able to focus briefly, as the ref separated us, on my counselors in the third or fourth row who were laughing hard at what was going on. And I noticed that if I staggered a little bit more than I had to, they laughed more and suddenly I realized that they were laughing with me at me, not at me without me. It was a survival lesson. I was lucky to be able to see that, when I took that moment to see that I could control it by making more laughter, I could save my ass. And it's the same damned thing when you go on stage and you say a line that, way down deep, is supposed to be funny; you say it in a way that, somehow, no one can spot, that says, "Hey, laugh at this!" There is an unconscious cue that says, "When I get to the end of this word, you're going to laugh!"

DC

How do you feel about the extraordinary rise and popularity in the last thirty years of improvisational comedy: Second City, Paul Sills, the Groundlings . . .?

TR

I worked with an eminent improvisational director in a play on Broadway that must remain nameless. It became the nightmare of my life. The rehearsals were the funniest ever held; it was brilliant in rehearsal. Unfortunately, it was never the same twice. We would improvise and invent marvelous things, and we'd all laugh and then we opened in Boston, and no one knew if they were supposed to enter stage right or stage left. There was no staged play. There was nothing to link on to. It was terrifying. I hadn't any training in that kind of work, and although I could improvise effectively in rehearsals, I didn't know how to achieve that kind of freedom in front of an audience and to do it night after night and make the *same thing* funny. I used to say to this director that acting isn't the first time, it is the illusion of the first time, and the techniques one uses are what give the audience the impression that this has never happened before when, in fact, every bit of it has happened before. That is the craft and the art of it. So, I guess I can say I'm not very big on the improvisational approach. You know, I seem always to know when something is improvised. There is a change in the reality, just as when someone drops a prop on the stage and no one knows who is going to pick it up. There is a sudden aesthetic change in the reality of the moment when it suddenly goes from preplanned work to improvised work. It's shotgun time.

DC

Somewhat relative to this is something I read that Duse said about improvisational acting. She felt that actors should beware of anything that turns out right the first time. She thought that only the mediocre could be improvised. And I remember, too, reading that the University of Pennsylvania's house organ, *The Punchbowl,* once had on its masthead: "Any damn fool can be spontaneous." How do you feel about this?

TR

I guess I feel that I have gotten benefits out of improvisation in rehearsals, when they were set up properly in order to explore one's behavior in a particular situation, and that some of the things you can learn from it, that you might otherwise never have arrived at because the words on paper would have inhibited you, are of value. But, as a form to place in front of an audience . . . well, I am not that kind of actor.

DC

How do you account for the affection audiences have for this kind of entertainment?

TR

Where?

DC

In Los Angeles, for instance. Improvisational groups are very popular.

TR

I don't think that's so true in New York. But then, the written word in L.A. has never enjoyed the respect it has east of the Hudson.

DC

Tell me, Tony, how do you deal with health problems when you are playing on the stage in New York. Do you suffer from colds, and sore throats and the flu?

TR

I suffer from them all the time. But there is a strange phenomenon: you never sneeze on stage. You can sneeze all day, in the dressing room and during the intermission, but your nose stops running the minute you go on. I don't know what it is due to: probably something to do with one's adrenaline. Fortunately, I've never had throat problems. I don't tighten up there. My father used to tell me, "If you have to sing a high note, think low, and if you have to sing a low note, think high." It keeps my throat open, and I never have to worry about that problem.

DC

You did *Promises, Promises* in New York, on tour in Los Angeles, and in London. I think of that musical as very much a latter-day American musical. How do English audiences react to that kind of material? Do they differ from us?

TR

They were very demonstrative at the curtain calls, most polite, and always gave a very generous round of applause at the end of numbers. They didn't laugh as hard as the audiences here, but that could very well have been because it was Neil Simon dialogue, and its rhythms are much more northeastern American than British. I played it in Los Angeles, and there the reaction was the least on both counts, because they thought it was a television screen. I'm not sure they laugh out loud without a laugh track. And they didn't know who was supposed to laugh first, they or the track. And since there was no track, it was very quiet when we played the show in Los Angeles. And most of the audience went for their cars as we were doing the finale, in the same way they leave a football game. It was not as thrilling, therefore, to do it there as it was in urban centers like San Francisco, New York, and London.

DC

I read something in an interview that Jessica Tandy gave to Dan Sullivan, the drama critic of the *Los Angeles Times*, that intrigued me. She said, "I admire young actors who essay *Hamlet* even when they're not quite ready for it. They take the risk and give it a 'go' and don't say 'I've got to make it me' or 'I've got to make it mine.'

You must make yourself '*it*.' " You played *Hamlet* early in your career. What's your reaction to Miss Tandy's remark?

TR

Unlike any other role I have ever played, Hamlet requires choices from the first moment you enter to the last breath you breathe as the character—choices that almost have to be based on something arbitrary, because there have been ten books written about every moment of the play and the character, each one building an argument about what it should be. And you cannot possibly satisfy all of them. And so you make the choices you will make out of the limits of your own imagination. If a high school student stood up to play the part, he'd get certain moments right that I couldn't . . . that Olivier couldn't. But some of it would be valid because it is like trying to inhabit a shadow. And so I don't think that is the best example to demonstrate what I think she means, because most plays do make certain demands on you that you must fulfill, and, then, she is absolutely right and I would agree with her.

DC

I have always thought that the Elizabethan theater and the musical theater share much in common in that the soliloquies are very much like songs—words without melodies, but with rhyme and meter—that are addressed "down front." Would you agree?

TR

I would never have known how to approach one if I hadn't studied your method of how to deal with a song. Because the approach to any of those soliloquies is the same. They are statements that do not exist in life. You don't suddenly sing in the street or in your room or wherever. Nor do you sit down in your room and think out loud. They are both devices that project a higher reality.

DC

I did think, when I read Miss Tandy's interview, that what she had to say about making yourself "it" (speaking of the role of Hamlet) was the opposite of singing, however. I teach the need to make the song "you" rather than the reverse—that the mark of a great performer is his or her ability to subjugate the song and to give the impression

. . . the illusion . . . not so much that it is being sung but that it has never been sung before until that moment when *you* experienced the need to create it. And, in that way, it becomes the performer's very own.

TR

Yes. But you know, most people sing a song and hope the audience will get from it what their reaction to it is. Which is, of course, wrong. But to short-circuit that approach is very difficult. Instead of showing me how sentimental you feel about this song, show me someone who isn't sentimental who is singing this song, and *I'll* feel sentimental *for* that person because I'm watching it.

DC

The important element of all this is that the singer must not become the reactor to the song. It is the audience who must do that. It is the desire for this result that causes the performer to sing the song in the first place.

TR

In a play, one would say: "Don't play the end of the scene. Don't come in to play the scene. You came in to get a cup of coffee, and got stuck in this situation, and you don't know what the end of the scene is." But, of course, somewhere you do—and that is the whole disguise.

DC

Tell me how you feel about contemporary music. Do you like it? Do you listen to it?

TR

There's a kind of lower common denominator about it that I find, after a while, a little boring. The rock scene, to me, is hot dogs at the ballpark . . . not out of line, occasionally. Hot dogs at the ballpark are fun and so, occasionally, I will listen to something contemporary. Billy Joel's things often have an energy and a musical wisdom about them, sometimes some of Linda Ronstadt's sounds are moving to me and personal, but they are the exceptions for me because this homogenization of everything so that we can all get it together, like chanting, has no meaning for me as an individual.

DC

Why do you think you're immune to it? After all, isn't it the music of your time?

TR

I never wanted to be a joiner. I always suspected everything everybody else liked, just on principle. You once said to me, years ago, in reference to something personal in my life, that we are all like islands unto ourselves, we overlap occasionally and touch each other with the same understanding for a moment, but then we drift back again into those little islands. So to try to make us share much more than that makes me feel depersonalized. I don't think I see reality the same way that others do, and I tend to think, too, that no one else sees it the same way, either.

DC

How do you feel about the general crepe hanging that seems to be going on in the theater and, even more, the musical theater? Critics, social commentators, and performers all seem intent on an early funeral service. Do you think this bleak prognosis is justified?

TR

They haven't seen a new musical they have liked, I guess. The people who write musicals seem not to know what to do. There is a terrible vacuum at the moment that is waiting for someone to come along and fill in a new way. I certainly don't think it is the money so much as the fact that no one has come along who knows how to use the kind of dramaturgy that has worked in the past and put it into a new and contemporary form that will reach people.

DC

Are there ways to get out of this bind?

TR

I'm a classicist in the sense that I think one can never get away from the need for characters and a plot and good dialogue and that these elements are as valuable today as they were for the Greeks. The unity of place and time can alter, you can go in and out, do flashbacks and go back and forth and you can have underscoring, but, finally, if you don't have people, a plot, and dialogue, you won't have a theatrical experience. I think that is true for a play just as much as it is for a musical. After all, there aren't that many good plays being written, either.

DC

But can it be argued that, perhaps, the tried-and-true tools of the trade that have worked in the last hundred years may be played out and in need of replacement?

TR

I don't think so. It will all begin again the next time they do *A Chorus Line* or if and when they figure out how to do *Follies* right. All of it is only waiting for someone to make it work. Because we know it works. You sit in a theater and get chills when it's right, and if you don't believe it works, then what do we have to believe in? We *must* believe that we have devoted our lives to an art form that has a place in the world for showing people something they have never seen before . . . that you can bring people into a theater to have a kind of religious experience. All we are waiting for is the arrival of a genius to show us how to put it all together.

DC

Those words of wisdom your father gave you when you were a teenager, do you think that now they would have to be altered to fit the times, or, more to the point, do you think it is a negative career choice today? What is your advice to the young player?

TR

Well, since my daughter is thinking of going into show business, I could practice on her. I would say that I think that the theater holds an important place in our world—a place in which the most basic truths can be communicated—that it started out as a religious experience in which people could sit around a campfire and act out whatever they needed to in order to be less afraid of the elements and the gods and things they couldn't understand . . . that it would reassure them and bring them closer together and make them feel that they had touched their fellow human beings for a moment before they went to their separate places to sleep through the night hoping that they would not be eaten up by a wild animal . . . and that you should strive, throughout your life as an actor or an actress, to make that kind of experience as common as you can. And in that goal is a reward of religious significance.

DC

And not to be fearful of it as a career choice?

TR

You make that decision based on how badly you want it and how much you are willing to endure the rejections and the humiliations. Someone once said it's a business for those who won't take no for an answer. Of course they are going to tell you no and, of course, it is going to hurt, and if you say, "I am determined and nothing is going to stop me," and if you have the right combination of luck, ambition, and talent, you will arrive. If you have only two of those without the third, you're never going to do it. It takes all three. But the work is, finally, its own reward. And if you feel that way and get rewarded by the work, then it is for you. But if you don't, you're crazy to go into it. Ultimately, you have to love the work. You certainly don't do it because the work is appreciated. It may sound highfalutin, but I do think you have to have some kind of an ideal about it.

DC

Have you realized that in your own career?

TR

In the challenge that I feel from good material—yes. That is to say, that I am challenged to be the best that I know I can be and that keeps me thin, it keeps me limber, and it keeps me trying to stay on top of it—because there is something, somewhere, that I believe in deeply. I believe in the power of the theater to change lives and to make people understand their fellow man and themselves . . . to send them out of the theater different than they were when they came in—whether they have seen a drama, a comedy, or, yes, a musical!

Bernadette Peters

Bernadette Peters is an ever-evolving artist. Her career evokes a quality of growth. I do not mean to imply that she has ever been anything less than the material she has been given to sing, and often she is more. But with *Sunday in the Park with George* and *Song and Dance*, she is now recognized as a performer of the first magnitude in the musical theater. She projects youth, beauty, glamor, and, in *Sunday*, even the simulation of old age. No excess is discernible, and yet one seems never to require more than what she supplies—so true is her tone. She possesses a voice that sounds so like the look of her that, when dialogue segues into song, she changes merely language, not gears. She has an alarming ability to sneak up on you with no apparent effort. When she sang "Children and Art" in the Sondheim piece, the heartbreaking effect was achieved with a minimum of visible tricks and, in consequence, a maximum of poignancy.

Although she has been singing on the stage since 1959, I think of her as an eighties performer. But I think, too, that that is because we are living in the eighties. When we are into the last decade of this century, I know I shall think of her as a nineties performer. No other artist of her generation projects this unique illusion of perpetual currency.

DC

Was the musical theater something you consciously set about to do, or was it something that came from the world of dreams?

BP

I wish I could say it evolved out of dreams, but it was my mother who put me into it when I was four years old. My older sister was already in it. She went to the High School of Performing Arts. My mother tells me I used to sing in front of the television set, and I certainly had a very outgoing personality as a child . . . as many children have because they're not self-conscious. So, I found myself in this world, and at one point, I finally realized for myself that it was a great creative outlet for me. That was when I was seventeen and began to study acting with David LeGrant.

DC

What compelled you to study acting?

BP

At seventeen I realized that I had begun to feel self-conscious when I would go to auditions. Even as I was reading the script, I would listen to myself and I knew that wasn't good. And I wanted to study. Especially at that age. You have so many emotions. It was a wonderful outlet for me, and by then I knew I wanted to be in this business.

DC

And outside circumstances were no longer responsible? It had become *your* dream?

BP

Yes. I had another dream when I was about seventeen or eighteen. I did a benefit down at The Village Gate*. I got up and sang three songs and I thought: "Wow! This is great!" And it *was* great. I guess the other thing was the live performing, which is such a thrill. Of course, a concert is different than nightclubs, where people are drinking. I've only done two or three concerts. In nightclubs you don't have their attention all the time because they're ordering a drink or they're talking to someone. At a concert, they're sitting there as they do in a theater, and you're doing what you want to do. I mean, it's *your* act and you decide what you're going to sing and how you're going to present yourself. On stage there is a fourth wall, but in a club, you come out and really look them in the eye. You're able to make real contact with them. And that's something I find easy to do, and I like it, too. Sometimes people are shy and they'll look away, but most of the time there is a connection and that's very nice. You don't feel anything like that on a stage, but, I must say, I felt a lot on that last performance.§. I felt that the audience was on the stage,

---

*A Greenwich Village cabaret.
§This is in reference to her role in the Sondheim musical *Sunday in the Park with George*.

and we were all one. Most of them knew it was my last performance, so they were all experiencing this extra thing.

DC

Was there any one performer, in that space between your fourth and your seventeenth birthdays, whose work you had seen that, in some way, inspired you and gave you a sense of direction?

BP

Well, I loved Margaret Leighton. I saw her in a movie with Julie Christie and Alan Bates—*The Go-Between*—and I thought "God! She's wonderful!" And I've always admired Katharine Hepburn. I remember seeing her in an old film, *Alice Adams.* She just broke my heart, and she wasn't even working on breaking my heart! She was working on what the character was going through. Those things were inspiring to me.

DC

They're not musical memories.

BP

I think I take that part of my life for granted. I've always sung. But I do find the most interesting thing is what is going on inside of me *when* I sing.

DC

You don't, then, separate the one from the other?

BP

No. I don't enjoy it when I see somebody separating the two. I mean, I know they're listening. I can tell they are listening by the way they sound. And I don't. I've never been in love with my voice, anyway. I think it's just a nice voice. Sometimes, I think it sounds pretty and I can use that. When it feels easy, I guess I live in that feeling— when I'm in good voice and it's coming out, easily produced, and I can forget about it and just sing what I want to sing *about.*

DC

Although you describe yourself as a natural singer, you must have had some study?

BP

When I was four, I was taking singing lessons, but, of course, I had to relearn how to sing much later. I guess I'm musical, and so I take it for granted a little. I just know that it's there and the other part is more interesting to me . . . what's going on underneath.

DC

Has the ability to produce sound correctly always been there?

BP

Well, no. I do have to work at that. I'm still learning all the time. I believe in studying singing. I know what I have to do. I have to keep it up if I'm singing in a show.

DC

It was almost ten years between *Dames at Sea* and *The Most Happy Fella*. Was there anything in between these shows?

BP

Let's see . . . *Most Happy Fella* . . .I was eleven. When I was thirteen, I went on the road with my sister and my mother in *Gypsy*. The second National Company with Mary McCarty. We started out with Mitzi Green in Las Vegas. There I was, thirteen and in Las Vegas. It was *very* strange. I don't much like being on the road, and I think that may be because I was thirteen and in Las Vegas, where there weren't any other children, anyone else my age. There was nothing to do, no outlet for me at all. I felt lonely there. So I did *that* when I was thirteen, and I came back and went to high school and didn't work again until I started studying when I was seventeen. I didn't miss it, because I went to a professional high school: PCS, Professional Children's School. It was really a private school, and I was involved with being a teenager, and going to discos, and being with my girlfriends, and keeping up my singing studies.

DC

You kept that going while you were in school?

BP

Yes, I did, because I was still auditioning. I felt like I was failing because I wasn't getting a job.

DC

You say "wasn't getting a job" so blithely. How do you feel about today's diminished opportunities for young people just starting out in the business? When I was a kid, you never thought you'd not be in a show because there wasn't a show to be in. If you weren't in one, it was because you couldn't *get* into one.

BP

I know. But, on the other hand, there is a lot of Off Broadway theater today. It's a great place for creativity.

DC

But it doesn't pay your rent.

BP

Yes, that is a problem. It certainly doesn't pay the rent, but if you have this dream in you and you want to create in this industry—in this business—then you get another kind of job to support yourself while you study and deal with it. One thing I learned when I studied acting was that there is your individuality—that there is really only one of you in the whole world—and that's what you should take advantage of. And once you do that, if they want *you*, they want *you*. As long as your talent and your technique are up to what you're about. I think there is always a place for people once they find their individuality—who they are and what they are about. It's getting the background and the experience that is going to be so hard right now because there isn't a lot of . . . I don't even know if there is much summer stock around. Not as much as there used to be.

DC

Bernadette, how would you define yourself: As a singer who dances and acts? As a dancer who acts and sings? Or as an actor who sings and dances?

BP

I would say that I'm an actress who sings and dances. I hope to say that more and more. I guess that's my dream—to hone my acting so that I can fulfill myself and show myself in just that way.

DC

Today, dancers and singers often hide their identification. They will say they are actors rather than risk being counted out before the fact . . . unless, of course, they want a career in the ballet or in opera.

BP

But don't you find that the industry pigeonholes you? Even the last work you've done—they'll only think of you in that kind of role. Or, I think because people do more than just sing or dance or act, that they don't want to be classified. Because once you're classified, they do just think of you as a dancer—and along with that goes a dancer's mentality—or a singer—and along with *that* goes a singer's mentality—which doesn't search out the whole person. When you say *singer*, sometimes you think of a person who only listens to his or her own voice.

DC

How do you feel about the passion everyone today has for study?

BP

Well, I don't know if you can ever know everything. You learn a lot while you're working, too, I must say, but you have to get to a certain place before you *can* work. So, I think it's like a dance class; it keeps your muscles stretched. And acting classes keep *those* muscles stretched, and singing lessons certainly do that. It's keeping yourself "up." I think that's terrific. I don't think you should ever have to say: "Now I've graduated. Now I know everything."

DC

And yet, it is a relatively new way of learning.

BP

Studying? Do you think so?

DC

Well, if you had asked Olivier or Astaire or Merman where they had studied . . .

BP

I see what you're getting at. But, I think Olivier is constantly learning, because you keep opening doors in your mind when you work on different characters. Study keeps everything flexible. It keeps all your tools at your fingertips, so to speak. And Ethel Merman . . . well, she was one of those people who had a God-given voice.

DC

May I bring up an interesting and a somewhat depressing point? You and Tony Roberts are the youngest performers I am interviewing. Everyone else is over fifty and, in some cases, a good deal older . . . and your being younger gives me a chance to discuss the contemporary music scene.

BP

Do you mean like the charts and *Billboard?*

DC

Yes.

BP

I know some of it, but I don't have the time to listen to it all. There are some contemporary writers I like. Bruce Springsteen, for one. I think he's a storyteller who writes wonderful stories. And I think Cindi Lauper is a real artist. I really do. Because she goes *into* what she does. She commits herself totally to a vision, a concept, when she is doing something. I think even someone like Madonna has something in mind when she is presenting herself. As far as the music itself, the one I enjoy the most is Bruce Springsteen . . . because, as I say, he tells stories.

DC

Is that the element of a song that makes it work?

BP

It's the kind of song I like. I prefer it to songs that have a beautiful melody and keep going back to the release. There are musicians like . . . Prince . . . I know one of the phrases in one of his songs—it may even be the title—that goes, "I would gladly die for you," and I never listen to the rest of it! I really should, to see if he's telling a story—also, what *he's* talking about. I have a feeling that more and more they are trying to tell stories in their songs rather than just going for sound.

DC

Would you say that, because of their particular style and sound, they are outlawed from the musical theater? Or do you think some of them could cross over?

BP

I think that now they are going to begin to cross over.

DC

You answered so quickly. I assume you feel that strongly.

BP

Yes. I was thinking that the music is really changing into more of a story behind what they are talking about. And that is the important thing. It's not just the sound. I can see Bruce Springsteen telling his story in a book show. I can see Cindi Lauper doing it, too.

DC

Do you think they want to?

BP

No. I think they could if they wanted to. I feel those two performers have integrity and they could perform a role on the stage in a musical. But I don't think they would want to. But, then, they might write their own kind of musical. After all, they are doing videos and they are thinking in concepts and about the way something should be said and what it looks like and how it is being presented. Cindi Lauper's first hit, "Girls Just Want to Have Fun," for example.

DC

But, aren't these songs and videos all vocalized? There is no dialogue. Do you think they can act?

BP

I think the ones I'm talking about could. I also think that maybe they'd write their own music that would fit better and not necessarily be like the music for the theater that we know. But, I do think, in the case of Springsteen and Lauper, that they could fit into our format. I don't think that groups that just go for sound could, however.

DC

In the case of a performer like Michael Jackson, it seems to me that, although he *is* theatrical, he is *not* in the way we define the word in the musical theater.

BP

Michael is so specific and so is his voice texture and his quality. It would have to be something very special for him.

DC

What are your tastes in music? Did you grow up loving the sound of show music . . . jazz?

BP

I grew up listening to Frank Sinatra and Frances Faye.

DC

And do you still like that sound?

BP

I love that kind of music! I think, though, that I just love music. I love all kinds of music. Classical music is so healing; you put it on and you start to feel wonderful. It's so uplifting and it makes you feel good.

DC

You've worked on the stage, in small and large nightclubs, in concert, on television, and on film. Is there any one scene you prefer above the others?

BP

Well, I always say that now the only thing that attracts me is not the format in which it is being presented but the piece itself. I'll even do a strange movie that I don't think will be a success if I like the role. I have to like the role. At this point in my career, I don't want to do something just to do it—another movie because I haven't done one in a while, or I should do it. But I do always think of conquering . . . and then there are more interesting things and even more interesting things to do.

DC

I know some people who would say, "God! I hope I never have to work in another nightclub again."

BP

But then, there's Tony Bennett. He loves to work in nightclubs, and he's a wonderful performer. And I admire Lena Horne. Someone once asked me how I see myself at sixty-five, and I said, "Lena Horne!" She's fantastic! But I am hoping my nightclub life will go more into a concert life.

DC

As a child did you have any musical training? Did you learn to play an instrument?

BP

I studied the piano, but I'm not good at it. I can read music, which is helpful.

DC

You don't require someone to play the song for you? No need to learn it from a tape?

BP

No. When they ask me, "Do you want the lyrics or do you want the music?" I take the music because I can read it. First, I learn exactly how it is written so I know what is correct. I mean what is written musically.

DC

Do you consciously plan how you will phrase a song?

BP

No. I only do what comes out of the sense of what I am saying and what I am feeling. Always.

DC

Rather than making a conscious effort to phrase a certain way?

BP

Not unless it is a stylized song that needs something like that.

DC

How do you go about choosing material for your act? Why do you replace one song with another, and how do you learn, in working out the act, what does or doesn't work for you and what might work better?

BP

Thank God you keep learning what doesn't work, what does work, and what you can keep. You always long for that terrific piece of material that you can depend on.

DC

Written especially for you or something published that you find?

BP

Either. I have a Harold Arlen medley that works for me—a wonderful piece that went from my last act to this one. And there is a wonderful song, too, about masturbation called "Making Love Alone" that I did on *Saturday Night Live.* I sometimes do that, and it always seems to work well. They said, "You can't do this on television," and I said, "Let me do it for the censors," and it was just . . . Cole Porter, not raunchy or anything in bad taste. You know, you learn that the first song you sing, the opening number, the audience is looking at you, getting used to you, and not really hearing what you're saying. Looking at how you look: "Is she thin?" "Is she fat?" "Is she old?" "Is she young?"

DC

"And what is she wearing?" Do you choose your clothes?

BP

No. Bob Mackie does them. I have input, of course, but he knows the kind of things I like, what looks good on me, and how the dress must look and that it may become something else later on. In one act, I didn't have anybody on stage with me; in the last act I had two men with me, but that time I didn't, and so I couldn't leave the stage to make any kind of costume change, so Bob made me a wonderful outfit: the top always stayed the same, but it started out with draped pants, satin, and at a certain moment I unhooked something that came off and I was in a dress with fringe hanging on it, and then, after that, there was something else: During a long intro for a ballad, the lights went down and, all of a sudden, I appeared in a gown! It takes someone with a terrific mind to be able to figure something out so that, never being able to leave the stage, I could still have three different costumes. He is a magic man! And I never have to worry because his clothes always fit beautifully. He also suggests colors I usually like. He'll see the act and realize what it needs and suggest "how about this into that?" Collaboration is an important part of it all and working with terrific people.

DC

Do you choose the material you sing, does someone choose it for you, or is it, again, a collaborative effort?

BP

All of those. I'll hear a wonderful song that I want to do, or I'll have an idea to sing "If You Were the Only Boy in the World" a cappella, or, at one time I was recording and I put in two of the songs from the record. And, sometimes, someone who is helping me put the act together will think of a song. It can come about in different ways, but the outcome is always the same: I have to sing it, and I have to like it, and I have to believe in it.

DC

How long is an act, Bernadette?

BP

That depends. If you are opening for someone else, you can do forty minutes and be very successful. If you entertain for the whole evening, an hour is very nice. In the case of a concert date they often tell me how much time they need. Once I did one that was going to be taped for television, and I think they wanted a lot more time and so I added more. And, then, you have to think of it being halved into act one and act two.

DC

Did you do that yourself?

BP

No, I did it with [*Tom Hammond*], my manager. He really helps produce the act with me.

DC

Why do you think the idea of "doing an act" seems to enchant so many young performers? There is no money in it, and a fairly heavy investment has to be made. Even in a small club like the Gardenia in Los Angeles or Freddy's in New York, there are still clothes to be bought, arrangements to be made and paid for, a pianist to rehearse with you and to accompany the act, and, often a further humiliation, the responsibility of having to fill the room with friends and casting personnel. And all of this for a split of the take.

BP

It's what we were talking about before. There are not enough places for young performers to work. Not enough shows are being done, and I think they need a place to work and to be seen.

DC

Do you think the investment worth it, then? To showcase yourself in an act?

BP

Well, I do think you'd have to feel in your gut that you would be good. I sang three songs downtown and met with a wonderful reaction and that urged me on to go ahead.

DC

Is being good in an act its own ball game, or do you think it can indicate one's ability to work on the stage or, for that matter, anywhere?

BP

I think it creates interest if you are good at it. It doesn't necessarily mean they'll snatch you up, put you in a film or in a Broadway show. But an act is a medium unto itself. You're in control of it, and you can present yourself in the way you want to be seen. And that can cause interest.

DC

A kind of personal advertisement.

BP

Yes. And you can sing songs that release a certain side of you that you want to be seen . . . that is interesting enough for them to say, "Well, let's bring her in and talk to her and let her read."

DC

Would you recommend doing an act?

BP

Creative people want to get into this business to create and to work, and I think it's important to do both. I know it's what satisfies me. I'm lucky because it earns money, too, although for some people it can also work as a real jumping off. Look at Bette Midler. Yes, I think it *is* good—another good place to investigate.

DC

Can we move on to *Sunday in the Park with George*? I'm sure you must know the extraordinary effect it has had on . . . How can I say this? . . . You are demonstrably on a new and higher plateau because of it, wouldn't you agree?

BP

I don't know the reaction it has had yet. I know people who loved the show and, for me, it was such a life-changing experience, but what its effect is, I can't say. When I speak to someone like you and get mail from people who saw me in a different light, I suppose that it did change people's outlook on what I can do.

DC

Was learning the score a difficult task?

BP

It was interesting because we did it first in workshop, and the first song I tried to learn was the first number in the show, and I was working with someone* I admired so much and wanted to please. I'd never thought I'd ever work with him, and I didn't know how he worked. I didn't know he would give me so much leeway in performing his work and finding what I need as an actress. I did have trouble, in the beginning, learning that first song: the nervousness, all the words, and the timing in which he writes is so different.

DC

Was that difficult?

BP

At first, yes. But when you finally learn it, you realize that the rhythms he chose make it easier for you, that he makes it a quarter-note for a very good reason. It is wonderful that he writes both the words and the music, because there is a perfect marriage of the two to help you say what you want to say. He is terrific!

DC

You were involved from the very beginning with the work. How do you feel about workshop productions?

BP

I love them. It's not a place where you earn any money, so you have to be able to afford it, but it is a wonderful chance for a show because the old way—going out of town, the money investment—if it isn't working, they say, "Close it." You're out of town, they panic and do all the wrong things. But here there is nothing lost. You can step

*Stephen Sondheim.

back and look at it. You can close it for a while and think about it. You don't have to do it *now*. When you're in Boston, you're there for two or three weeks and . . . that's it. You have to bring it in. You can postpone the opening and stay in previews, but then you'll have everyone in New York watching you. You're working under the gun. Whereas, in a workshop, you can sit back and reflect. You have time. I really think it is going to save the theater.

DC

Did *Sunday in the Park with George* change appreciably during its workshop performance? I suppose I mean, did you think at the time, "Now, this is an example of why a workshop is valuable," or, after the fact, think, "Here's an example of a show that could have gone out of town and come into New York in the usual way"?

BP

It was so valuable! It gave them the courage to go on with it . . . the belief that their idea would work: "cutouts" coming up and going down, people coming to life and forming a painting and what it was saying. And also the chance to see what would have to change. In the workshop we did just the first act and only three performances of the second. We got a good idea of it, though. The second act changed—the modern section—from the workshop, although we had a lot, I must say. I always played an old lady in the second act, but the machine* was different. It became more of a piece of art that he [*George*] invented and designed. And the music wasn't there, either, and we didn't have the songs in the second act.

DC

So, between the time the workshop came to an end and you went into rehearsals for the Broadway production, that second act was perfected?

BP

No, because there were two songs added the last week of previews that really pulled the show together. "Move On" and "Children and

---

*A reference to the mechanical device that appears in the second act and is George's creation.

Art" lock up the show in a beautiful way. And my character became a much stronger one. They realized that they had been telling it just from the man's point of view and that they'd left out the point of view of the woman . . . how she'd feel. I had always thought that these two people would have had to be powerful to be so connected, otherwise there wouldn't have been any connection at all. He sings about the woman in "Finishing the Hat," about the "woman who waits for you is not the woman you want to find waiting" and that the woman who leaves really knows what you're about and knows she can't have all of you and that it's not enough for her. I'm paraphrasing but, you see, when the woman you wanted goes, you can say to yourself, "Well, I give what I give," but the woman who will stay with you knows that 'however you live, there is a part of you always standing by'. So, I mentioned that I didn't think the woman's case was dealt with. When they added "We Do Not Belong Together" for me, I could sing about how *I* felt about the whole thing. It made her a much stronger character.

DC
None of that was in the workshop production?

BP
No. It was amazing how those two songs, "Move On" and "Children and Art," tied everything together from the first act.

DC
How do you feel about those people who maintain that the work is essentially a one-act musical . . . that the second act is not necessary and, in fact, even out of the tone of the piece?

BP
Sometimes people like more conventional things. They like everything easy to follow, wrapped up in a nice little . . . Don't give them any curves.

DC
And yet, whatever inching ahead is achieved in the musical theater is, I imagine, due to Steve's courage to push away from formula. Tell me, is there a significant difference between receiving a fully realized

script that one can go into rehearsal with in the usual standard procedure and creating a role in the more investigative environment a workshop production allows?

BP

I think you're always creating a part of it, somehow, in either case. There are always things that you add to, that are suggested to you, and that you go to work on.

DC

I suppose I'm thinking of a musical like *A Chorus Line*, which seemed to have accrued rather than to have been written before the performers ever saw it.

BP

Apparently the first ones, like *A Chorus Line*, were done that way. Everybody came in, and it was written on the spot. But I don't think they are done quite that way anymore. In the case of the one I am doing now*, it is pretty much there, but we are making changes and the line of the show is changing.

DC

How long is a workshop?

BP

I think there are new rules now. I believe it can only be six weeks from beginning to end.

DC

I would suppose that one aspect of doing a workshop of a musical that the actor prizes is that the role is more or less shaped on you, rather like a dress fitting?

BP

That was very much the case with Mandy§ and me. The roles were

---

*At the time of this interview, Miss Peters was in rehearsals for a workshop production of *Song and Dance*.
§Mandy Patinkin, the George referred to in the title.

written for us vocally. I think we happen to be right for the roles, because the script was there, but they were also made for us.

DC

What is it like to play and sing "old age" for someone so distant from it?

BP

I said to the director that I thought I was crazy to do it, that I'd be skinned alive, and he said, "Please, don't get crazy on me. It's really going to work." He wouldn't believe me, and so, well, I just went ahead and did it. At the time, I was staying at the Mayflower Hotel and there were a lot of elderly ladies there. I used to watch them and listen to them. They have high, little voices. Kind of like my voice quality.

DC

Is singing "old" difficult?

BP

It's an amazing thing. I know old people don't have a lot of energy, and by the time we were finished working, I didn't have any either. And I had a wheelchair. I did have to try to keep the energy level low and to be aware of that all the time. Steve was helpful, also. He placed the music in the cracks, so to speak. Old people are tired; everything is slower. But you have to find the spirit, too. That's the thing I admire about old people. By the time they get to be that age, they can just say whatever they want, do whatever they want. And, of course, "Children and Art" is such a beautiful song for her to sing.

DC

In a show as difficult as *Sunday*, how do you pace yourself for eight shows a week?

BP

I finally got it down to being able to go out once a week on Thursday night because I had no matinee that day and didn't have to do one the next day. I could go out on Sunday, too, because we had Monday night off. And I had to stop myself from talking too much on the telephone. That's one of the big things. And, you know, when we first started, the score seemed rangy, but then it gets into your voice. It's like using muscles you haven't used, and then you begin to stretch into it. It's in your voice, and you don't have to work as hard. You find out where the trouble spots are. In "Everybody Loves Louis," I know if I am angry—if I punch the beginning of that—I lose it for the rest of the song. You learn those things.

DC

Do you have a personal warm-up system?

BP

I have a tape I go through. One thing my singing teacher taught me. People see me around the city with gauze on my tongue. I pull my tongue out, and move it from side to side to release the throat muscles, to relax them . . . and it does. It's wonderful. You can do some vocalizing, too. I do that between numbers, too. People who see me backstage . . . Well, I only do it in the basement with the door closed. Otherwise, I just pull it silently.

DC

What about winter in New York? Colds? The flu? Sore throats?

BP

I had three or four colds this year. I hadn't lived in New York for ten years. I was trying to remember if I'd had that many when I had lived here or if I was just getting used to the climate. It was terrible. Actually, everyone in the show had multiple colds. It was a bad season.

DC

And that's not an easy score to sing.

BP

Well, this year I finally learned. I used to go on, no matter what. Do or die. I thought I just had to do it, that I owed it to the audience. But what really happens is that the audience starts to worry about you when you're up there, hoarse, and you can't produce the sounds. And I learned that, well, you're a person, too, and then I had to say:

"Look, it's humiliating for me. Why should I do it if it's humiliating? Let the understudy go on." By then she had learned it, and the audience could enjoy the show rather than worry about somebody up there dying and sounding terrible.

DC

Where do you think the musical theater is heading, Bernadette? It is clear that the $5 million musical is not a healthy answer for what ails our part of the theater.

BP

I don't know if it is a matter of how much it costs, but it *is* a matter of what it is saying, what is up on that stage. I remember when we did *Mack and Mabel*, which the audiences enjoyed very much, even loved, but the critics did not, and I didn't know what they wanted. Then *A Chorus Line* came along and I thought: "Oh, they want something innovative. They don't just want a love story that is done very well. They want something happening on the stage." That was about ten years ago, and I think we may be going through another period like that. Maybe something frivolous with pretty music is just not enough.

DC

And yet you said earlier that some of the audiences that saw *Sunday in the Park with George* were thrown by a musical that didn't have tried and true plot lines.

BP

Yes, but a lot of people came back and saw it again. They understood it and loved it. Audiences are not used to listening the way they used to. Television has gotten us into a thing where you turn it on and don't have to concentrate on it. It's all so easy. They're home watching television and talking. At the movies they talk back to the screen. And even in the theater, the sound is so overmiked you don't have to work very hard. The audience doesn't have to be ready to listen. So, they are just sitting down being entertained and it's easy for them. But, a show that tries to go further, one you really *have* to listen to, have to *hear* what's going on in order to understand it . . .

DC

. . . An audience might tend to resent?

BP

Of course. And *Sunday* is not an easy show. First of all, they're not easy lyrics, no easy melody. And you have to get into the framework of it. But it is such a beautiful show that people don't know why, unconsciously, they are moved by it. Now, I, on the stage, have a different experience than the audience. Even after doing the material for two years. It only grew for me. It never got tired for me, and I don't know how often one can say that. When I first sang "Move On"—I'm thinking of the lines, "If you can know where you're going, you've gone"—it meant one thing to me. All of a sudden, a couple of months later, it meant something else to me. I thought: "I'm going. Something will happen in my life and it will mean more to me, even have a deeper meaning." And so . . . I left the show. I believed the song so much, I moved on. I loved the show so much I could have have stayed in it forever. And that's when I knew I had to move on. The "move on" lesson was a wonderful thing that I learned. And there are other wonderful things in the show that I learned. It's hard to describe. The last scene can mean all kinds of things. I mean, all those people there . . . Are they really there? Are they in his mind? Has he died? Has he had some kind of revelation? What is going on?

DC

All of this gives me the distinct impression that you hold out great hope for the musical theater. After all, if it can offer life lessons— and even sing them—it surely cannot be concerned only with its death?

BP

Oh yes! Music is so uplifting and powerful. And in the theater it is combined with words! It is soaring! And this is a time when composers and writers can stretch more, not just write a couple of peppy tunes. There is a place for all kinds of musicals. *Mack and Mabel* and *Sunday in the Park with George*.

DC

How do you feel about the future?

BP

For me? As a performer? I think it's important for me to have a role that requires more than just singing a few happy tunes.

DC

Well, as you said, you have done that. Now it's time to move on.

BP

[*With great enthusiasm*] Oh yes! Exactly! That's exactly it!

Richard Kiley

Richard Kiley is an actor who sings. He shuttles back and forth between legitimate and musical stages with the ease of a dancer. Like Ethel Merman, George Gershwin, Coca-Cola, and baseball, he is quintessentially red, white, and blue, and yet he made his most memorable mark playing the quintessential Spaniard—Cervantes's Don Quixote. That alone should define him as the stunning actor he is, and because that incarnation of the knight-errant had to sing, the display of his skills is even more apparent. Along with a splendid speaking voice and a passionate love of language, he evidences an abiding sanity that would make him the perfect spokesman for actors and singers were one ever needed to speak for the many.

He was the first actor in the immediate post–World War II years who moved from the classicism of plays like *The Trojan Women* and *A Streetcar Named Desire* into the musical theater; the first to prove that actors without vaudeville experience could find a common playing ground on both sides of the line.* Since then, the traffic across that border has been steady, but Kiley was the first.

---

*Walter Huston, in the thirties, scored a significant success in Kurt Weill's and Maxwell Anderson's *Knickerbocker Holiday*, but he had been a successful vaudevillian early in his career.

DC

Who's Who claims the title role in a high school production of *The Mikado* as your first appearance in a musical, but I would rather skip from that year, 1938, to 1951, when we met during *A Month of Sundays.** Since you had been known exclusively as an actor until then, how did that come about?

RK

It was very funny, because I had never sung on a stage in my life until then. I did come from a very musical family. My mother played the piano, and we all stood around and vocalized and did harmony, but other than that *Mikado* in high school I had never been on a stage before—singing. I'd gotten out of the navy and worked for a year as an actor in radio in Chicago. I made myself 600 bucks and came to New York, not knowing a bloody soul.

DC

With only the intention of being an actor?

RK

That's right. No singing at all. I never really thought there was a buck in it. I thought it was something like . . . juggling or . . . some little thing you could do. But as it was in the case of a lot of us, there were slim times. I'd been in New York about a year, gotten married, and there was a baby on the way, so when my agent called and said, "Don't you sing?", I said: "Well, I don't know. I guess so." He said, "Would you like to audition for the chorus in *South Pacific?*" Well, I got myself a song—a terrible song, a rousing song that I thought would go well with an evening full of a lot of fellows shouting and being sailors. It was called "The Song of the Open Road." When I got to the Majestic Theater, I went out onstage, and if there was one guy there, there were 200. It must have been five-deep around—a cattle call. You were given a number and when your number was called, you stepped forward. I must have listened to about ten really glorious men's voices, and my number was coming up, and the guy immediately before me, so help me God! got up and

---

*Written by Burt Shevelove and Albert Selden and based on Arthur Kober's play *Excursion*. It starred Nancy Walker and Gene Lockhart.

sang "The Song of the Open Road"! It was like Sherrill Milnes squared! Glorious! "Well," I thought, "I have a choice. Nobody knows who I am. They can call my number and my name and I can look around like everybody else and say, 'I've never heard of the guy' and sneak out," but, since I was desperate, I crept forward, trembling in every limb and said, with a kind of shit-eating grin on my face, "Ladies and gentlemen, that's the way the song *should* be done. Now we're going to get the comedy version." And, of course, it was terrible. I started in the wrong key. I couldn't hear the piano and my knees were knocking. It was an absolute disaster. But, rotten as it was, I had sung onstage and broken the ice. Later, I got a job as an understudy to Anthony Quinn in the National Company of *A Streetcar Named Desire* and when we got back to town, I was recommended to Burt Shevelove and Al Selden and that's how I went to audition and got the part.

DC

The memory of that audition seems a good deal less painful than the first one for Dick Rodgers.

RK

Well, I knew some people by then and I had done a lot of singing. I thought, "If I'm going to do this again, I'd better try to get to where my knees don't knock and my voice doesn't tremble." I had studied with a woman in Chicago when I was nineteen, but I had dropped it. Now I began to do some of the things, the little warm-ups, that I had been taught, and I guess I performed well enough for them to feel that I was capable.

DC

I was involved in *A Month of Sundays* assisting Burt, and I remember that you always seemed easy and comfortable when you sang.

RK

That's acting.

DC

I know, but I teach a great many actors who live in terror at the very idea that they may be asked to sing.

RK

I think the reason is that, although I was never a professional singer, as I said before, we always sang around the house when I was a kid. We were a very musical family. A lot of actors have literally never sung before other than to hum *Happy Birthday*.

DC

By the way, do you read music or play an instrument?

RK

No.

DC

How do you go about learning the material you have to sing?

RK

I have a very quick ear. And I have people play it for me and put it on a little tape.

DC

Before tape, did you work with a pianist?

RK

Yes. Dick Rodgers, in *No Strings*, played it for me, and I could almost pick it up after one or two playings.

DC

Subsequently you have learned how to sing?

RK

Yes. I have studied.

DC

What drove you to do it?

RK

Vocal troubles. When you have no technique, you don't know how to save yourself. You get a cold or you're tired and your voice can go just like that. Sometimes, if I had not slept the night before, for whatever the reason, or from simply tossing and turning and worrying about something, I'd get up and I'd do a matinee and it would be like . . . [*He runs his hand across his throat.*] Particularly in *Kismet*, in which I was singing a tenor role. And again, it was fools rushing in, because I thought: "Oh, I can do that. It's pretty music and 'Stranger in Paradise' is a lovely song and so I'll do that," never realizing that I'd have to pull up my socks. Then I began to study and I learned to sing in a light way. But it was singing with a technique; one I had never had before. It helped me a great deal. Where I got into trouble with that was that it was a kind of light, easy Broadway sound and when I got into *La Mancha*, I discovered that I had to get a more open, so-called legit sound. You see, I had this concept of what I wanted to sound like. There is a line in Cervantes's novel where he says, "This one has empty rooms in his head," and I thought that would mean a kind of wonderful hollow sound—something like this . . . [*He drops his voice and speaks in a cavernous rumble. One can easily understand the difficulty in sustaining this vocal quality.*] There I was, trying to get a sound I was not physically equipped to get as yet. I hadn't developed the voice enough to get what I was reaching for.

DC

But you heard it in your head?

RK

I heard it in my head, yes, and I knew what I wanted. I could get it occasionally, except, again, when I began to tire or we were doing long weekends—a Friday, two Saturday, and two Sunday performances, I would find a lot of vocal fatigue and I didn't know how to save myself.

DC

You wouldn't describe the sound of your voice until then as "legitimate"?

RK

It was a good sound. It was a very bright, white sound rather than a full-out open-throat sound. But then I found a teacher who was absolutely wonderful, and I began working with him, on and off, for about fifteen years. I know what I'm doing now.

DC

Would you suggest that every actor take on vocal study as part of basic training?

RK

It depends on where you are in your career, I think. If someone is starting to be a singer, obviously you have to start much sooner than I did. But I got into singing through the back door, through desperation. I needed work, and I would have tried to juggle or rollerskate or whatever the hell they wanted me to do. But, you know, once I got into it, and because I loved music, so, I realized, "Hell, this is a wonderful extension of my acting, if I can learn to do it properly." I made some wonderful discoveries in *La Mancha*: Where the Knight of the Mirrors was driving me crazy, right to my knees—and all these mirrors are around me, and I say "I am Don Quixote, Knight-Errant of La Mancha," and then he goes completely crazy, finally unable to face the truth. He stares into the mirrors and begins to weep. Shortly after this, I had to sing again. Well, I found that there was so much tension from the yelling and the shouting that I was getting into trouble and losing the voice placement. I found I could get rid of a lot of that tension; I thought, "There's got to be a way to channel this tension out of one area into another." So, I just let it all hang loose and, suddenly, *I could scream the bloody house down!* You know, I started out as an actor, a Method actor, as we all were. I thought to myself, "I've got to have that naturally." It's a natural part of the emotion, and when you're emotional you really have no control. And then I thought, "Dammit! Certainly I had control! If I'm weeping and saying, 'God! Oh my God!' no matter how realistically I'm playing it, I'm still thinking of my legs. There is no one holding me up. I'm not collapsing, so there *is* always a degree of control.

DC

What you are saying is that you were forced to learn a way to *dramatize* effectively what you had to do in order to *sing* it effectively.

RK

Absolutely. So you *can* do anything if you focus on it. You don't have to blow the hell out of your voice to achieve an effect that will be self-destructive. You can play an emotional scene and keep your throat free.

DC

The role of Joe Rose in *A Month of Sundays* was very close to your or, for that matter, anyone's real life. Was it difficult to go from the commonplace to the gaudy satins and pizzazz of the Caliph in *Kismet*? And from straightforward show tunes to the demands of a Borodin-based operetta?

RK

That part didn't disturb me at all because I approached it as an actor. And I always loved period things. In *La Mancha*, I felt I had always worn a cape. There is a good strong streak of ham in me that took care of the turbans. I thought it was all marvelous. I'd studied the classics to a degree and felt at ease in those costumes. Actually, the more costumes and makeup I have, the better I am, anyway. I feel more comfortable.

DC

More hidden?

RK

Yes, more hidden. More able to forget myself and devote myself to the character I'm playing.

DC

Essentially, then, you are saying that Joe Rose is more difficult to play.

RK

Tougher for me. Very, very tough.

DC

Would that still be true today?

RK

I think so. Even David Jordan, in *No Strings*, was tough. They were both very close to me.

DC

Why do you think this should be so? Is there freedom in disguise?

RK

I know a lot of actors who feel this way. I remember talking to Olivier about this. I had a wonderful afternoon with him in London when I was playing there. We talked about "voice" a lot. I was fascinated with the things he had done vocally in *Oedipus*. He showed me some of his vocal exercises. He does them religiously before a performance. But Olivier always hides, if he can. Behind a nose, eyebrows, false hair, shaved head—something. Of course, his greatest romantic role was Heathcliff, in which he was naked to the world, and I thought it was glorious.

DC

Does that say something about the whole theory?

RK

Well, it does blow it out the window, but he himself said: "I was never comfortable as Heathcliff. I wanted to play him with heavier eyebrows and eyelids." There are certain actors who say: "Don't look at me. Look at what I am trying to do."

DC

Of course, the Caliph and Don Quixote are not in the same league.

RK

You're right, the Caliph is not much of a part—not much there, other than having two or three of the greatest songs to sing. They were much lovelier than the ones Drake had.* Drake worked all evening, and I came out singing "Stranger in Paradise" and that's what people went out whistling. But that was what seduced me into doing it. I thought it was glorious and old-fashioned.

*Alfred Drake played Hajj the Beggar in *Kismet*.

DC

Part of a time when families stood around the piano and sang?

RK

That's it. That wonderful kind of lyricism that was the beginning of the end of lyrical songs. Music for music's sake. But I did get bloody bored with the role. That's why I left early on. There was nothing to play other than the joy of the music, and when that went, I stayed with it three or four more months and left.

DC

The interesting thing I remember about *Kismet* was that it opened during a newspaper strike, and, because of that, the critics couldn't attack it early enough to kill it. By the time they did review it, it was a solid hit. Do you think that because the critics were barred from reviewing *Kismet* until much later, audiences were able to find it and in increasing numbers?

RK

Yes.

DC

Would it have been so successful had it been reviewed?

RK

If they could have held on, I think it would have happened. Bad notices would have had a terrible impact on the first few weeks of business, and probably audiences would have been scattered and sparce. But I think word of mouth would have got around. It is, after all, a lush, wonderful, old-fashioned musical.

DC

Kismet was renowned, too, for its staging and its dancing. You went from the world of Jack Cole* to Bob Fosse's *Redhead,* with Gwen Verdon. Did working with a leading lady who was essentially a dancer require some kind of adjustment?

*Choreographer of *Kismet.*

RK

What Fosse did with Gwen was to use things that she was capable of doing. She has this nutty, elfin, slightly wacko sense of humor. She also has a faculty for being very sexy—indeed, verging on the lewd, sometimes, in some of her costumes—and yet she gives it all a kind of innocence, a "Who *me*? Oh, I didn't do that!" which, of course, is its fun. It's fun, too, to be with her on stage. There is a lightness about her, and she is an intuitive actress. I don't think she ever really studied it, but she has a good instinct. For example, she enjoys improvising within certain limits. I have worked with people who are trained either as singers or as dancers who, in an acting situation, where—God forbid!—you are three inches off your mark, will suddenly say, in horror, "Aaaaaaaah!" And they're "up." I early on discovered that Gwen, when I threw her an ad-lib, would pick it up, and she was marvelous at it. So, in that regard, she was very refreshing. We ran a year and a half, and then we took it on tour for another six months or so. It could have been a bloody bore because the story, again, as with so many musicals, was slender and tended to be unbelievable. But if we hadn't had those moments, those funny things that happened, it would have been damned tedious. Yes, I must say she was really fun to work with.

DC

You sang the lyrics of one my favorite lyricists, Dorothy Fields.

RK

I adored her. It's very funny, because when I went up to see about *Redhead*, Gwen had seen me do a couple of plays and *Kismet*, and she wanted me to play opposite her. The part was really wrong for me. He was supposed to be a great big, barrel-chested strongman in the circus. I told my agent: "Look, I've co-starred for the first time in a straight play*. I've had my name up in lights, and I don't want to go audition for something. I don't want to go on doing that forever. If they want me, they want me. There are records they can listen to, and they've seen me in plays." So, I went up to see them and finally, of course, after they said hello, someone said: "Would you just sing.

---

*Time Limit, with Arthur Kennedy.

We haven't heard you do anything that's kind of off the beat and light."

DC

They were referring to *Kismet*?

RK

Yes. And I said, "Well, I'll wing something," and so Albert Hague*, who was sitting at the piano, said, "Do you know 'On the Sunny Side of the Street' "§ and, God help me, I didn't know Dorothy Fields. I'd been introduced to this lady very quickly. I said, "Well, sure, I'll try it." So we started with "Grab your coat and get your hat . . ." and I'm reaching for the words and she's throwing me cues . . . "leave your worries on . . . uh, thank you . . . on the doorstep." Well, I'm going through all the dum-dee-dums, and she's giving me the words and I thought, "What a darling woman." I was that stupid! At the end of it, they said "Oh, that was lovely, that's wonderful," and I said: "Wow! You're incredible! You must have total recall." And she said: "With that one, I do. I wrote it." I felt like a complete horse's ass. I muttered somthing like, "Oh my God, I'm sorry!" But she was adorable, and we became great pals.

DC

And then you moved on to another first—*No Strings*, with words and music by Richard Rodgers. He had never done that before.

RK

I don't think so. He may have had a little input somewhere along the line, but I think this was the first time he wrote an entire score. Dick was always very tough. He wanted everything on the beat, no bending notes or anything like that. I think he did pretty well with the lyrics.

DC

Did he ever tell you what impelled him to do it?

---

*The composer of *Redhead*.
§Written by Jimmy McHugh and Dorothy Fields.

RK

I think that, in his heart, he probably always wanted to do it. His experience with men like Hart and Hammerstein made him secretly feel, "Sure, I could do that." As undoubtedly they must have felt . . .

DC

About writing tunes? I wonder.

RK

I had some funny experiences with Dick. My first meeting with him was kind of marvelous. He asked me if I would come over to the Majestic Theater and chat. So I went over to the theater and there was a work light on and he was sitting by himself in the audience. Maybe one other person was there. I came out; we had never met before. He'd seen things that I had done. He said: "I'm in the process of writing a musical with Sam Taylor. It's a story about a black girl and a writer, a white guy, in Paris. It's a romance. We're talking to Diahann Carroll about playing the role and I'd like very much, if you're interested, to have you play the man." I said, "It sounds very interesting, Mr. Rodgers," and he said: "I really haven't done all the music yet because I wanted to talk to you and get the feel of your voice and how you feel about lyrics and things like range and keys. Just kind of a general feeling." So, we fooled around and he played a little bit and I sang a couple of things—just lightly and easily— and I said, "I'm comfortable in that general area" and so forth, and he was wonderful. Then, he said something about 'It's nice to meet you after all this time" and I said: "You know, we really have met before. In fact, we met on this stage we're standing on."

DC

South Pacific, the "Song of the Open Road"—the comedy version.

RK

Well, I told him about that, and he seemed to recall it. He said, "You're the fellow who made that crack about 'now you're going to hear the other way of doing it?' That was you?!" And I said, "This is a much pleasanter way to talk to you, Mr. Rodgers."

DC

No Strings was the first interracial musical and was, in fact, ahead of its time. And yet, I remember being discomfited by its self-consciousness and its refusal to deal with the subject.

RK

As you say, it was a bit ahead of its time. We opened at the Fisher Theater in Detroit, and on opening night when I kissed Diahann Carroll, maybe 75 to 100 people got up and walked out—en masse.

DC

What year was that?

RK

1962.

DC

In that respect, why do you think the lyric theater is so far behind the operatic theater? Nobody ever thinks that Leontyne Price, Grace Bumbry, Shirley Verrett, or Simon Estes should not sing opposite white singers—and often in far more intimate plot lines.

RK

That's very interesting. I guess that, in the opera, if you can deliver the voice, and the voice is great enough, people have blinders on. It's as though you can be the size of Pavarotti, who is as big as this room, and sing Rodolfo, who should be a slender handsome young artist. It's something you accept, and you listen only to those glorious sounds. Whereas, in the more mundane world of musicals, one is closer to the play with music. The music doesn't soar quite so high.

DC

If *No Strings* were created now, do you think it would be a different show?

RK

I think it would be a much more courageous show. Although, in a way, it's too late. It wouldn't make any sense. Everybody would say: "So what? Big deal."

DC

The theme of miscegenation?

RK

There was an interesting thing that happened when they talked about the movie version. A year or so after the show had closed on Broadway, I spoke to Dick Rodgers about it. We met and I said: "Dick, what's happening? I understood that the film was going to be done." And he said: "Well, they came up with a very interesting idea. They changed the story." I thought: "Sure. Typical movieville. They're going to 'improve' everything and screw it up." But the change was very interesting. He said: "The idea is to make David Jordan [*the leading man*] a young, progressive senator—kind of a Jack Kennedy type—from the south. A young Turk. A wonderful, sexy guy who really is able to woo the voters, has all sorts of progressive ideas in his southern constituency, and so forth. He goes to Paris on a stint, meets this girl, and falls deeply in love. He wants to marry her. Now he has a problem that's a real problem. His career is at stake." You see, in the show, David Jordan was a writer, and so what? So a writer brings a black girl back to the States. So what else is new?

DC

To Maine?

RK

OK, so it's a problem in Maine, but if you don't like Maine, you can live down in Soho. If you love each other enough, who gives a damn where you live? But, now, here's a man who is presidential fodder, a kind of idealist, which allows him to fall for this girl. He doesn't see the color. And I said to Dick: "Christ! That's a wonderful improvement! I can see that happening. It's an agonizing decision."

DC

After *No Strings* came another first. You replaced the leading man in *Here's Love*.

RK

I was a big fan of Meredith Willson's, and everybody made it very pleasant for me, but . . . Well, I'd just moved into a big house in

Tuxedo Park and I was between jobs. Nothing was happening, and this came along and I grabbed it.

DC

Did they give you free rein?

RK

No, they didn't. It was very quick. I think I rehearsed for two weeks or maybe less. There just wasn't time. When I got into it, I found there were little places I could make my own, but in the dances and all of that stuff, I had to . . . Well, let's just say it wasn't a happy experience.

DC

And then came *I Had a Ball* with Buddy Hackett. I seem to be dwelling on the extraordinary variety of people you've worked with in musicals. Worked with, and I imagine, dealt with. I remember that Hackett wasn't impelled to stick very close to the book. Do you think you have a gift for "fitting around"?

RK

Oddly enough, people have frequently asked me that question. They've said: "How in the world did you ever work with someone like Buddy Hackett? He's never given you the same cue twice." I said it was the only thing that kept me sane. Buddy and I would improvise every night. Although some of the songs were very good*, talk about puerile scripts! Yes, Buddy is mad. Stark staring mad. But, I must say, he was funny. He kept me on my toes because every night we'd do something different.

DC

Perhaps weak shows may require loose performances? Did you go along with all the improvising in order to keep your sanity or because that is the nature of things when one works with a comic personality like Hackett?

---

*The score was written by Jack Lawrence and Stan Freeman.

RK

If I had tried to maintain the story line, which was nil, I would have opened a vein in my bath.

DC

Going from Hackett to O'Casey must have made your head spin. A musical of *Purple Dust*! Does that play sing?

RK

Not at all. It was in 1965 at the Goodspeed Opera. Bob Rounseville and Ray Middleton were the leads in it. We had opened the season with *La Mancha* for four weeks and followed it with that [*Purple Dust*]. Of course, in the fall, we came into town with *La Mancha*.

DC

Had you an inkling, from the start, that this was going to be the watershed musical it subsequently became?

RK

Alby* had brought the script backstage to me during the Buddy Hackett show. I knew instantly it was what I had to have, what I'd been looking for. It was three things: It was an acting role, it had size, and it was a character role, which was what I was ready to get into—character work. I was forty-three years old, and I was still playing dumb leading men. And I wanted to be, in fact, I always felt I was, a character man. And this was an opportunity to do just that. When I read it, I said yes immediately!

DC

Did it change greatly when it moved from Goodspeed into town?

RK

The stage design was quite a bit altered. Alby and Howard Bay§ conceived a sort of floating platter look with the idea of people creep-

---

*Albert Marre, the director of *Man of La Mancha*.
§The musical's designer.

ing out and coming up like rats out of the hold. That was all brand new.

DC

Was the score difficult for you to learn, or did you use the same system as before—listening to the composer [*Mitch Leigh*] play it?

RK

I listened to tapes. The toughest song of all for me was "The Golden Helmet" because of the strange kind of rhythm. It was a strange, offbeat rhythm like a *paso doble*. And, as I told you, what I wanted to do was to sing it like an old man. I didn't want to play Quixote this way [*He stands and, shakily, speaks a line from the play.*] . . . and then suddenly sing [*He straightens, and in archetypical baritone, belts out a phrase of "The Impossible Dream."*] . . . as a young man.

DC

Although there is some kind of time-honored tradition to do just that.

RK

Yes. But I was determined to sing in the same voice I spoke in.

DC

La Mancha is one of those musicals that seems to speak to audiences in a quite special way. What do you suppose there is about it that is so provocative?

RK

You know, the tradition of the holy fool is a very ancient one. In Russia, Rasputin was an example. And years before that, the wandering mendicant monks. In India, there is a very ancient, deeply rooted concept that madmen are the children of God. Sometimes the world itself seems so mad to people that I think the idea of a madman as a spokesman who is striving for things which are obviously impossible, despite his nutsiness, has a certain nobility about it.

DC

You make it sound like a Jungian musical.

RK

That's right. It is. You see, the idea was that the holy fool—the court fools who held a sacrosanct place—could speak the truth and couch it in a strange language and not be jeopardized, never be punished. That was the rule. You could kick a fool and throw a leg of lamb at him and tell him to shut up, but you could never punish him. He was the one who always had the king's ear, even in Shakespeare; *Lear* is a perfect example.

DC

It was, I believe, the first time a leading role was sung by two men.

RK

Oh, that happened much later. I played eight performances a week for the first year and a half. When they brought me back to do the revival at Lincoln Center at the Vivian Beaumont Theater, I said: "Fellas, look. I'm ten years older. I'm in my fifties now, and I ain't gonna play eight of those a week." So, that started it and, as I recall it, it was the first time it had ever been done in a musical. Uta Hagen did it in *Virginia Woolf*. They had a matinee company.

DC

You've played Quixote in England and throughout the United States. Is touring a blessing or a curse?

RK

Well, the last tour I did, which began in 1978 and went into '80, just about two years, I sort of wrote my own ticket. It was a wonderful tour because we would play long periods of time, twelve weeks, in each place. When I really had had enough, and I finally did, I said: "Listen, I'll play it twelve weeks wherever you want to send me and then I want two weeks off. Just disband the company." Well, they did it, and they made $23 million on that tour. That was the tour that started the revival of *The King and I* with Yul, and Rex's revival of *My Fair Lady*. Just five, six years ago none of that was happening. People were only concerned with doing new musicals.

DC

Did you find audiences pretty much the same, or did they change significantly from one part of the world to another?

RK

London was strange, at first, because I was used to playing it in the States. I was used to a great deal of laughter at the beginning. Then, of course, as the play progresses, there is a pivotal place, a kind of fulcrum, where the play and your feeling for Don Quixote has to inch over into a more serious connection. In London, I was rather shocked because, although we were a huge bloody success, audiences did not laugh that much. They were tremendously enthusiastic at the end, but . . . Well, the result was that we played the damned thing like the Russians were in Newark. But they adored it. And, as I say, it was tremendously successful there.

DC

Does one become overly concerned about health in long runs? Colds? Sore throats? The flu? How do you protect yourself?

RK

I have a whole regimen I do. It's a boring life. If you didn't have the two or three hours in the evening, it would be like life in a monastery. It's terrible. I sleep late. I get up. I have breakfast. I jog. I do yoga. I do my warm-up vocalizing—that I do early in the day, maybe three or four in the afternoon. I like to do it far enough away from the performance so that my voice isn't tired.

DC

What about matinee days?

RK

On those days I try to do the vocalizing around noon. No later than noon, so that by two, two-thirty, or three—whenever the performance is—my voice will not be gone from the fatigue that occurs from the workout. I will be just right again. I do my jogging, my vocalizing, my yoga, and I usually do some work on something like French. I go, point by point, from one step to another. I come back and do something a lot of singers and actors do not do—I nap for about half an hour. I remember Alfred Drake telling me he could never do that because his voice would drop down. For some odd reason it doesn't happen to me. My voice, with just a couple of little things, becomes bright again. And then I go to the theater early, and I usually do a slow, easy makeup.

DC

You must alter the routine in some way when you have a cold?

RK

Yes. Number one: The first thing in the morning, when I open my eyes, I hum. I usually do that lying in bed. If that is there, then I'm OK. If it's bronchitis, tracheitis, or something iffy, I will lay off all the jogging and probably start with a steam and break it up and get rid of as much phlegm as I can. I'm in constant touch with the theater—the usual thing: "Are you going to try it?" "I'll try it."

DC

You always had the safety factor of knowing that someone was there to spell you if things got bad.

RK

Except in the beginning, when I had no safety net at all. I went on. You wouldn't believe the shape I was in. It was agony. When there is a theater full of people and the show has caught on and the understudy isn't ready, it's agony. Sometimes, I've gotten halfway through a performance, and the voice—when you have bronchitis— just goes.

DC

Getting back not only to good health, but to another unique experience you have had, Dick: In Edinburgh, in 1979, you did a poetry reading with Grace of Monaco. Leaving aside the obvious, could you talk about poetry and how reading it differs from singing verse?

RK

You know, in an odd way, there isn't that much difference. I did this thing with Grace—it was the beginning of an idea I had had—and then I did it on PBS on a program called *First Person Singular*. It was my own one-man thing. I took out a stage version of it about a year ago, and I added some rather romantic poetry along with the things I'd done before. For example, I did Alfred Noyes's "The Highwayman," which people had asked for. Now, that's very interesting because when I did it, we had some wonderful lighting and I fooled around with it a little bit and I discovered that it was a quintessentially romantic poem. When I did Prufrock*—this is me as Prufrock . . . the collar, the tie, the clipped speech, the whole thing. But then, I got up on stage with "The Highwayman" and I thought, "I have to *play* this; really play it. This is romantic poetry." And I almost sang that poem. It had its own melodic thing. And I thought, "Christ! I sound like some old ham English actor!" And then I thought, "Wait a minute. No!" Because I heard playbacks of it, and it was exactly what I'd wanted to do! And the audience was rapt, I must say.

DC

Do you think that may have been the secret of Kean and maybe Booth? A willingness to go with the musical sound of the line? A method of dealing with speech that became unfashionable and, even worse, an indication of the "indicating" actor?

RK

That's a fascinating question. There is this gray ground between naturalistic acting and either singing or wildly exaggerated line readings. But there is an area where it is perfectly fitting to do those attentuated sounds.

DC

Are you saying that words possess their own kind of music?

RK

Absolutely. It's a fascinating subject. Because with this poetry thing, I went from being very clipped into another completely different sound for a Stephen Vincent Benet poem, "The Ballad of William Sycamore."

---

*T. S. Eliot's poem *"The Love Song of J. Alfred Prufrock."*

DC

Do you think your sense of musicality contributes to the heightened response you have to language?

RK

Yes, but it is very interesting. I have never known why I wanted to do poetry. It's one of my old dreams. I find comfort in it. As a matter of fact, I talked to someone just the other day. I said: "Look, I will do a radio show. I'll put on tape the poems I love. Someone can add music to it, and let's try to sell it, syndicate it." And they said, "Well, poetry, you know . . ." *Poetry* is a naughty word in this country.

DC

We seem to be living through a time when everyone is intent upon announcing the death of the Broadway theater in general, and in particular, the Broadway musical theater. Just as young people mature, they are being confronted with its disappearance. At least our generation was assured that there was a business there for us to get into.

RK

Yes. There is this feeling that the big musical productions as we knew them are in their Götterdämmerung. I think they've had it. It isn't going to be possible to mount them as they were done in the past.

DC

Do you think there are other ways to do them?

RK

Yes. Number one, away from Broadway. Number two, those big grinding sets are like dinosaurs. I hate to say it, but it's true.

DC

Will another form arise in their place? After all, people will always want to sing, and there will always be people who want to hear them.

RK

Right. But when you look at something like *Cats*, with a set that's absolutely staggering, it really is like a dinosaur. It will get so big that it can no longer move, and it will die, locked into its own massive weight. Whereas, something like *A Chorus Line* is so simple. It was tremendously jazzed up, but in its original production downtown, it was pure entertainment and dance, combined with an ingenious view of the hearts of those kids. I do think the days of the "big" musical are gone. Either that, or it becomes an elitist thing only the rich can afford.

DC

Then you are not saying that young people should turn their backs on the future of the American musical theater?

RK

Oh, no, they can't! But they will have to invent their own. Take Off Broadway. When it became as expensive as Broadway, theater got more off and off and off. Look at Chicago. The plays that have come out of that city and other regional theaters! Some of these kids who come to New York now have done Shakespeare, they've done Molière, they've done Congreve! New York, now, truly is a heartbreak place unless you are one of the lucky, lucky few. If you are not, go somewhere that is not New York, that is not Hollywood.

DC

And if you want to sing?

RK

If you really want to sing? Well, you know what I think will happen? I really feel we will force ourselves, through greed, into retreating back to the fundamentals, to the voice itself, to the acting itself. I believe that. I believe young people nowadays, young singer-actors, are extraordinary. When you and I started out you were either an actor, a singer, or a dancer. No such thing, now. They're marvelous! They do everything! There was this wonderful old actor I knew, David. One time, in the dressing room, I was talking to another actor about sex, and this old fellow turned to me and said: "Sex? Nonsense! Give me a board and a passion!" And I always thought, if I ever write my autobiography, I'd call it that: "A Board and a Passion." That's finally what it's all about.

*N*ancy Walker

Nancy Walker may be celebrated and admired by millions as a clown, but by her own admission, she began and still would be happy to be thought of as a singer. Her comic spirit and her unique sense of timing: (*Time* magazine once suggested that it was more trustworthy than Greenwich time) first were seen in a Broadway musical for which she had auditioned as a straight singer. What had been evident from the start was the absolute honesty and deadly sense of humor manifest in her singing—singing that can still stop a show, as those who saw her and/or listen to her clarion vocalizing of Stephen Sondheim's "I'm Still Here" know.

　　When I first heard her in the theater in the very early forties she was the first major star of my own generation to establish a foothold among the front echelon of the musical theater. Ethel Merman, Bea Lillie, Martha Raye, and the legendary Fanny Brice (banished to radio and Baby Snooks) were the stellar performers of a generation or more before us. In 1941, when the nineteen-year-old Nancy Walker in "Best Foot Forward" arrived as the blind date at the Winsocki Prom weekend, those of us in our teens and twenties could relate not only to one of our own but to the living proof that it could happen to us. She was an evident "authentic," lavishly validated by critics everywhere, who was funny, who could dance and sing and work a stage all on her own. No white singer I had heard before could phrase with such originality; no one I had ever seen could physicalize what she sang with such originality of body language. Despite her renown as a comedienne, I still think of her as the last of the red hot mamas. She has been laughed at by millions of theatergoers and television and movie buffs for over forty years; she has danced and been choreographed by the greatest choreographers of her time; she has acted on Broadway in plays as alien to her reputation as those by Chekhov, T. S. Eliot, and George Kelly; she has directed Off Broadway the first one-act plays of Nobel Prize–winner Saul Bellow and directed, too, on Broadway, on television, and in film. She is surely one of the most protean of women, but it is to her life as a singer that I have addressed this interview.

DC

Although audiences all over the world think of you as someone who works only in comedy, this isn't true. You began as a straight singer of songs, didn't you?

NW

Yes, I did. I think I was ten years old when I decided I wanted to be in musical comedies. I'd been seeing shows as far back as I can remember. If that sounds precocious, you have to understand that I came from a show business family, so they were looking at me with a gimlet eye. By the time I was ten, although I didn't necessarily have to go into the theater, I had to have a goal.

DC

Did you see any plays?

NW

I saw everything—musicals, plays, Martha Graham—but my eye and my heart completely were taken by Ethel Merman—and my ears. Suddenly the theater was filled with music and a sound I had never heard before.

DC

What do you think there is about a musical that, in particular for someone like you, strikes an early chord?

NW

Looking back, I think I must have known that my freedom lay in a musical. You see, when I announced that I wanted to do musicals, my father [*Note: The eminent vaudevillian Dewey Barto*] said, "Well, you're going to have to be able to do everything." And I said, "Why is that?" He said, "Eventually, people are going to be asked to do everything, and I think it would be wise if you start now." For the next ten years I studied everything—dancing, singing, languages, sculpting—and I realized, then, that singing was an extraordinary act for me. You see, I had all kinds of inhibitions about the way I behaved and the way I looked. I was extremely shy, but not when I sang. And not when I sang if I couldn't see you. Even when I studied with somebody, I'd stand in back of the coach because I was so frightened, but once I got onstage, that didn't exist any longer. Now that I think about it, it's rather like people who stutter, but when they get on a stage, they can sing or speak with no trouble at all. I guess I was an emotional stutterer who wouldn't let anyone catch me at it, and nobody who ever taught me ever saw me. *I* knew it was working and, through the years, I have become my own editor. George Abbott taught me to be my own editor and my own judge of what is going on.

DC

You don't consider yourself an entertainer like the stand-up performers who work in nightclubs and in small rooms and whose purpose is to beguile the audience?

NW

Oh, in no way. I would love to be able to do that, but, you see, I do it for *me* . . . particularly, for me.

DC

That is not true for a great many performers, wouldn't you agree?

NW

I don't know. I think I'm much too egocentric. When I see performers pushing onstage, I think they must be doing it for the audience and, as a way of thinking, I believe that to be a large error, because an audience will take you to their level and I don't think that's a wise way to go. I don't mean this in any derogatory sense, but masses of people are made to laugh by very little, whereas, if you can say, "Don't laugh at that, wait for something else, because it is going to be better," that's what I think should be done. Most people go for the one, two, three but if you give up the one, two, the three is much bigger.

DC

How old were you when someone finally hired you and paid you to sing professionally? And what kind of work was it?

NW

I think I was fifteen or sixteen. Madge Tucker hired me at NBC. She had a radio program called "Coast to Coast on a Bus: Madge Tucker's Children's Hour." Anyway, I got an audition there. It was some time before I figured out why I was there, because it was all radio stories about fairies and fairy godmothers, and, you know, with my voice, I was the fairy godmother. But she let me sing the most sophisticated songs, and I wanted to sing so badly! I was doing all the wrong things, far too sophisticated for me, but not for my sense of rhythm. You see, I had taught myself by sitting up at night until three or four in the morning learning records, learning entire orchestrations; every part I could hear, I learned. It must have driven my poor family crazy! But I couldn't go to sleep until I had learned one number each night. And then, for a finale, I'd cry myself to sleep, all because I wanted to be in a musical!

DC

I remember reading that you were fired from one of your first jobs. Is that correct?

NW

That was when I was sixteen or seventeen years old. I was hired by a gentleman who had a . . . He yelled at me once for calling it a "chili joint" . . . Well, maybe it was better than that. There were two acts. There was another lady who danced, and there was me. I was so unknowing I had to copy the makeup by watching her at her dressing table. I didn't know what I was doing. But, again, the desire to sing was overwhelming. I was bursting in all the wrong directions. He said, after the first show, "That will be that," and I was out on the roadway near Washington, I think, or Maryland, hailing down a Greyhound bus at two in the morning.

DC

Didn't he like the way you sang?

NW

I don't know. I was just unknowing. There I was, up there, seventeen years old, singing "Moanin' Low." I didn't know what town I was in, let alone what "Moanin' Low" was about!

DC

It seems so interesting that no one recognized a talent that, only a year later, when you were eighteen and appearing in *Best Foot Forward* on the Broadway stage, was hailed by the critics as well as the public as extraordinary.

NW

I don't know what it was. In those months before I auditioned for *Best Foot Forward*, I played a small town—I think it was New Haven—on a vaudeville bill with Eddie Lambert. I don't recall how I got the job; it must have been with my father's pull; but Eddie was a brilliant comic to whom I owe a great deal. It was just for one evening, but I went on for two shows, and each time he'd say: "It's just going to be astounding when you hit—where you're going. This is not important. Where you're going is what's important! And I can see it. I can't tell you about it except to tell you it's going to be all right." I'm not sure that the people around me didn't have a clue, but it is very dangerous to tell that to someone—to tell somebody that she's funny—and they were all very wise. That's why we have so many "empties" today. They're really empty Coca Cola cans. It says Coca-Cola, but when you open the can, there is nothing in it. You can never tell someone, "you are funny. Go be funny!" Because, if you are truly funny, it will stop you dead in your tracks, because you won't know how to "be" funny. "Doing" funny is not "being" funny. I mean, we laugh at seals, but seals, per se, are not funny—they're sweet. Somebody who clonks in without knowing it, clonks into a wall—that's amusing. Or somebody who falls on a banana peel—that's funny. It strikes something funny in all of us. We're relieved that it wasn't us. But the minute you say, "Go be funny," that's the kiss of death!

DC

But so many comics today do very well with "doing" funny. Doesn't that, somehow, refute your theory?

NW

Very few people today are funny. They are given funny lines, or what passes for funny lines, or they are put into bizarre situations, but, you know, we had our Three Stooges. But they were funny. The Ritz Brothers were funny men, if you knew them. They were funny gentlemen. Funny things happened to them in their lives. Willie Howard was a sad but a funny man.

DC

But these men "did" funny, didn't they?

NW

They "did" funny because they *were* funny. They didn't "do" funny to "do" funny for a cheap laugh. What *happened* to them was funny. I never saw Willie Howard do a comedic thing. He did knowing things, but he didn't do comedic things. There's a big difference. Knowing is timing.

DC

And you?

NW

I have done some things very seriously and gotten laughs, so I learned to use that, too. That's another wire that I walk when I want to get a particular effect. If I am terribly earnest about something and suddenly do a "take" on it, on myself, it takes the curse off its being serious and turns it around and makes it funny.

DC

Going back to your first musical, *Best Foot Forward*, that audition of yours is historic. Could you tell me how it all came about?

NW

The day before the audition, my father said: "Why don't you change your name? Perhaps having the name of Barto is not wise because I'm well known in the business and somebody may dislike me, take it out on you. Who knows? Why don't you strike out on your own?" So, we put six names on pieces of paper, tossed them into a hat, and I picked out "Walker." The next day, my pianist and I went down to the audition, and there must have been 200 people waiting to get into the Barrymore Theater. I looked at them and became very discouraged, but I thought, "I'll wait." All I wanted was a chorus job —anything, as long as I could get into a musical. In a few minutes, a very elegant lady walked out and said, "Isn't Miss Walker here yet?" Nobody else raised their hand, so I did. I was a new Walker, but there I was, and she took me past all those people.

DC

You didn't stop to wonder how she knew a name that was only a few hours old?

NW

I didn't care how she would have known it. I just wanted to get into the bloody theater. Then, she said, "Are you going to dance?" and I said, "No." Why in heaven I thought I could ever get into a chorus without dancing is a puzzlement but, you see, singing—that was it! I said that I could dance but they had told me this was a singing audition. So, after the next person had sung, I went on and sang a rhythm, not a comedy, number.

DC

Do you remember the name of the song?

NW

Not until the other night. I was in New York to attend a tribute to George Abbott, and he remembered it. He's ninety-seven and he remembered it! It was "Beat Me Daddy, Eight to the Bar." There was nothing funny for me in that, but Mr. Abbott—although I didn't know then it was he—said, "Please sing another song." Now they were really laughing and I was heartbroken because, you see, I thought I was being ridiculed. I ended up singing four songs, almost in tears when, thank God, he stopped me and said, "Will you come out into the auditorium?" It was very dark out there, and I was able to dry my tears, and then this very tall man came over, loomed over me, I should say, and said, "Well, there's nothing in the show for you, but Richard Rodgers is going to oversee the music that Hugh Martin and Ralph Blane have written and he says he won't do it unless I put you in the show. So, I'm going to write something in it

for you. We just think you're marvelous and we'll see you in October."
That was in May and I never spent a summer like that in my life. It
was terrible and it was wonderful! And I shall never forget it.

DC

And so *Best Foot Forward* happened and everybody knew who you
were. Except, in a sense, you.

NW

Well, you know, I didn't know what I was doing was "comedy" until
we opened in New Haven. They never told me. I guess they thought
I knew. It is amazing. I think, too, they were shocked at my shock.

DC

You were such an original on the stage. Do you think now that you
might have unconsciously modeled yourself after others you had seen
in those musicals you had attended as a child? I don't mean *modeled*
in the sense of *imitated,* of course.

NW

I'll tell you who was influential in my feeling about how to walk across
a stage, which, if you know how to do it, is one of the most important
things you can do in the theater. I know that sounds ridiculous, but
if you can do it and "catch" people, you've got them by the tail. It's
embarrassing how few people know how to do it. I'm one of them.
Harry Richmond and Billy Gaxton knew how. You would pay twice
what you have to pay now to see a show just to see them walk across
a stage. It was a magnificence! It was their art. They were works of
art. Me? I have joy when I do it, and I give joy because it is so
splendid to feel that rhythm that hits the stage from left to right . . .
just walking. There isn't a show girl alive who can touch you, and it
has nothing to do with outer style. It's all inner. And I say this with
no boasting whatever. I did nothing to create it. Nothing. Except that
I recognized it in other people, and it is one of the things that helps
me to stand alone with other people who stand alone. Does that make
any sense? There are other people on other mountaintops and we can
all wave at each other, but we are isolated on our own mountaintop
because . . . we can walk across the stage. I defy anyone to challenge
me in that. It certainly saved my fanny in *Best Foot Forward* because

we had done a number that was the ultimate disaster. I was in the center of it, and it was just terrible. So Mr. Abbott said to me, "Listen, what would you do with that song?" and I said: "I don't know, sir. I really don't, but I'll do whatever you want." He said, "Well, why don't you try it all by yourself, or with one of the other boys if you need him . . . Whatever you want to do." It was . . . something I'd waited for all my life. I was nineteen! Oh, the joke of it! But I had yearned for it for what had seemed like a lifetime. And I got to do it in the first show. I couldn't believe it.

DC

Which song was it?

NW

"Just a Little Joint with a Jukebox." It's a great song to walk to and that's what we did. We just walked back and forth . . . back and forth . . . singing it. And that was it. It was all over.

DC

There is such a great swinging quality to your singing. Do you think you and possibly our generation were influenced, again unconsciously, by the big band sound of the forties? And not only by them but by the quality of Merman's voice, which was, well, never a swinging sound. I'd never heard anyone like you, in a musical, who combined the old and the new in so original a style.

NW

It's interesting that I don't think singers influenced me as much as the great jazz musicians I listened to. Did you ever hear of Slim Gaylord? He was a fantastic bass player. The first time I heard him, I thought he was playing two instruments at the same time. He wasn't at all. What he was doing was jive singing along with the bass, and, well, everything he played sounded like a swing waltz! I used to listen to him for hours on end. And two others musicians—Django Reinhardt and Stephane Grappelli. The rhythms those men created against the melodies were so diverse, like an underbelly that supported the song. It was like wonderful wine poured through a roast, and I would try to pull out the different rhythms, and that's when I really started to sing.

DC

Best Foot Forward, in a sense, brought the two together. The score allowed for the swinging vocalism, and you were performing in a musical. And the comedy?

NW

It was a dollop of whipped cream.

DC

You had not been aware of it until then?

NW

No, not at all.

DC

You went to Hollywood to film *Best Foot Forward.* Was this a new work technique you had to learn? Performing for the camera?

NW

Well, what you learn you certainly don't learn in one film. You record, and then, many days later when that recording is refined and balanced, it is blared out to you over loudspeakers and you lip-synch, and suddenly you find yourself thinking, "Oh, this isn't what I wanted to do at all!" In the choreographed numbers this isn't so important, because there is someone watching you, but when you're out there, presenting yourself on Thursday, it's never quite what you did on Tuesday . . . not vocally.

DC

Does singing on television more closely resemble working on a stage?

NW

It's the same thing and yet different. There can be a prerecording or you have a backup.

DC

How long did you remain in Hollywood?

NW

I was out of California every time I had five minutes. I found Los Angeles extremely dull. It was a film-oriented town, and I wasn't much interested in that. Not after I saw how films were made. It's a very slow process and it's very boring. I sat around for six months and then we did *Best Foot Forward* and *Girl Crazy** at the same time! That was something I never quite figured out. After that, I began begging off. I kept saying "Please, may I leave? Please, may I leave?" I finally got permission two years later, in 1944. Meanwhile, of course, I had been back to New York many times to make personal appearances for the war effort, but, in 1944, I went back to do *On the Town.*

DC

And, again, you were directed by George Abbott. Can you describe how he helped you in those early years?

NW

He's such a precise man, and he doesn't tolerate fooling around when you're working. You couldn't *not* learn from every direction he gave you or anybody else. He wasn't out to teach, but he couldn't help doing just that—at least, in my case. He has the most fantastic eye and ear and, as many great directors are able to do, he can turn his back and, three lines later, say, "Don't do that." You weren't aware you were doing anything at all, but he was. Then, he'd say, "Do exactly what you did before," and so you would do exactly what you did again, and he'd say, "Why did you raise your hand on the punch line?" And you'd think, "God, I could kill myself!" He would want to know why you were moving against the sound of the words. And then, you'd say, "Well, I just can't stand still through a joke." He'd say, "Find a way." So, if you couldn't invent it, he'd show you a way. But he always left it open for you to invent it for yourself. For instance, he'd say to me: "You have these two lines coming up, sweetheart. When you're through with them, I want you over here." Well, the first time he did that I thought I'd faint! How do I get over there? And I said, "Well . . . how . . . do . . . I . . . ? And he said,

---

*With Judy Garland and Mickey Rooney.

"You'll manage." And I did. He wouldn't want anything to get in my way—in the way of me.

DC

At the same time that he wanted what he wanted.

NW

He wanted you over there because, in getting you over there, you were going to service the next line for wherever it was coming from. It just opened gates! Floodgates! I was so crazy about his notes; he'd give you a note—he had paper coming out of his ears, little chits— and then he'd crumple the paper up and throw it on the floor. I went around picking up all the papers because I knew human nature would always lower the level of the performance he demanded, and I always kept those notes to remind me of what he had wanted originally.

DC

On the Town had a score by Leonard Bernstein and Comden and Green and Jerome Robbins did the choreography. It was each one's first Broadway credit. Having sung only pop scores on the stage and in film, did you find Bernstein's music difficult?

NW

I'd say to Lenny, "Why am I singing this?" And he'd say, "Because you're a clarinet." Since, as I told you, I had studied from recordings by learning all the parts, I'd say "All right. Gotcha!" And I went on singing. It never occurred to me to argue with him on those terms.

DC

I heard about a quartet in the second act that gave you trouble. Is that true?

NW

Yes. It was during "Some Other Time." For all my bragging about learning parts, I have never been asked to sing two of these parts together. You see, I cannot do harmony. Period. Everybody has long since stopped asking me, but in those days Lenny, with great rosy optimism, was always asking me to sing the harmony part, and I couldn't convince him or anybody, so every night I'd make a terrible

mess of it, and we'd end up with four people singing three-part
harmony. I just joined the melody. He'd come back after the show
and say: "No, darling. We're going to have dinner and I'll explain
the way it should go." I got to the point where I'd say, "I don't want
to have supper with you anymore because all you're doing is banging
the fork on my plate and singing the harmony." I never did get it.
There was a Steinway showroom right next door to the Colonial Theater
in Boston, and they gave him the keys, God help me, and each night
he'd take me there, with people passing by at one o'clock in the
morning wondering what those two idiots were doing in there! Well,
it was fine while he was singing with me, but the next performance
I was off and away singing right along on the melody.

DC

Do you read music or play an instrument?

NW

No to both. I had years of piano lessons when I was a child, but
music is still a mystery to me.

DC

How do you go about learning new scores?

NW

I have somebody play it, banging out the melody, until I get it. I
used to be very quick. I'm a little slower, now.

DC

As we said a moment ago, Jerry Robbins also made his Broadway
debut in that show. Did you have any idea, then, what lay ahead for
him and Mr. Bernstein?

NW

Oh, yes. No one had ever seen or heard the likes of them before.
And they were adorable. They came out to California to meet me and
to continue writing and working. Jerry was performing with Ballet
Theater and had already choreographed *Fancy Free* for the company.
On the Town, the musical they were writing, was based on the ballet.
They expressly asked to meet me. It was a strange meeting. I think

we were all a little in awe of each other. Again, it was that strange feeling I had; we recognized we were on different mountaintops. We were all so young. I was twenty-two then, and we had a common dream and a life force that you couldn't beat. As I look back now, I think it was that everything we were about was "theater," and you could feel that. George [*Abbott*] felt it, I know; he spoke of it many times—the talents of all the people involved. He was then fifty-one years old and was extraordinary!

DC

Following *On the Town*, you did *Barefoot Boy with Cheek*. Again, a George Abbott musical. Was there anything you learned from that show?

NW

Yes. We shouldn't have done it.

DC

Well, then . . . Your next show was the first one written expressly for you: *Look, Ma, I'm Dancin'*. For someone like yourself, who still had one foot planted in the "old" theater system, being starred in your own show must have been an extraordinary experience. Today, of course, it happens all the time, but, then, one had to work long and hard for it.

NW

All one's life one has crazy, soaring dreams about the kind of reviews one would like to get, but I never dreamed anything like those. Even more meaningful was that I had gotten to a point with Mr. Abbott where I had learned so much from him that one day he came into my dressing room and said: "Here, would you correct this for me? Just see if it works and if it doesn't, make it work, would you? The scene is not for you; it's for two other people." I don't believe I have ever felt so honored! It was a short scene, but I was so thrilled that he trusted me with it.

DC

And, again, you were working with Jerome Robbins. Would you talk about the dancing in *Look, Ma*? The musical was about the world of

ballet, and I imagine the choreography was more difficult than anything you had danced before.

NW

We had a difficult time getting the show on, and I think now, that
in the major plan of my life, there was a reason for that. Jerry had
said, early on, "Look, kiddo, if you want to do *Look, Ma* you had
better put on the ballet shoes." And I said, "Right-o!" I studied for
a year and a half, both in class in the daytime, and privately at night.
En pointe. In toe shoes. The longer the show was postponed, the
better I got. And I realize now that, without those delays, I could
not have done what Jerry asked me to do.

DC

You suffered a major trauma in that show. Can you talk about it?

NW

I began to lose my voice. We all attributed it to a cold. It wasn't. I
didn't know the reason for it when it happened. I only learned that
two years later, but it totally closed my throat. It was emotional. I
finally had to say, "Please let me out of this show." Now, you must
understand. This was a show I had worked for all my life . . . and
for those reviews. I'd written them in my dreams, but not as good as
the ones I got, and suddenly, eight months later, I was no longer
able to perform in it. I don't want to speak about the nature of the
emotional trauma—it was quite set apart from the show—but it affected the show, and I was deeply sorry about that.

DC

Can we talk about singing? How important do you feel the study of
a good vocal technique is, and would you recommend that a young
person learn it earlier or later in a career?

NW

Well, my early training was just in . . . style. And I do not recommend
that because it relies almost exclusively on energy and, sooner or
later, energy wanes. Then, when anything occurs to threaten you and,
by extension, your voice, you have no technique to take arms against
the new enemy. It is important to find someone who will teach you

how to produce your voice correctly and not destroy it, and *you*, in the process. Then, when you do find that teacher, study! Because you should be able to feel as if you threw a note out into the audience, walked away, fixed your makeup, fixed your hair, came back, opened your mouth, and took the note back.

DC

Regardless of the sound systems that now amplify all musicals?

NW

I haven't worked with those, although I will in the new show I will be doing. I have worked with sound systems in the "foots," but I was never aware of them. When there were poor ones, in summer stock, or only three of them, you had to race forty feet to get from one to the other. But in well-miked houses, I was never aware of having to project. However, I repeat: Study is the only way to go. If you don't have the technique, you are always prey to your emotions. And your energy level.

DC

You followed *Look Ma, I'm Dancin'* with *Along Fifth Avenue*, the first of many revues for which you became well known. Do you think that clowns like you, and before you, Brice and Lillie, will always be fated to appear in revues because of the lack of book material for women who, by definition, are born to be funny?

NW

The form really doesn't exist today. They call those variety shows on television, revues, but they are only just variety shows. The main job of a sketch writer is to find the punch line or the end line of the sketch. I make that a specific definition because most writers don't know how to do that. The punch line is where you end a sketch that has a beginning, a middle, and an end. It has to make sense, no matter how zany or bizarre the sketch may be. In television they use the blackout or music or they simply fade out on another person.

DC

I imagine revues are the most difficult kind of theater to create. They don't have the protection of a book, characters . . .

NW

Well, they have characters, but the characters only last eight minutes. But, to get back to your question, I don't think funny women are fated to appear in anything different than other women in the musical theater. We're all on a stage. Books and sketches are the same. A sketch is nothing but a short playlet. With luck, it's funny. If not, you take it out and replace it with another one. I like the revue form, although I started to do them fairly late in my career. As for Brice and Lillie, I don't believe they ever did book shows, whereas I have been lucky.

DC

You have done one revival, *Pal Joey*, on Broadway. Did you enjoy singing a great classic score?

NW

Well, it's a great comfort to know that you're going to open your mouth and sing a hit. You barely need to do anything because everyone is there either because they want to know the score better or because they know it intimately and are so pleased that *you* are doing it this time. But, you have to work hard to top all of that and think, "Yes, I know you know this, but I'd like you to hear *my* way with it."

DC

You learned you were pregnant in *Pal Joey*. As far as singing is concerned, is there a problem with breath under those circumstances? How late into your pregnancy were you able to perform?

NW

Up until the fifth month in a, well, brief costume, for those days. It wasn't a hip-high bikini, but I wore shorts and a little shirt over a bra. I was able to work with nothing "showing" and no loss of breath. In fact, quite the contrary, I had a great amount of energy. Tremendous energy! The people who worried most were the show girls. They used to stand in the wings with cookies and say, "Are you all right, sweetie?" They couldn't get over the fact that I wasn't on my knees. But I had never felt that wonderful in my life.

DC

Your first Off Broadway appearance was in another revue, *Phoenix '55*, a show I was a part of. I wonder if we can talk about the range of roles you played—wider than anything you had attempted before.

NW

I think that's one of the great joys you have working in revues. Songs, dances, sketches . . .

DC

You have been described as a clown—as opposed to a comic or a comedienne—by certain critics. I have read that Walter Kerr said of you that "the greatest clown today is a woman."

NW

Yes, but I never felt like a "clown" until I put on whiteface in *Phoenix '55*. How can I describe this? I always do everything everyone else does, seemingly, but I'm the one who catches her sleeve on the doorknob. I think that's why my comedy, for such a long time, came as such a great shock to me. I did exactly what everyone else did, but the results were funny and I didn't understand why. Even with Mr. Abbott's help, it took me a long time to realize the intricacies and the fundamentals of comedy. I just never thought of myself as funny. I still don't. When I am being my most serious, it gets laughs. I've learned not to be hurt by that. But, I never feel like a clown. My body does funny things without my intending it to.

DC

Could you talk about Bea Lillie, another great clown?

NW

Bea, because she was English, was permitted a wider scope of comic characters in her sketches than I had been, that is, before *Phoenix '55*. She was very arch, and so she had farther to fall. I'm . . . almost there. My comedy is very definite, so I can be made to look the fool more easily. It's a totally different approach. When I read some of her material now, I realize I couldn't do it at all because I don't understand that arch quality. I'm more streetwise . . . the bee hovering around the elephant. I can kill him with a sting but . . .

DC

Your performance of "I'm Still Here" at the Sondheim evening is generally considered to be definitive. Even the recording gives me some idea of how dynamic it must have been to have seen it.

NW

It was a chaotic evening. We were all so nervous because we were going to be singing for the master and we all wanted to be so good for him and so right. I hadn't been able to remember the lyrics, straight through, throughout the six weeks I rehearsed the song. They . . . just escaped me. The day before the show I had sung the song for Steve at his home. I hadn't remembered the lyrics, and he said: "Uh, listen. I'd like to add sixteen more bars." And I said: "Why not? I don't know these, so why not add some more?" I got, as did everyone, one run-through with the orchestra and was told that was because they were pressed for time. I didn't get the lyrics right then, either, and I haven't gotten them right since.

DC

But you certainly got them right when the light hit you!

NW

It was an extraordinary evening for me, and everybody was just brilliant! I had absolutely no idea what I was going to do with the song. It was getting nearer and nearer to the moment when I knew I was going "on," and I thought: "Good God! What do I do?" But I'll tell you what happened when I started singing. Halfway through the first chorus I heard or felt—I'm not sure which—a great rumbling. And I knew that if I didn't get out of its way, I would be pushed right into the orchestra pit.

DC

Coming at you from behind?

NW

Yes. All I knew was that I had to get out of its way. And so, mentally, I just stepped over a foot to the left, and I just let it roll past me. It was the first time I ever got out of my way in my singing. And I thought, "I've been free before, but never this free!" And it was a great freedom!

DC

You can hear it on the recording. Particularly in the powerful build to its climax. *Phoenix '55* was followed by a rash of straight plays from Noel Coward all the way to Chekhov and then, the move to California where, for fifteen years, you performed on television with very little singing along the way. Now you are returning to Broadway in your own show, singing and dancing and clowning. I imagine it will be some kind of an emotional experience for you to be back on the stage, in front of a living audience again.

NW

I'll be free again.

DC

According to *Who's Who,* you are 65. Do you foresee any problems in singing eight shows a week?

NW

I don't plan to be singing *Parsifal,* so I don't think there is anything to be concerned about.

DC

You were a smoker throughout much of your life. Were you ever worried that it might hurt your voice?

NW

It never did. I used to smoke right up to the moment I stepped out onstage. My last step was the stepping on a cigarette to put it out.

DC

But you don't recommend that any more?

NW

I don't recommend smoking, period. But, I did do it, and I never paid for it vocally. I paid for it physically but never vocally.

DC

If you had to say something to young women who are now going into the world of comedy in which men have habitually reigned, what would it be?

NW

I don't know. It is such a different ball game, now. First of all, today women can—do—say anything that men can say. I don't know but that there hasn't been a certain loss of femininity. I don't even think that word has any meaning today. Someone in pants and a shirt can say things that someone in a peplum and an organdy skirt cannot say. And it doesn't have to be a man in that shirt and pants. It's a completely different visual thing today.

DC

Do you think your kind of comedy, the classic clown, is giving way to the new stand-up comedienne and, by doing so, moving into history?

NW

Well, are you asking me whether the clowns in the circus will ever be passé? I don't think so. But the clowns in the circus have an innocence about them. That is why children relate to them. And it is why grownups love them—it is something to which they'd like to return. We all have that innocence in us, but we cover it up with a lot of smart jokes and . . . Well, I've never been able to do that. I still consider myself a very innocent person—considering what I say, you might not believe it—but I cover it up a lot of the time. But I have never lost my naïveté, and I pray to God I never lose it! I don't find that in too many people today. People on the street aren't naive. There isn't an innocence; there isn't a vulnerable moment, or if there is, you can't find it.

DC

Is that integral to comedy?

NW

You bet it is!

George Hearn

George Hearn is an actor-singer without whom it is difficult to imagine musical theater as it is defined today. Just at that moment in time when musicals began to strain at their leash and pull further away from formula into the operatic, there he was. Anyone who saw his work in *Sweeney Todd* was witness to the perfect amalgam of what a singer looks like and sounds like when he is homogenized into a singing actor. I think of him as the Alec Guinness of the musical theater. From Todd, to Torvald-Johan (a dual role) in *A Doll's Life* to Albin in *La Cage aux Folles,* he seems utterly to erase himself and become the identity given him in the theater program. And he does this with such skill and modesty that were the real George Hearn to step forward, who might he be? Although his voice is elegant and true, one is, upon hearing him, further aware of the delight he takes in making words preeminently important for the listener. In my memory, no singer in the musical theater, with the possible exception of Rex Harrison, can make words so clear, so lucid, that one is simultaneously able to hear what they say and know what they mean. This unique talent is granted very few performers. One need not see his work to comprehend this gift. His singing on cast albums of the shows in which he has appeared displays the same generosity with a lyric. Irving Berlin once remarked of Ethel Merman that one had to write her a good lyric because, Lord knows, everybody was going to hear it. This is true of George Hearn, and one could add, everybody is going to understand it as well.

DC

You have done so many interesting things as an actor and as a singer. Did you intend for your career to have this bilateral focus from the start?

GH

I think it swerved back and forth a lot. I remember Colleen Dewhurst said once, "Somebody said to me what a marvelous career you've built for yourself . . . choosing." And she responded, "I've taken every job that was ever offered to me:" Well, I think what I have done is pretty much the same thing. I came to New York in '63 from Memphis, Tennessee. I studied voice in Memphis and then in Aspen, Colorado, for two summers with Mack Harrell, and then I went to Washington University in St. Louis, where I studied opera. I performed several operas in workshops and did some lieder singing.

DC

Then, at that time, your sights were set solely on a singing career?

GH

Well, somewhat. My degree was in philosophy. I didn't know what I was going to do. I think I was just trying to pick up everything in sight. And I love words and language, but I didn't like—and still don't like—sacrificing language to a melodic line. It may be that there was a certain prejudice there that led me away from the world of opera. There are some marvelous actor-singers, but there is also a tendency to use the voice as an instrument. The other day I said to someone that Olivier's voice is not inferior to Horne's. It's just a different use of the instrument, a form of speech you must have to cover that kind of language.

DC

Is it your interest in language that so informs your singing, or is it a part of your actor's credentials?

GH

I don't really know. In the old bardic tradition, the singer was both a writer and an interpreter of the oral history of the country. And they certainly were united in Homer's time. And, of course, there is the Irish tradition, and I'm Irish. It seems to me that they have only become separated in modern times. The remembering and performing of language, the singing and the incanting of it, is an old, old tradition.

DC

Can you read music? Play an instrument?

GH

Yes. And I play the piano a bit.

DC

When you go about learning a score, do you use the help of others or do you teach it to yourself, by yourself?

GH

In recent times, with *Sweeney Todd* and *La Cage aux Folles*, I've learned it with the composer. We sat at the piano, and they played it for me, and I listened. In the case of *Sweeney Todd*, I listened to the recording a few times. Jerry Herman and Don Goodman taught me the songs from *La Cage*.* I'm learning an opera now that I'll be singing at the New York City Opera next year along with a revival of *Kismet* that I'll do there first. I love *Kismet* and I've never done it. Now, that's a language play! There's a mixture of a lot of splendid language with a lot of singing. And there is that kind of mixture in me. When I first came to New York, I did sixteen plays for Joe Papp in the first two or three years. I think I did thirty-six Shakespeare productions—two or three of them, two or three times. And I love it.

DC

I've always thought Elizabethan soliloquies are much like arias. All they lack is a prescribed melodic line.

GH

Johnny Collum§ and I used to talk about that. There were two things that bugged me at the time. One was that we had both arrived about the time the Beatles arrived and people weren't asking for legit baritones, at least not for a few years. And the other . . . Well, he had this theory that growing up with Baptist ministers, you got into a sense of music and incanting. [*He gives it the Elmer Gantry reading.*] "Come down and rededicate yourself to Christ!" And they got used to that kind of incanting of language. People often ask why there are so many good southern Shakespearean actors—and there are quite a few of them—and it may have something to do with the musicality of that tradition.

---

*Jerry Herman wrote the score of and Don Goodman was the Assistant Director of music for *La Cage aux Folles*.
§Actor/singer who replaced Richard Burton in *Camelot*, he also appeared in *Doubles* and in *Shenandoah*.

DC

You do feel strongly that music and words are bound together and neither one is more important than the other?

GH

Yes. I think it is most wonderful when they can inform each other.

DC

W. H. Auden, in an interview, said, and I quote him exactly: "One great thing about opera singing is that you cannot pretend it's naturalistic." How do you feel about that?

GH

It's complicated. I read somewhere, recently, some film critic, I believe, who said that stage acting was embarrassing because it was so unnatural. It infuriated me because I dislike filming a lot and find it extremely artificial. Seventy people in a room, setting every light meter. There is nothing natural about it. You might think, if you're an innocent sitting in the theater, that those people on the screen are naturalistically acting, but they're not. Movie people cannot believe you raise your voice in anger or for any basic emotions. You see, *naturalism* is a strange word. If you're born with that enormous Pavarotti voice and your name is Pavarotti, you talk that way, naturally.

DC

Often the young actors I teach who have been raised solely on the teachings of Stanislavsky are surprised to learn that their voices are not, in any way, adequate to the demands of singing.

GH

"Naturalistic" acting does not communicate to the audience. When you talk to really old-fashioned actors—and I love to talk to them— it's "I don't care what *you're* crying about, *I* want to cry!" I think, too, that there is a lot of misguided Stanislavsky going about. And, then, there is the obverse, which is kind of awkward. I have trouble when I film. Film directors say: "George, there's too much body in your voice. It's too fruity, it's unnatural." Well, it's not unnatural to me. This happens to be the way I talk. So they want me to talk artificially in order to be "natural" on their film. They don't want me to vocalize or hit the cords at all. But human beings, when they argue or scream and yell at each other, *do* vocalize. It's a funny reverse snobbery about how to use your instrument. The really good ones do it all. The really wonderful opera singers, the really wonderful actors, they can do a film; they can do it all.

DC

Auden, in the same interview, spoke about his experience writing, with Chester Kallman, a translation of Mozart's *The Magic Flute*. He said, and again I quote: "We decided to put the spoken interludes into couplets. Nearly everybody in the cast were singers and had never spoken verse before. There was only one part played by an actor. With the singers, we could teach them immediately how to speak verse and they could get it in ten minutes because they knew what a 'beat' was. But we had awful trouble with the professional actor."

GH

That is strange, isn't it? It could have depended on what their tastes were.

DC

I thought, perhaps, that the singers found more comfort in the 'beat' because they were used to the rhythmic prison of music.

GH

I think that couplets are very hard to act, anyway. I did the Wilbur* translation of *Tartuffe*, which is very good. But there are traps. It's like reading Alexander Pope. And those traps are in those rhymed two lines. It can become very doggerel-like. And, I think, in this case, maybe the actor was on the right track and Auden was not. I mean, you go, da da da da da da da da . . . which might have been what they wanted to write and would probably work because *The Magic Flute* is so formal an opera and its set music, too, is formalized. But, I think, in most cases, if you wanted to do rhymed couplets,

---

*Richard Wilbur, poet and translator-adapter of many of the plays of Molière.

you'd want to break over the line, the way good Shakespeare is read, which is not to *disguise* the fact that it's written in iambics but rather not to allow the iambics to wear *you*. After all, all theater exists to tell a story, and the better you can tell that story, using every skill you have—vocal, physical, dance, mime—the better it will be. But couplets and recitatives are tough. I'm studying a new opera now, *Casanova's Homecoming* by Dominic Argento, that I'll be doing with the City Opera next year. It's very difficult and it's in English. There are a lot of recitatives, but he has a wonderful kind of middle ground of odd harmonic changes that keep you from, well, you know, that thump, thump of Mozart's recitatives.

DC

I read something when I was a kid—it was by either Joseph Addison or Beaumarchais—that said, "Anything that's too stupid to say you can sing about." Of course, the person was talking about eighteenth-century Italian opera. But often, when I hear a contemporary song, I think it still holds true today.

GH

Well, you know the rule of thumb about writing for a musical: a song must occur at the moment when speaking it will no longer gratify you. And, when it is really well written, as in the case of a good musical like *Kiss Me Kate*, or *Guys and Dolls*, or *Brigadoon*, or, hopefully, *La Cage aux Folles*, the moment comes when the emotion is pitched to such a height that it is perfectly natural to step into music, and if the introduction into the song is naturalistic, the audience will buy your moving into it.

DC

Of course, so many scores that were written during the twenties and the thirties were written more to entertain than to move the plot forward or to reveal character.

GH

You could say, then, that the flip side would be that when the statement is universal, it may possibly sound stupid *until* it is sung. When you have to say "I love you," it's wonderful to be able to sing it.

DC

How do you feel about text that isn't very good?

GH

And still has to be sung? You do the best you can with it. There's a beautiful song called "You're Nearer" by Rodgers and Hart. It's beautiful until the ending. I guess they couldn't think of a right ending, so they wrote " . . . for I love you so." It kills the impact of the whole song. You do the best you can with that. You can gloss over it, or if you can justify it, perhaps the character runs out of words? Billy Bigelow says, "Oh, what the hell! What if it's a girl?!"* I guess, as an actor, one can deliberately try to say it. That's probably the best way to do it. But, by and large, a bad lyric is a bad lyric.

DC

I also uncovered an interesting quote of Arthur Miller's. It is in reference to a girl who, in one of his plays, was inaudible. When this was pointed out to her, more than once, she became furious and said that she was acting the truth and was not going to prostitute herself for an audience. When Miller told this to Walter Hampden, that actor's comment was, "Those kinds of actors play a cello with the most perfect bowing and the fingering is magnificent, too, but there isn't a string on the instrument." I bring this up because I often wonder whether the techniques the actor studies are, in many ways, oppositional to those the singer learns. Whereas the actor deals, from the start, with the significance of the text, the singer learns the importance of sound and its correct production.

GH

A lot of that is so.

DC

Do you feel that both studies can come together?

GH

I think they'll probably come together less and less from now on because acting for film and television is . . . Well, sometimes I feel

*From "Soliloquy" from Rodgers and Hammerstein's *Carousel*.

even the theater now is a museum piece—at least, a little bit. I hope that it will never come about that we are so entirely. But when a young actor comes to me and asks, "What should I do?" I tell him, if you want to get into television or film, don't study speech and diction. Try to get rid of localisms in your speech—study that—but you don't need to project at all. If you want to go through the theater system in New York, or wherever the theater system may be, or into the opera world, then of course you must study how to project your voice over space. But it is only a liability to a film actor.

DC

If, as you say, it sometimes seems as if the musical theater is becoming a museum, how do you account for the enormous interest young people everywhere appear to have in it?

GH

It is kind of marvelous, isn't it? It is being insisted upon by them, and they haven't even started yet. Every now and then when we commiserate together, someone says: "Yes, but the theater is very resilient. It will live through this. It will rise again." And it does still exist and there is, thank God, Stephen Sondheim, and there are wonderful people working in it. It may be that the audience is not that enormous, but maybe it was never that enormous. There was a time when theater crossed the country in tent shows, and that was the entertainment. That is what, perhaps, television and film serve now. In addition to the fact that, at its best, it serves high art. But the theater, I think, may not be as dead as we think.

DC

Can we make a right turn here into another subject? I wonder whether you consciously go about phrasing what you sing. There always seems to be such an abiding intelligence behind what I hear you "saying" —especially in *Sweeney Todd*.

GH

Well, I never mark anything in my script or in my score.

DC

Do you find yourself doing it the same way each time?

GH

Mostly. I hear of some actors who are so fresh and different every day, and I envy them. If I find a pattern that works, I generally stick to it. Of course, repeating a play for two years—as I did with *Sweeney Todd* and *La Cage*—after a year, I begin to flirt occasionally with an idea that is totally spontaneous, never thought out, a fresh way of phrasing it a little differently. Not because I'm bored, just because it occurs out of whimsy. You can make some bad choices, some second-rate choices, but if your work is good around it, I don't think people will stick you for it.

DC

Do you find there are different imperatives for you when you approach a play, a musical, or an opera?

GH

It generally depends on how we are going to rehearse. We rehearsed for two months for *La Cage*, which was wonderful. I was used to a month's rehearsal, and I keep the book in my hand as long as humanly possible so as not to make choices any earlier than necessary. I think there is a selfishness in people who go in with all their choices already made, a lack of communication with other people, because so much depends on what the other actor gives you, and you want to stay as fluid as possible. But, then, there is also the question of good manners, and you must begin to freeze it yourself. It always depends on the piece. *La Cage*, for example, is very simple dramatically. Once I got the trick of the female mime stuff, I got off the book. I got off the book very quickly without ever sitting down to memorize it. Whereas, with Shakespeare, even a play I know, or *Watch on the Rhine*, for instance, I would stay on it quite a long time.

DC

Do you feel the same way about learning the score?

GH

I usually get the score pretty quickly. You can't play around with music. You either know the notes or you don't.

DC

Is there a big difference between learning a Jerry Herman score and learning *Sweeney Todd?* It would seem to me that they come from two very different countries.

GH

Very. It's a joy to sing Jerry's tunes. They're so available and they please people a lot, but, as with the Argento piece I'm working on now, with *Sweeney Todd*, well, I had to know it cold before I began rehearsals. If I hadn't, it would have been time wasted that I needed for the dramatic performance of it. While you are sitting there hammering it out with the piano player, you're not learning the acting. So you have to know the music.

DC

There is, too, a difference in depth and height between a duet like "Pretty Women" in *Sweeney Todd* and "Song on the Sand" in *La Cage?*

GH

Stephen is up to much more complicated things, and it is much more intriguing, therefore, to me as a performer. The pleasure of *La Cage* has been a different kind of pleasure, because I love the material. I love the fact that we've hit a stroke for the liberalization of people's feelings about homosexuality. I think it is important, and I'm glad to be on what I call the side of the angels at a time when the country is swinging so hard to the right.

DC

Taking something of a cue from that, may I make another turn to the "right"? Is a long run particularly difficult for you, in the sense of keeping the show fresh?

GH

It hasn't been with this [*Note:* La Cage] too much and it wasn't with *Sweeney Todd*, ever. I'm fifty now and I've been in the theater for twenty-two years or so. I've done over 115 plays, and the last two or three have been long runs. I like long runs because I like repetition.

There is a lot to learn in repetition. You sift down through many levels of consciousness. You start wondering, looking at a fellow actor, "Why is he here?" Not the character, of course, but why is that man standing on the stage right now? What are we saying? And feeling the audience and approaching the same moment over and over again. Knowing the ground and being able to make theme and variations on it night after night. It reflects your own life to you. Your health. Your happiness.

DC

Do you consider it good fortune to have a change of co-stars during the course of the run, or is that another difficulty one must do battle with?

GH

I think it was good in *La Cage*, for example. The parts are wonderful and simple compared to *Sweeney Todd*, and the change is nice. Of course, *Sweeney* had an "infiniteness" about it. It drove me crazy. You can get crazy about saving yourself, and then you can endanger yourself from the other side and get crazy about spending yourself. I was in *Sweeney* for a few years, but now I think I have a sense of balance about that energy level.

DC

Singing *Sweeney* is rather like having a tiger by the tail, I would guess.

GH

It was. It was. You know, it's a perilous thing we do for a living, and you go through various ways of dealing with it during different periods of your life. And this period I'm living in right now is the most civilized.* There is love and a sense of family in my life and that has not always been so. I'm Irish, and when I go to excesses, I get a little crazy. But I got through *Sweeney*, although how, I don't know.

---

*Mr. Hearn was getting married a few weeks after this interview took place.

DC

I'm sure you know that Stanislavsky worked exclusively in opera, with singers, during the last years of his life. I'd like to quote something he said: "Stop trying to paint a picture of emotion. The music does that for you. It is the prompter of your feelings and ours, as well. All you have to do is go into action." What is your reaction to that?

GH

I like it. It is easy to layer another attitude over the material, and then you're acting two or three times on top of the other. That's another thing about doing a show over and over again. You can't simplify down to using, as a film person would, an artificial technique like the singing voice. For instance, I wish I could rerecord *La Cage.* When I hear the end of Act One, it seems to me now that I overacted "I Am What I Am." I'm tearing at my voice, leaning on it too hard. I wanted that vocal gratification for that moment, and I realized later that in a sense it is written there. You don't have to comment on what is already there, which is a mistake we make a lot. I imagine that's what Stanislavsky is referring to. Stephen and I used to go round and round about a couple of things, in a sweet way. His notes were very meticulous. It's not . . . [*He sings, in broad Italianate style.*] "Pretty women, fascinating . . ." It's . . . [*He re-sings it in a clipped, unsentimental fashion.*] And I loved singing it the way he had scored those notes because it's very useful. And he checked me in "The Epiphany." [*He speaks out in his best hell-and-damnation voice.*] "Not one man, or ten men or a hundred men can assuage me! I will have you!!!" And I used to growl it out. It never hurt my throat, but people used to say, "Oh! You'll hurt your throat!" And Steve would say, "Sing the notes! Sing the notes!" Then Hal* would come back and say, "I like it when you growl." You see, the director wanted more acting, and the composer wanted his notes.

DC

We seem to have come full circle round from where we began this interview. But the important point you are making is that they must be laminated, one on top of the other.

*Hal Prince, Producer-Director of *Sweeney Todd.*

GH

Yes, indeed. Let's say this for both of them and for Jerry Herman and Arthur Laurents[§] they also realized that *I* needed a certain emotional fulfillment from the piece in order for it to be mine. Because I honor these men, I wanted to please them, but finally in the long run, you have to trust each other's taste. I once had a fight with an English director and we'd gotten down to it, the leading lady and I against him. We weren't, really, but we did want to do something in a certain way and he disagreed. And he said: "All right. We do it your way or we do it mine. What do we do?" And I said: "We do it my way. Because you're the director, but you walk away on opening night and I have to produce it for the entire run of this show, so we do it my way. I'm the one who has to crank it up every night." And I think there is some truth in that. A director and a composer finally have to say, "Well, the performer has a point of view." They must. They hired you, your taste and your judgment. And I think all these men respect my judgment and know that I am not going to distort their piece any more than necessary to get what I need from it.

DC

But you all share a common purpose, certainly?

GH

Yes. And, also, I'm not there to draw attention to myself, the actor. I think we must always serve the play, but I also need whatever gets my energies working through what I believe to be the lines of the character.

DC

Here's another Stanislavsky quote for you. He said: "The composer provides you, the singer, with one most important element . . . the rhythm of your inner emotional life. That's what we actors have to create out of a vacuum." Do you think that music, by placing the singer in a kind of corset within which choices are made, makes it a little easier for the singer than it is for the actor, who has no perimeters of this kind?

[§]Director of *La Cage aux Folles*.

GH

There is something to that, I think, although the word *easier* doesn't come to mind. It is *easier* to act a good line than a bad one. I can't do soap operas because I cannot learn them. I cannot learn the lines. They're all the same to me. Colleen Dewhurst and I did a play, and somebody said to her, "When are you going back to real acting instead of this light-weight writing?" And she said, "This is the hardest work I've ever done." A comic role is as hard as any actor ever works. It's as hard as Cymbeline or Lear or Hamlet, because you don't have those "hands" holding you up.

DC

"Hands" like music?

GH

Yes. People think when you play Hamlet, you're as smart as Hamlet. It just means that you learned the lines. They confuse *your* intelligence with *his*. They say, "I love the way you thought that . . ." Well, I didn't think that. Somebody else did. And so, I think the more that is given to you—and this would be true of opera and ballet—the more you have that is valid and useful and the further ahead you are. But then you must consider "interpreting." Interpreting requires another kind of intelligence. You have to be damn good at learning notes and applying them to your own emotional self. You hear a lot of tenors singing "Che Gelida Manina" and, of course, what makes the difference is the one who sings the best high C.

DC

But he's selling his talents in a different marketplace, don't you think? Bad acting is less discernible, since it is not measurable. Everyone can hear a bad high C.

GH

Yes. And that is a huge subject, and I love it because my life and my career fall right in the middle of it. Well, further away from great singing, but I care about the language of acting. Norman Treigle was a singer-actor who had it all. Dammit, he was good! He was an actor! He was all over the place. He could tumble, do back flips. He had huge hands that could surround a woman! Everything was suggested by his physicality. And his voice was marvelous! So nothing was lost anywhere. I think Dick Kiley's got it, too. He is a wonderful actor-singer.

DC

Yes, I agree. Speaking of other performers, was there anyone you saw, as a youngster, whom you admired and even unconsciously may have patterned yourself after?

GH

I don't think so. Until I saw Treigle, however, I hadn't seen what I thought was even adequate acting. In the theater it's pretty much the same. Of course, this year we saw Derek Jacoby's Cyrano, and that was wonderful. Talk about singing! The use of the voice, the very forward, spit-out, white sounds that Leonard Warren could never have made.

DC

Is there anything you would say to young actor-dancer-singers that would give their studies a sense of direction?

GH

Well, if there is going to be a theater that is not electronic out there where living actors do living plays, there has to be good speech and good diction. It's not all technical, but you have to have the technical skills. There has to be a passion to communicate with an entire theater, to "hit the back row." I don't mean that in a hammy sense. There are film people who say there are certain actors who "make love" to the camera. I'm not one of those. But there *are* performers who make love to an audience, and the only way you can do that is with speech and diction. You've got to be clear, and you've got to project to the back, and it has to sound natural, and it can't be, as I said earlier, the audience saying to the actor, "I'm sorry you're crying but I wish *I* were." It's got to be about giving them the chance to react.

DC

How do you feel about electronically amplified sound in the theater?

GH

I don't like it. When I did *A Doll's Life*, Hal Prince said: "You can all sing enough to fill that theater. Let's flirt with the idea of . . ." But they didn't. I think audiences expect that amplification. They're used to watching the big screen. They want that immediacy, that vibration.

DC

But not in the opera house?

GH

Not necessarily. When I went to see *Sweeney Todd* at the New York City Opera, Beverly Sills told me that the first night, just before they went on, Hal [Prince] and Steve [Sondheim] came to her and said, "You're going to hate this, but you cannot do this unless you put in a 'system'." And she said, "The system we have in the City Opera is I go back and say, 'And the part of so-and-so, usually played by so-and-so . . .' and the red arrow goes like that and . . . Well, that's all we have." So, they put in a $10,000 system with those microphones, and people still didn't hear too well. *Her* theory was if the singers and the actors have bad diction, you're just going to get louder bad diction. Stephen's concern was not so much to be understood in the big arias but to get the ambiance, the intimacy that the audience gets used to wherever they're sitting. And it is very hard to keep that ambiance of intimacy without electronics if you are making heavy acting demands on the performers and the sets are moving back and forth.

DC

How did they do it before electronic amplification was invented?

GH

I have a couple of ideas about that. For one, they had smaller theaters most of the time.

DC

But the Palace Theater is very large. Even the back wall is phony. There are seats behind it that have been closed off. And yet, think of all those vaudevillians who played and "filled" that theater.

GH

I think people wrote much simpler stuff then and, by and large, it was all "down in one." And, in opera, the acting is minimal because you have to come down front. Harry Theyard used to say there's a spot on that stage where everybody will hear you. It's down left a little bit and it's a spot that's magical, where your voice can be acoustically heard. And, also, they used to use better materials: real plaster and real wood. You can't hear anything in the new theaters they build because it's all beaverboard or wallboard and it's not going to make a sound. And the theaters are too large. The Met's too large and so is the City Opera. The operas we hear weren't done in big houses originally. La Scala is not that big. And the Mozart operas were done in court. They've got to be smaller. The only people who can survive are the big voices: the Sutherlands, the Prices, and the Pavarottis. They can get by at the Met, and although you love the voice, you'd love it even more in a slightly smaller house.

DC

But then don't we get into the economics of the business? Opera and the musical theater must make x number of dollars in a theater that seats y number of people to make z amount of profit needed to put it on and keep it running.

GH

Yes, but if you care about the music and the form and care about marrying it with acting, then there have to be some compromises made in the size of the house. They're just too damn big! I don't have specific, useful things to say about this, but I do have a passion for the subject. That's why, when *Sweeney Todd* came out and the reviews said Broadway singers can't sing the way opera singers can, it made me angry. Marilyn Horne, my dear friend, said, "I couldn't do it, and I don't know anyone at the Met who can sing your part eight times a week." Because that's a different use of the instrument. But the critics dumped all over the tackiness of Broadway singers! Well, the opera singers knew what we were doing. They knew the use of the voice. The other day I was talking to Harry Theyard, who has sung at the Met, about the Argento opera I'm preparing, and I was complaining to him that I had thirty or forty Fs, a couple of Gs, a bunch of F sharps. It really lies "up there." And he said, "When you go 'Whoop!' you're hitting E flats and Es when you're talking. Don't worry about the opera!" I thought that was very interesting. As a singer, he knew what *Sweeney* was costing me. Another thing they never do in an opera is talk. They don't use speech patterns. They won't. Because speech is very costly in a different way than singing is. Just learning *Kismet* a little bit has done more good for my voice. It's been amazing because that's where my voice naturally lies.

DC

But it does have that G sharp at the end of "Rhymes Have I."

GH

Yes, but I can do it when I'm singing right because my voice belongs in that groove.

DC

How badly threatened are you by the winter weather in New York? Do you worry about your health and how it will affect your ability to sing each night?

GH

I worry a lot! The only bad time I had with *Sweeney* was in San Francisco when the climate got to me. Every town has its version of it, but there they call it the "San Francisco throat." It was not good for my sinuses, and I went to a throat doctor and said, "Save me." He said, "The cords are great, but you can't get to them." I said: "You got it. I just can't hit the cords. I've got so much of that . . . you know." And it's very painful. Up to a point you can sing through it, but then you have to say, "I can't do that," or you'll hurt yourself. You can damage your cords permanently. This year, knock on wood, I haven't been sick all winter, but last year, with *La Cage*, I had to leave the show a couple of times. And, of course, you get through a lot of them when you're not singing right on top of your mark, where you have to croon. There are many times when have to finesse every angle.

DC

But I imagine you must be able to do that with a good deal of grace?

GH

I try, but you know you've worked when you've done it. I used to say to the young kids who like football, "It's not how you play football but how you play 'hurt' that counts." Come to think of it, it's the same in the theater. You've got to be able to play hurt because, well, you're going to be doing it eight times a week!

Lee Remick

Lee Remick's career flows with a continuity that is the joy and envy of her friends, and yet she is often, too often, taken for granted. In actual fact, she has been giving performances on the screen, on television, and on the stage that, for consistent excellence, cannot be duplicated by any other actress of her generation. The awesome variety of the roles she has played is stunning. She can be patrician and just as effectively limn a middle-class housewife, a WAC, and an obsessed alcoholic. She has played Winston Churchill's mother, Jenny Jerome, in nineteenth-century brocade and Eleanor Roosevelt in sensible shoes; then, costumed by Sears and with equal comfort and fidelity, she has played the prisoner of a crazed rapist.

I first knew her as a student, so it is saddening to me that the subject that brought us together—singing—is one in which she feels, with no justification whatever, under par. The contrary evidence indicates that her work in musicals, both on the Broadway stage and on television, is as laudable as her career in those other parts of the show business forest. It is not difficult to slot her. She is quite simply a great beauty who can do anything and everything: the quintessential professional.

DC

When we were young, we thought of our parents as the older generation, the one ahead of ours. Today, we're told that a decade is all that separates one generation from the next. There must, then, be multitudes of people who love you and have no idea that you began your career in musicals. And as a dancer.

LR

It is true. Originally, as a young girl of eight—and until I was sixteen years old—all I ever wanted to be was Nora Kaye and Maria Tallchief and Margot Fonteyn. Every day of my life I went to a ballet class.

DC

Had you seen any ballets?

LR

Well, I did ultimately see them, but at the age of eight I was sent to ballet school. We lived in New York, and my mother thought it would be good for me. All little girls go to ballet school. She thought I would learn awareness and knowledge of one's body and music and how to move. And that's what started it. But then, you know, I got that bit between my teeth and I fell in *love*. I *fell* in love with ballet and with my teacher, which is, of course, what it's all about. Mr. Anatol Vitzak. This was at the Swoboda Ballet School in Manhattan. I fell in love with it all to the extent that I didn't want to go away to summer camp—I was always sent off to summer camp—because that would have been two months away from ballet school. I went every day after school all through my school years and twice on Saturdays. I lived and breathed it, and I never gave a thought to anything else.

DC

How long did this obsession last?

LR

I guess until I was about fifteen or sixteen and then, well, life started to happen. Boys showed up, and I started to skip Friday night class because my hair was all fuzzy and my cheeks were too red if I'd been to class for an hour and a half and I was about to go out on a date. So that began to wane a little. But, more to the point, it began to wane when I started to work as an actress. I was sixteen and I answered an ad in *Show Business* magazine.

DC

Did your mother know about it?

LR

No. I saw the ad and went to an open call for dancers at the Hyannis Music Circus. Oh, there was method in my madness. I chose Cape Cod, cunningly enough, because my father lived in Boston, and I knew that if I was allowed to go anywhere and work by myself, it would be the Cape because he would be near. So I went to this audition in my little leotard, leaped around, did a lot of kinds of dancing I didn't know a thing about because I was a very classically trained dancer and I did a little modern, which I didn't know anything about either. I was afraid to bend my knees.

DC

May I interrupt? Had you seen any musicals as a child?

LR

Oh, yes.

DC

Then you knew what you were up to?

LR

Yes. And I had been around my mother, who worked in television and in the theater. She worked in the summers in stock, so it was not an alien world to me. People had been over to our house. People who were involved in the theater, so I knew about it, and I knew my mother would not be averse to the idea. My father might be a little bit more of a problem. He was considerably more conservative, at the beginning, about all this. Well, I went to the audition, lied about my age, said I was eighteen, found out later they didn't believe me, and then the audition got honed down to us three girls and three boys who were going to be the rest of the dancers in the company.

DC

I remember those choruses.

LR

Yes, you've seen them. So, I got the job and was told I had to join Chorus Equity, which I did. I went home and told my mother and she was absolutely dumbfounded that I had had the nerve to go off and do this, and then tell them. And my father did agree, said it was fine, for they had obviously talked it over at some length. "Where will she live? And how? Sixteen!" That was a lot younger then than it is now. I remember that I was not allowed to live with the other singers and dancers because my family did not consider them "OK" people to be around. They were all of them older, and it was not a good idea. I was made to live, happily enough, with a family who rented their rooms to the apprentices, who were all nice, clean-cut college kids. My family thought that was OK. And that's where I lived that summer.

DC

Can you remember the first show you did?

LR

No, but I do remember my father dropping me off the first day of rehearsal, so nervous and so excited. I couldn't believe that they were going to pay me, because it was so much fun! It was so thrilling, and they paid $60 a week! I couldn't believe they were giving me this money for doing something so terrific! I still find it somewhat difficult, half the time, to be paid for something I love to do. I mean, I insist upon being paid very well. I like to be paid very well, but it is still . . . To do something so wonderful . . . I couldn't believe it. The whole thing, the rehearsal, ten to six and then you run and grab a hamburger, get to the theater, put on your makeup, much too much, of course. At that stage, everything went on this face! Everything! And it was all just perfect, and I was in love from start to finish.

DC

You probably began the summer at 16 and ended it at 116.

LR

Well, I was still very wide-eyed about the whole thing. I was so in love! That was the big part of it. It was so romantic, so very romantic, working in the theater.

DC

It's part of your heritage, in a way. You just mentioned that your mother had been an actress.

LR

She was always involved in it and loved it and was encouraging about it.

DC

Was she successful?

LR

She was very good, but she chose not to do it. She lived, primarily, in New York, and she wanted to be a mother to my brother and me, and so didn't pursue it as a full-out career. When she remarried, she stopped. From that summer, I went back to school for another year. It was Miss Hewett's, which is quite another world. A very small private girl's school.

DC

You must have been queen of the May after such a worldly experience.

LR

I was, sort of, but I was involved with school and very keen to do all that well. I was always keen to do things "right," then. To please was very important to me. But, in that year, in that winter of that last school year, I was with my mother in Sardi's, and we stopped to say hello to some friends of hers, Reggie Denham and Mary Orr. He said to me, "Can you act?" Just said: "How do you do? Can you act?" And I said, "Yes." Of course, I had no idea of it at all. None. But it seemed a good idea.

DC

And at that moment, the dancer surrendered to the actress?

LR

Pretty much. But then they sent me this play called *Be Your Age* and I read it and read *for* it. It was the only job I ever got from a reading in my life. But I did do the play.

DC

Was this for Broadway?

LR

Yes. And, in a way, it was the beginning of a charmed-life syndrome. I mean, I was still in school, but, because Conrad Nagle had a radio show or something to do in the morning, rehearsals didn't start until one o'clock, which was the luck of it. If it had been a regular rehearsal schedule, I probably would not have done the play because my mother and father and the school would not have allowed me to do it. So I went to school all morning and then raced down to wherever it was to rehearse from one until eight.

DC

Did you go out of town?

LR

Yes. We went to Philadelphia. I can't recall any of it in detail because, in the first place, the play was not wonderful. It was like *Time Out for Ginger*, which opened the same week and was much better. Better done, too. We closed in three or four days. The school nearly threw me out. They had a meeting of the trustees or whatever, because it had never happened before. A student at Miss Hewett's classes called away to be on Broadway! My mother made pleading speeches at the board of director's meeting, and finally they allowed me to remain. I think they were all happy because I had done Broadway. Anyway, I slipped back into school, graduation, white dress, all of that, and went back into stock in the summer. I went and did . . . I think that was the summer I did *Brigadoon* on the circuit.

DC

Just dancing?

LR

I was dancing and playing a teensy-weensy part, Jeannie. So it was dancing and a bit of opening my mouth and speaking as well. I also did *Paint Your Wagon*. I studied with Paul Godkin and Charles Weidman, and I was a good dancer. But I knew I was never going to be an absolutely wonderful dancer. There's no question about that.

The passion was not there by that time. I don't think I ever would have been a fabulous dancer.

DC
You didn't have to sing in both shows?

LR
No. But very soon after that, I did "I Caint Say No" when I played Ado Annie in *Oklahoma!* and I sang "Life Upon the Wicked Stage" in *Showboat.* Just those two.

DC
Then you were considered a soubrette and not an ingenue?

LR
Well, yes. I guess so.

DC
Starting with *Oklahoma,* dancers had begun to take over soubrette roles.

LR
I never, never *sang,* because I didn't know what I was doing. I just opened my mouth, no vocalizing or warming up, nothing. I didn't know how to. It must have been just after that that I started taking singing lessons.

DC
Before we leave your summer stock days, how many summers did you play in musical revivals?

LR
Really only three. And then I went out in a play. It was called *Jenny Kissed Me.* And *The Seven-Year Itch.* I did both of those in one summer. The same summer I went off and did the film of *A Face in the Crowd.* And that began a whole other life.

DC

I still think it strange that no one has ever thought of you as a dancer and a singer when you have done so much of that on the stage.

LR

Well, you know, people in movies get so "slotted" so quickly. You show up doing a little sexy drum majorette in *Face in the Crowd*, albeit a fancy movie with a wonderfully strong director, and then I made *Anatomy of a Murder, The Days of Wine and Roses*, and . . . nobody ever thought of asking me to dance with Fred Astaire. I was very lucky not being pigeonholed as much as some people.

DC

And then came *Anyone Can Whistle**. I know there were people in New York who knew you could dance as well as act, but who knew you could sing?

LR

I'm not sure if it was Arthur's or Steve's idea.

DC

Had they heard you in a living room?

LR

Never, never. And I don't know why, but I do think that what they were looking for, in that piece, were actors, which is clear from the casting. Angela Lansbury, at that time, hadn't done a musical either. They wanted actors. And it was, to be sure, the experience that put Steve on to the idea of not having actors singing ever again, because although Angela could sing it very well, I couldn't do it full justice at that time. And Harry Guardino couldn't sing it, as well. We couldn't handle it or sustain it. Angela always could.

DC

Although *A Funny Thing Happened on the Way to the Forum* had been done two years before, I think of that show as a musical comedy.

*By Arthur Laurents and Stephen Sondheim.

Anyone Can Whistle was a watershed musical in the sense that it was the first time we heard Steve's more, well, "serious" sound. Did you have to audition?

LR

I certainly did. I had just come back, after having made a film in Spain, to Los Angeles and there was a call from my agent and the script, which, of course, was magic. It read like a dream—gangbuster, fabulous, witty, funny, outrageous. And they said, "Can you sing?" And I said, "Well, I'll let you know." They put me on to a teacher, and I went to him for lessons. He got me to the point where I could audition for Arthur, and Arthur said, "Why, my God! You can sing!" I sang, "Bewitched, Bothered, and Bewildered," and I suspect I sang it very badly. You see, I always felt I could learn anything and, to an extent, it's true. But it isn't entirely true.

DC

But true enough so that you were not put off trying?

LR

Right. And, somehow, convinced that I could if I worked hard enough at it, I put my mind to it. It's, "Yes, I can." It wouldn't have occurred to me to say . . . Well, it's like when Reggie Denham says, "Can you act?" The first thing I say is yes.

DC

You wouldn't do too well in the army.

LR

No. "Do not volunteer." I haven't volunteered for anything, But I studied diligently. I always go over the top with anything.

DC

Did you sing for Arthur on a stage?

LR

No. In the singing teacher's living room. And that might very well be the reason I was invited to attend. I don't think I ever got a job from an audition. In a room, yes. On a stage, I don't think I ever did. I did very few of those because I didn't work in the theater until after I had made a lot of movies.

DC

And so you sang in that living room?

LR

And Arthur said, "Terrific!" and I went back and I studied and studied some more until rehearsals started. It was an extraordinary experience. The whole thing was terrifying and exciting because the material was so wonderful and so were the people. Meeting Steve, knowing him, loving him. But I was bewildered. You see, I had no editorial eye about it. I know that sounds very Pollyanna, but that's the way it was.

DC

Anyone Can Whistle was the first musical you had done from the ground up.

LR

That's right. And it was a killing schedule for everybody to maintain. And wearing all those hats that were new hats. Singing. I developed this incredible tonsilitis. I don't know too much about psychosomatic illness, but I think something like that was responsible. I did have tonsils the size of small grapefruits apparently, and, once we closed, I had to have them removed. It was all terrible. I do think that singing is one thing you can't do if your body is not up to par.

DC

Do you think that that experience is, at the root of it, responsible for your fear of singing?

LR

Yes, I think so. I never felt on top of it.

DC

Up until then, it was always gung ho for anything anyone suggested. Now you seem to have pulled back a little.

LR

I have. I have.

DC

Anyone Can Whistle was a commercial failure, but it has become a cult favorite. Do you think the gorgeousness of the score keeps it alive, or was there something the script was trying to say that touched people in a way that may have lacked finesse but was, nevertheless, telling?

LR

It was wonderfully raw. But it does seem to me that the so-called sophistication of the piece was, in fact, naïveté. The favorite thing people say about the show now is that it was ahead of its time. I don't think so. When you read the book today, it seems very naive and almost childlike in its "it's the crazies who run the world" philosophy.

DC

Whereas the songs have retained their currency. One hears them all the time. Especially the title tune.

LR

Yes, and although Steve's work had begun before, it was the beginning of that wonderful romance in all he writes. So juicy, full of love and wit. They don't have to be hung on the script.

DC

Audiences had heard his lyrics in *West Side Story* and in *Gypsy* and his music and words in *A Funny Thing Happened on the Way to the Forum*, but *Anyone Can Whistle* established his unique signature. People were asked to listen to music that wasn't easily assimilated. And yet, I am always surprised when I hear someone complain that he cannot write a melody. *Anyone Can Whistle* is brimming with them.

LR

Oh, yes! One day, in rehearsal, we were working on a song, and this singer—she was in the chorus and she had a wonderful, big voice, an operatic voice—she said to me: "I've just got to tell you something.

I've been listening to you in rehearsal"—and, I thought, "Oh, yes?" cringing in horror at what she might say—and she said, "I went home last night and sang that song myself, and I just have to tell you that it is one of the most difficult songs to sing." I said, "It is?" Never having sung anything else, really, except Ado Annie, I was so relieved. I had no idea of how a song "lies."

DC

Did you keep studying throughout the show?

LR

Oh, yes. Every day. All through rehearsals.

DC

And did singing every night present particular problems?

LR

As I say, I don't know how much of it was psychosomatic, but I did have a bad throat infection which just got worse because I was so uptight and strained.

DC

Had the show been a success, that would have been something you would have had to deal with.

LR

Yes. But it wasn't. And the tonsils came out after we closed. Right after that, I came to work with you. That was in the fall of 1964. The following year, you remember, I did *Annie Get Your Gun* because, by then, I had come to think that I loved doing it—all the singing. I was worried, though, that I might not be able to do it. I mean, I hadn't been able to sustain *Anyone Can Whistle.*

DC

I remember we chose *Annie Get Your Gun* because both of us thought it would be a good stretch for you.

LR

Yes. And it was very demanding. After all, Merman sang it. But I managed very well and never lost my voice all through the eight-week summer. And I wasn't so uptight. Now, this is not to say that I certainly elevated the score!

DC

Had *Anyone Can Whistle* been responsible for creating this fear of singing or had you always been plagued with that terror?

LR

Well, I would so love to know why, really. I think it is because singing is so bald. You see, acting is something people can be very opinionated about—what they think is good or what they think is bad about an actor.

DC

You mean the actor's work?

LR

Judging the work. And I do stand back and judge—myself. We all do it. You can sit in the theater or in front of the television screen or the movie screen and say, "Why didn't that scene work?" or "I didn't think that was good." But with singing, it either sounds good or it doesn't sound good.

DC

You can say that about dancing, can't you? It either looks graceful or it doesn't look graceful.

LR

Yes, but singing somehow, to me, has less fuzzy lines about it. And when it doesn't sound good, it really sounds terrible.

DC

The miss is the mile.

LR

Oh, yes. It is just that little millimeter off key that is so agonizing. It's strange, but as actors we will strip ourselves emotionally and reveal all kinds of depth and raw emotion, but there is something more naked about standing up and just opening your mouth and having music come out.

DC

But have you ever stood in the center of a song and, while you were singing, thought, "This is a turn-on I have never experienced as an actress, or even as a dancer"?

LR

I have. Now, that is interesting because I have felt it when I was really acting the song, when it wasn't just . . . music. A couple of times in *I Do, I Do** when I was doing a song that was a character song that was funny, when I wasn't just sitting down, sitting still and singing. That is what scares me, the feeling that it is me serving the music.

DC

As opposed to a song that serves the character?

LR

Yes. That is when I'm comfortable. I like that. I feel good, then.

DC

But I mean much more than that. More than feeling good. A sense of being the instrument through which the music is created. You've never felt that?

LR

No. I don't have that confidence in my own ability to make music.

DC

But you do it very well indeed. And you've received awards for doing it.

---

*Miss Remick won an Emmy for her performance in the cable television production of *I Do, I Do*.

LR

I feel like I get away with it. I don't know why it is that I cannot or have not enjoyed it as much as . . . acting.

DC

Do you think it may be because you approach music as something set apart and sacred?

LR

Yes. It is separate and apart.

DC

But I have heard you talk about sitting in the theater at, say, one of Steve's musicals, and the passion that it arouses in you is quite set apart from film and television.

LR

It's true.

DC

Is it *that*, do you think, that makes actors more aware of their inadequacy? This raised "musical consciousness"?

LR

It is special. It's another language. But I can't speak for other people who have this problem.

DC

Because, of course, they do.

LR

God knows they do! I know they do. Not only people in our business. I have a very good friend who, I think, would fold up and crumble into a heap if she were asked to stand up in any room in front of anybody and sing. It just tears her apart. She can't do it. Luckily, nobody asks her to, which is the difference. She doesn't have to put herself on the line and say, "Yes, I'll do it." Here I am dashing off

to New York to do Steve's thing with a bunch of musicians*. You
see, *they're* musicians. They understand the language.

DC

And somebody may find you out?

LR

Somebody will find me out and I'll look silly because I won't understand what the symbols are on the piece of written music, what they
are all about.

DC

Was this a problem even when you were in school, being found out?

LR

Occasionally, yes. And I don't like not being on top, being "up" on
what there is to know at the moment. I don't like being a person who
whines, "I don't understand that." I want to be . . . [*She snaps her
fingers.*] "up"! And a step ahead all the time.

DC

Whenever you are asked to sing, you run to a singing teacher.

LR

Yes. And I get myself all wound up, and then it's all I want to do!

DC

And then, after you've done it, it goes to sleep again?

LR

Yes, it does.

DC

Dancing, too?

---

*A concert recording of the complete score of *Follies*.

LR

Yes. I haven't danced much at all. I did a little bit in *I Do, I Do*. That's even harder to get back into. We all know about that. So I don't go to class anymore because I'm not about to dance in something.

DC

It's a better way to stay in shape than, say, aerobics.

LR

Anything is better than an aerobics class! But you see, I'm lazy. It's either this incredible over-the-top burst of energy or none. And you have been saying this to me for years. "It would be so much better if you just kept it up. Take a singing lesson twice a week, all the time, whether you're working or not." Of course, it makes more sense. Now I shall go back and crash it. Crash-course myself. But, you see, I love that.

DC

Part of the event?

LR

Yes. And I love that kind of immersion in whatever the event is. And it's so good to have that twenty-four-hour-a-day saturation in whatever it is you're up to. I suppose it's that type A personality that they talk about that causes heart attacks, God forbid! And my twenty-odd years of migraine headaches. "Gotta, gotta, must . . ." It's a compulsion. I think that that's what makes performers do what they have to do and what makes us as crazy as we are. There's nothing safe about it, you know. And, for all this nervousness over the years about singing, I hardly ever say no if somebody asks me.

DC

In your case, musicals seem to be the opposite of "you can't fire me, I quit." More like "you could hire me if you asked."

LR

It's true. It's true. There must be something about being terrified that is attractive to me. Because if you're terrified of something, you stay away from it. Right? And if you don't like cold water, you don't jump in. But there *is* something. Whether it is the challenge of it all. Because it's not my milieu, it really isn't what I'm known for. And still . . . I got that letter about the concert recording, and it didn't occur to me to go back and listen to the score again first before I thought, "Can I sing that or not?" I didn't do that. Just picked up the phone and screamed, "*Yes!* Oh, yes. I'll be there!" There's something about that frightening part that gets me there. Not to class every day of my life or to singing lessons every week, but to be a part of that event that one day.

DC

Wherever I go to teach, Lee, I am always asked by women over forty the usual questions: "Why aren't there more roles written for us?" "Should I lie about my age?" You know the sort of problems women of "a certain age" are forced to cope with in the business. How do you feel about them and how did you deal with them?

LR

It's most complicated. In the first place, it seems to me that it's a funny little cusp-y time there when you get used to being over forty. You get used to being regarded as someone who is no longer that person you have always lived with, that young person. It's very difficult. When people start asking me to play a role and I pick up the script and then I realize that it's this *woman* and not the part of the girl, anymore, and then you think, "Well, it does take a long time to get to be this woman." But it happens in a minute.

DC

A minute measured in show business time or on the calendar?

LR

Oh, a minute measured in show business time. It happens in . . . one day. In one day, you suddenly get a piece of material where you realize that someone is thinking of you as this mother of a twenty-year-old. Now, I'm the mother of a twenty-six-year-old, but it never occurred to me, professionally, that anybody would send me a script saying, "You play this one, not that one over there, not that young woman. You're playing the more mature . . ." Oh, that wicked word! ". . . woman."

DC

Is that a difficult moment to deal with?

LR

It was for me. It was like, "Wait a minute!" It was hard. But I suppose all men and women go through it.

DC

Why do you suppose there is this shortage of roles for women over forty? There isn't a shortage of women over forty.

LR

But what movies are there for us to go and see? All teenage or college movies.

DC

And yet, think of all the "womanly" roles in the musical theater: Auntie Mame, the mother in *Gypsy*, Mrs. Lovett in *Sweeney Todd*. And certainly women, and not girls, have played most of Rodgers and Hammerstein's work.

LR

But that's not true in the world of movies and television.

DC

Well, then, how would you feel about playing *Follies* if it were revived? Another over-forty role.

LR

What about it? I'd be there!

DC

And *A Little Night Music* . . . Desiree?

LR

Oh, I'd love to play her!

DC

And in other media?

LR

Well, the movie business is different. There are exceptions because there are movies that involve grown-ups, but an awful lot of them don't. The last couple of films I did were *Tribute* and *Competition*. They were not seen very much. They were terrible as far as their box office was concerned. But the saturation of television is amazing! People come up to me and talk to me in great earnestness and seriousness about *The Women's Room*, which they loved. They even thank me. It's really nice. Sometimes it can be irritating when people stop you, but one of the things I like about doing what I do is the recognition part of it. Someone passing you on the street just looks at you and smiles and it's like a hug. Especially when you work in front of machines as I do.

DC

How good it would be if they could tell you they heard you sing somewhere.

LR

Every once in a while someone will come up and say, "Oh, I saw you in . . ." And I think they're going to say some movie, but instead they say, "I saw you in *I Do, I Do*," and I go, "*You did!?* Who are you? How did you get there?" And that is wonderful! All this talk has me worked up. I really do want to do it some more. One thing is certain: I must have this push-you pull-you about singing, because, although it terrifies me, I don't ever say no to it.

Gene Kelly

For far too long, Americans idealized an archetypal concept of the dancing-singing-acting man. He was possessed of one body and two faces, and this Janus-like creation was called Astaire-Kelly. Only in the recent past has this image been allowed to split into its rightful component parts: Fred Astaire and Gene Kelly, two distinct and separate men who share the same allegiances but have little else in common. Mr. Astaire remains a black and white perfection in top hat, white tie, and tails, while Mr. Kelly endures, in technicolor, as a sailor, a rain-soaked singer in the rain and a blue-jeaned American in Paris.

For my generation, Gene Kelly was the first dancer to cross over from the musical to the legit theater and back again without suffering the suspicious tolerance in which the average person on the street tends to view the dancer. This is his abiding legacy, and it has permitted dancers who came after him to walk in his footsteps out of the ghostly ghetto in which dancing men, for so many years, have had to reside.

His great stage performance in *Pal Joey* left so indelible a stamp as to resist the notion of anyone else in the role. The part was thought to be unsavory, but he gave *unsavory* a new and charming meaning. *Charming* is not a word men tend to tolerate happily in other men, since, on the sexual battlefield, its possession places the lucky soul who manifests it one up on those who do not. And yet it is the quality we most admire in Cary Grant. Add to that a virile dancing style and a piquant singing voice and you have . . . Gene Kelly.

DC

Your career has been a diverse one from its very beginning. Did you plan it that way?

GK

I came to New York in my middle twenties. I'd always planned to be a choreographer and, later, a director, but only on the stage. I never considered pictures. In Pittsburgh, where I grew up, I staged things for the Pittsburgh Playhouse, for colleges, and for various local organizations like the Junior League. They were the best jobs you could get in Pittsburgh if you were a director-choreographer. I often found myself participating as an actor because I couldn't find someone else to do it, but it was never my intention to be on the stage. When I went to New York, they laughed at the idea of giving me a job as a choreographer, and so I got work as a dancer in Cole Porter's *Leave It to Me*. I heard the singers in the show, and I had already come to realize, even in Pittsburgh, where I had staged shows and nightclub and vaudeville acts, that there are real singers who are trained, like opera singers, and there are popular singers who are real singers, and then there was the dancer-singer who can carry a tune but must make up for the deficiency of his voice. So when I was in *Leave It to Me*, I got a Russian basso in the show who took students and I went out to Astoria to his place and I took some singing lessons. He was a good singer who knew what he was doing, but I realized that if I followed what he told me, I was going to try to become a real singer in those late years and this was not in my milieu at all. So I quit. For those young people who will be reading this, let me explain the difference between real singers and dancing singers. The dancing singer is moving all the time, and he has to get his "tones" from his chest. There is no way for him to stop and breathe down into his diaphragm and let a rich, full tone come out—that is, unless he stands stock still, which is not what he is being paid to do. Not that I believed I would ever be able to develop that kind of voice starting at the age of twenty-six, but I was willing to improve what I had because I was determined to stay in New York and get better parts. Since I never gave a thought to anything but musicals, I stuck to singing and dancing and did the best I could. In those days there were no microphones. When you sang, the people in the first row had to get it but so did those in the top balcony. You had to do a lot of practicing.

DC

Practicing how?

GK

Well, in empty theaters after rehearsals, trying to reach the back wall and not make ugly faces the people who were in the expensive seats would see.

DC

Was there a particular performer you'd seen when you were growing up who represented some kind of goal or role model for you?

GK

No. As I said, I wanted to be a choreographer, and I wanted to know all there was to know about that. I studied most of my dancing in Chicago and some of it in New York. Men rarely studied classic dance in those days, especially since male "classic" dancers were very much looked down on. But because it wasn't the fashion then, you didn't have to walk to school and get into a fight just because you went to dancing school afterwards. And I did study hard, and I became a good classic dancer. But in the thirties there were no American ballet companies. The Ballet Russe of Monte Carlo came, I believe, in 1933, and I auditioned for them and was accepted for the chorus at $35 a week, but I was making a couple of hundred in my dancing schools and, knowing I would never be given a major part in the company no matter how many years I stayed with them, I turned it down. The next American group that came along—if you discount San Francisco, Atlanta, and Catherine Littlefield's Philadelphia Ballet—was the Kirstein-Balanchine group, but they never got past about twelve dancers, and by that time it was the end of World War II and Balanchine was spending half his time choreographing musical comedies. The state of American ballet was at its nadir, so the place to turn to was musical comedy. Also, right from the start, I had what a lot of people thought was a dumb style of dancing because it was different and very athletic and not well suited to ballet. But I had two mentors, Robert Alton* and John Murray Anderson§, and they encouraged me. The big thing in the late twenties and all through the thirties were the dance teams.

DC

Veloz and Yolanda and the DeMarcos?

GK

And, of course, out here, Astaire and Rogers, and they could sing and act and they made it all an art form on the screen.

DC

But wasn't it unusual for someone as homegrown as you were and are to have had this impulse to dance so early in your life?

---

*Mr. Alton staged many of the successful musicals of the thirties and early forties.
§The eminent director of a string of revues that ranged from *The Ziegfeld Follies* to the equally successful *New Faces*.

GK

I don't know why, but I loved athletics. I loved movement and I loved speed. I loved to play hockey better than anything, even though it's a contact sport, and I loved, too, to run. I used to run for miles, and . . . well, I think it all drew me to dance. My brother Fred got me into tap dancing because we could make some money in American Legion halls and in speakeasies, and, frankly, my father was out of work. My mother was managing a small dancing school she had started in partnership with a man, but when he flew the coop, my brother and I stood in and assisted. I learned a lot more from teachers she hired from New York. I never sat down in a theater at the age of seven and watched Pavlova or so-and-so and forever after knew I wanted to dance—in the way I've read about in so many books.

DC

You mentioned that you were in the chorus in your first two shows, *Leave It to Me* and *One for the Money*. Was it difficult to get into a chorus in those days? As difficult as it is today?

GK

Well, they were funny chorus jobs. In *Leave It to Me*, Bob Alton had put together five boys and five girls who were supposed to be the sons and daughters of Victor Moore and Sophie Tucker. Naturally, it was inevitable that the American boys and the Russian girls* would get together, and behind us there was a chorus of pony girls§ and behind *them* were eight or more show girls who were tall and lanky Texas beauties. And behind *them* was a huge singing chorus. It was a jam-packed, old-fashioned, terrific New York Broadway show with a good book by Sam and Bella Spewack.

DC

The dancers in today's choruses are more skillful, wouldn't you agree?

---

*An allusion to the plot of the show.
§A descriptive for chorus girls who were chosen because they were short, as short as the show girls were tall.

GK

Yes. They're more eclectic. They have to be able to do all kinds of dancing. In *One for the Money* there were sixteen of us in the chorus, and we all had to be able to dance, sing, and act. So, in that sense, there was no chorus. It was in that show that I first had the chance to do a half-chorus of a song, "Teeter Tatter Tessie," and do a sketch. Later, they wanted me to go into the sequel of that show, *Two to Get Ready*.

DC

How did you get from the desire to choreograph into singing and dancing on the stage and, then, into a legitimate play, Saroyan's *The Time of Your Life*?

GK

They wouldn't give me a job as a choreographer.

DC

But did you simply turn up and do a reading for the play?

GK

Yes. Marty Ritt* had been set for it and actually rehearsed in it, but at the last minute at the tryout in New Haven, they felt the part needed a dancer. I auditioned, and they signed me, and Saroyan wrote some additional stuff for me.

DC

Was it interesting to find yourself in a straight and serious play?

GK

It was very interesting. Bill [*Saroyan*] stuck some music in there, and he said, "Now, you're not able to dance, but go out there and stop the show." Unbeknownst to him, he taught me a very valuable lesson. I never knew how to characterize dance before that. If I was doing a ballet number, I'd do a ballet number. If I'd do a tap number,

---

*The eminent stage and film director, who in his early years was an actor.

I'd do a tap number. Maybe it was in my own style, but still, it was balletic or it was tap or jazz. But in this play I'd go out every night and I'd fumble around for steps, and the audience loved it.

DC

You were playing the part of "The Hoofer" rather than a man who hoofed.

GK

It was much harder work than doing the "speed" stuff.

DC

Had you ever acted before that, or studied acting?

GK

I acted in Pittsburgh a few times, but I never studied. Not a "note." I did some summer stock. I worked at Westport for the Theater Guild, who produced the show. In fact, they were the ones who wouldn't audition me originally because I had a done a role for them in which I wore a tuxedo.

DC

And they couldn't see you as a down-and-out hoofer?

GK

That's right. They probably thought, "We'll put him in the Plaza."

DC

But you were still working toward that one goal, to become a choreographer, and these jobs were just marking time?

GK

Yes. I was working it out on myself, you see. I did finally get to do Billy Rose's Diamond Horseshoe*, and I choreographed *Best Foot Forward*, so I did get my licks in before I left New York.

---

*A successful supper club in New York during the forties.

DC

Are the problems of directing a musical more, rather than less, demanding than those of directing a play?

GK

They're compounded in a musical. In the first place, you have to tie in the songs and then tie in the dances. And musicals on the stage are easier than those on film. On the stage, turning around, a pause, a sting chord* in the orchestra, a light change which, in films, would seem like a power failure up in the booth—all of these work on the stage. What I find objectionable in musicals is when someone steps out of character to sing or to dance. It's a big mistake to do that just to get a hand. I found out, in *The Time of Your Life*, that you can stay in character and still stop a show. All this is comparative. We're speaking about hard or easy, but it's all tough. Every time you face an audience, you're proving yourself.

DC

Can we return to your singing in musicals?

GK

As I told you, I was always moving and always breathing from the chest—completely wrong, as any singing teacher will tell you. But because of that I paid a lot of attention to the lyrics. The audience heard every word, and I always played in character. So a lot of song writers, conversely enough, liked me because they knew the words would be played. Whereas, some very good singers would blur, even though they were expected to get all the notes. So, I always stood in good favor with song writers for that reason.

DC

I have heard that it was Dick Rodgers who saw you in *The Time of Your Life* and gave you the *Pal Joey* role. Is that true?

---

*A sting chord is a harmonized single note which announces something that needs attention, usually a song.

GH

Yes. He came, and then he brought Larry Hart and John O'Hara and George Abbott, and they all agreed.

DC

Did you have to audition for the part of Joey?

GK

Yes. I went out on the stage and committed the unpardonable sin of singing "I Didn't Know What Time It Was," which was a Dick Rodgers song. The reason I did it was that I thought I was still proving myself. I wanted to show them that I could handle a ballad . . . a real ballad. But it turned out well.

DC

Did you have to read for them?

GK

No. They had seen me in the Saroyan play.

DC

You mentioned Bob Alton. How would you define what he did? He was surely a much less sophisticated dance director than the choreographers we have today, like Jerome Robbins, Bob Fosse, and Michael Bennett.

GK

He wasn't like them because he came from the old school of dance, but he staged numbers better than anyone I've ever known. Every number he ever staged with a chorus stopped the show. He was and is the only one you can say that about. For example, in *Too Many Girls*, the conga number he did for Desi Arnaz and the chorus—it was just a conga line, but he did it in such a way that it stopped the show! And that was the finale of the first act. He did it consistently in *Pal Joey* and in *Leave It to Me*. He didn't have Balanchine's sophistication, but Balanchine's popular work was never as good as Bob's. He came out to MGM, found out that he hated the camera, and discovered that he had an aversion to doing all the numbers with the leads. For some reason he never whipped the camera. He'd put on the same chorus numbers, and the producers would come down and go "Wow!" Then, when they were photographed, they'd have to be seen in small chunks because the environment is not the same as the two eyes that see them on the stage, and, well, I guess that's as simply as I can put it.

DC

What has happened to the genus: Bob Alton?

GK

Oh, he's still around. Peter Gennaro*, for instance.

DC

Then one shouldn't separate someone like Alton from the kind of choreographers whose work we see today?

GK

No. It's just a different style of dance, and since dance follows music, they follow the music.

DC

How did the job of choreographing *Best Foot Forward* happen? You were still in *Pal Joey*, I believe.

GK

Yes. They had hired a choreographer, but after two weeks of rehearsals they knew they were in trouble. I had just two weeks more in *Pal Joey*, and in between shows I'd come over and help with the choreography. Dick Rodgers had asked me. Hugh and Ralph§ were new, you know, and George Abbott used to say, perhaps foolishly, that he didn't know anything about music. He'd always worked with a Dick Rodgers and a Larry Hart or a Bob Alton. So he had asked Dick Rodgers if he could be what they call in Hollywood an "Executive Producer." So Dick would come over and sit in the audience, and Hugh and Ralph would come in with these great songs, and he'd say,

---

*Distinguished Broadway choreographer.
§Hugh Martin and Ralph Blane, the composers and lyricists of the show.

"George, they're great!" and George would say, "Yeah?" And after
I started to stage them, Mr. Abbott got comfortable, and we all got
pretty much laid back.

DC

When I interviewed Nancy*, she talked about a walk-across she did
in "Just a Little Joint with a Jukebox."

GK

That is a great example of something that started out as a big number
but turned out to be too big for the show. Danny Daniels, who had
lied about his age—he was fifteen—in order to get into the show,
was brought in one day by my brother while I was doing a matinee
of *Pal Joey*. Danny was a great tap dancer—he still is—and he could
do things none of the other kids could do, so he was spotted in the
number. I had had a meeting with Jo Melziener[§], and we decided to
make it a fantasy with a huge jukebox in the back, and everybody
loved the number in rehearsal, but when we got it on the stage, we
couldn't get in and out of it without the whole show coming to a dead
stop. So after one night, we killed it. We retained a few things from
it but that was all.

DC

So many dancers experience a difficult time moving from a world of
silence into one of vocal expression, either in speech or in song. Did
you ever have that problem?

GK

Always. Always. But that's why you have to give dancers a motivation
to get past that. Sometimes you say: "Let's just cut out the song.
Let's just do a couple of lines because, after all, all you're saying in
the song is 'I love you,' so if you're having difficulty with it, let's just
say it without the music." Sometimes I'll start with a little scene and
use some of the words of the song. Sometimes they could do with
less mechanical help, but often they can't, and then, for example,
you have them run up-stage and the stage darkens and two spots hit

---

*Nancy Walker, who was in the show.
§The eminent set designer.

them just as they turn around, and now they are in another world as they come downstage back into this world, and they're over that obstacle. I call that "mechanical help." As you know, good performers can make that transition quite easily, but people forget what it means to dance. I once told some producers a story, and they said, "We'll get so-and-so." And I said, "But she can't dance." And they said, "But you've got a month to six weeks, haven't you?" And I told them, "If Jascha Heifetz came in and somebody said to him: 'Teach this person to play the fiddle. You've got four to six weeks' . . ." And they said: "Oh, but this is different. This is just singing and dancing."

DC

Why do you think people feel this way?

GK

They've always thought dancing is easy. Now the way dancing is done to popular music, people get up and do anything they want. But you can give trained dancers a routine, and they'll follow that kind of music and stay together. But they have to be trained dancers. Yet, a solo singer will get up, and she'll shake around and the "illiterati" will say: "Hey, look at her! What a good dancer!" And she's just doing what she wants to do and, in the next show, it will be different and, in the next show, still more different.

DC

You know, Gene, whenever I see your films, it strikes me that your voice is as much a part of my image of you as your dancing. Is that because the years have accustomed me to it?

GK

No, but they should all be tied together. Often in my films, if I had control, I'd have Judy Garland or Frank Sinatra sing the ballads. But sometimes I'd get trapped. In *Cover Girl*, Jerry Kern said that the leading man was going to sing "Long Ago and Far Away," and I went over to Ira's* and I said: "You know I never sing ballads. I'll be

---

*Ira Gershwin, Mr. Kern's lyricist on the film.

frightened to death." Solly Chaplin* rehearsed me in it, though, and it went very well. When the day came to record it, I went into the booth, and after the first take, I burst out of it and said, "Mr. Kern, I can do this much better." And he said: "I don't think you can. It's very good and that's fine." And I said, "Please, let me do another one." So, I started to do another chorus and then I said, again, "Please, one more." Morris Stoloff§ asked Jerry to let me do one more, and afterwards I came out pleased as punch and said, "There! I told you I could do it better!" And Jerry Kern and Morris Stoloff said, "It's the first one."

DC

I suppose the moral of that story is that we're not always the best judges of our work. I just found myself thinking, however, that perhaps you got better through the years—more proficient at it—or maybe people began to hear your voice as part of your . . . "fingerprint."

GK

I sang much better on the New York stage because I sang every night. Here [*in Los Angeles*] I didn't sing much at all. But I did "Our Love Is Here to Stay" with Leslie Caron by the quay, and it was soft and sweet, and the dance and the music and the arrangement and the singing and the ambience were all soft and sweet—you couldn't break one from the other—and they all blended one into the other.

DC

They must have liked your singing right from the start because you were never dubbed.

GK

No, I was never dubbed, but the first picture I did with Judy (*For Me and My Gal*) was a sort of vaudeville picture, and that was the

*Saul Chaplin, celebrated composer (*Bei Mir Bist Du Schoen*, *Until the Real Thing Comes Along*, and *The Anniversary Song*; and Associate Producer of many MGM musicals (*Les Girls*, *CanCan*, *Merry Andrew* [wrote the score with Johnny Mercer], *Man of La Mancha*, *West Side Story*, and *The Sound of Music*).
§The Music Director–Conductor.

kind of singing I used to do all through my teens and to pay my way through college, and so it was easy.

DC

When you played on Broadway, did you find it difficult to do eight shows a week?

GK

Yes. Often I wouldn't talk all day Sunday and Monday until showtime, but I believe that was due to no microphones and I was still breathing from here [*He indicates his chest.*] I wasn't breathing properly. I still don't. I did a musical with Olivia Newton John, and those girls, Barbra and Olivia, sing . . . [*He whispers a musical phrase*] so tiny . . . [*Haute voix*] you can't hear them. So when I work that way, when I'm told to sing quietly, I find I have no trouble. I don't have to project. It's a cheat way of singing, but it does the job. I'd go into the studio with those girls, and suddenly [*He belts out a full, rich sound.*] they come out like that. It's marvelous!

DC

When you left *Pal Joey* to go into film work, you never went back on the stage again. Was that on purpose or because time didn't permit it?

GK

No. In fact, I had conversations with Gadge Kazan* about doing *Death of a Salesman,* and I would have done that, but he never reoffered me the part. He had me read it, and I said, "Yes, I'll do it." He just changed his mind, I gather. I went back to direct *Flower Drum Song.*

DC

But never to perform? Why?

GK

The movies were so interesting to whip, and I was still searching for new ideas. You couldn't repeat in a movie. It was much more interesting and more difficult to direct a movie. It's like the landing on

*The director of the original production.

D day. You have to have everything there, and you have to know everyone's part, and you have to know what the grip is doing on the set. I thought that going back on the stage was a rocking-chair job. I was never crazy about performing. Never. I was always more interested in the creating of it. As soon as that was over, I would be on my way. I like putting it on—the staging of it—so essentially what started way back in Pittsburgh stayed with me always. Not performing may have lost me a lot of money in Las Vegas, but I didn't want to do it.

DC
You were a part of the golden age at MGM. Were the studio heads responsible for that time, or did performers like you force it to happen?

GK
I think we started it—inside. We were very lucky. They had a studio orchestra, and the producers would listen to us because I think it was a question of their own pride. They felt they had hired us because they believed in our talents. We'd say: "Get that guy from New York. He's the best arranger," or, "Get this other fellow. He's the best vocal coach," or, "Get this actress. She not only can dance but she can act," and they would listen.

DC
It was like a stock company.

GK
Yes, it was. The only musical stock company in the world. And we all did things for one another. No one was credit happy. When Jack Cole got hepatitis in the middle of *Les Girls*, I finished the picture for him. My name was never on it. Nowadays that would never happen. It would say, "So-and-so created and conceived by so-and-so . . ." In *Cover Girl*, although my name wasn't on it, everyone in the business knew I did everything but the first couple of numbers.

DC
You have never done cabaret in Las Vegas or during the 50s and 60s, a one-man show at the Palace Theater. Was that due only to a lack of interest in performing?

GK

When I was working my way through school, my brother and I played cheap nightclubs and speakeasies, and I vowed if I ever got on a Broadway stage, I'd never play a club again. After I got married, I'd always say, "If my kids need money, I'll do it," but it's just not satisfying. And it's not creative. You get it set, and then you do it and do it and do it.

DC

Gene, would you say your dancing owes more to ballet than to tap?

GK

I don't know how to define it. It's an athletic kind of dancing. It's my own, but I am pleased, in my later years, to see some of the younger guys copying it and the style, so I know it's caught on. It's a wide open style that, of course, is based on line and form and a lot of ballet and some modern and tap dancing, but tap dancing was never my favorite. Because of the characters I played, it was somehow obligatory.

DC

This is an awkward question, but why do you think dancing has always been a discomfiting career choice in this country, in particular, for a man, despite the fact that men like you and Fred Astaire are so honored and admired?

GK

I don't know if that's true anymore. It's certainly much less true than it used to be. One thing I do know: a man has got to look ahead, or he's going to be frustrated. Once he turns forty, he'll have to get a job or he has to teach, and a lot of good dancers aren't necessarily good teachers.

DC

Arlene Croce, in one of her *New Yorker* magazine articles, said something to the effect that although tap studios are full, the popular art of it barely survives. I believe she called it a "subcultural expression like jazz." Would you agree with her?

GK

I guess that it emanated from the people and not from the royal houses, as ballet did. So, in that sense, I'd agree with her. But I think that jazz is no longer a subculture. It's a cultural force, and a hundred years from now it could be our Mozart, our Beethoven, and our Bach. As for tap dancing, it will rise and fall as any popular art does. It sits well with men, you know. They never feel sissified or in any way put down when they tap-dance, in the way they might when they see or do ballet. Every guy I know, whether he's fifty or twenty, says, "Gee, I always wanted to tap-dance!"

DC

Why do you think that tap dancing is thought to be, if not an exclusive, certainly a preeminently black statement?

GK

That's a myth and a misnomer which is promulgated and promoted by well-spoken and eloquent blacks. Tap dancing didn't originate with the blacks here in America at all. It came from Ireland. They had danced the "clog" for centuries, and when they came to this country, jazz music came along, and that kind of dancing fused with the black "shuffle" and the soft shoe. They borrowed from each other. The reason, I believe, why the blacks have kept tap dancing more alive and popular is because there are so few opportunities for them to dance any other place. Of course, there are Alvin Ailey's and Arthur Mitchell's ballet companies but, other than these, the possibilities for employment are practically nonexistent.

DC

Gene, you've worked with three celebrated writers who have not been heavily "biographed," I'm thinking specifically of Larry Hart, Cole Porter, and Jerome Kern. Would you reminisce about them?

GK

Larry was a great friend. I knew him personally long before I knew Dick Rodgers. He was an amazing writer. I can give you an example. In *Pal Joey* we needed a second chorus for the girl who played the journalist and sang "Zip." He took a piece of brown paper and wrote down obscene endings for each line like, "Zip! Da da da da da da da da da da fuck. Zip! Da da da da da da da da da suck," and then he went out into the lobby of the theater, and in fifteen minutes he came back with the second chorus! "Zip! I consider Dali's paintings passé. Zip! Can they make the Metropolitan pay?" But the original was all obscene.

DC

I remember hearing a dummy lyric of his for "My Funny Valentine." It was about a plumber's daughter. I was told that it was his way of retaining the prosody of the musical line when he was away from Rodgers.

GK

He was a stickler for meter. That's how he fell into those inner rhymes like, "I'd go to hell fa ya in Philadelphia."

DC

And Cole Porter? What was he like?

GK

He was the first writer-composer I met. It was during my first show, *Leave It to Me*. I was reading Huxley's *Point Counter Point*, and every time there was a break in the dancing rehearsals so that Bob [*Alton*] could work with the singers, the dancers would go off and stretch or whatever, and I would always go off into a corner and read. One day, Cole said to Bob: "Who is that young man who's always reading in a corner when there's a break? What's he *reading?*" So, Bob said to me, "Would you like to meet Cole Porter?" and I said, "Oh, I'd love to." He took me to the back of the theater where Cole always sat, and we met. He said to me, "I'm just curious about what you're reading." And I said, "It's *Point Counter Point*," and we started to discuss Huxley and other books, and then I was invited to Cole's for dinner. I saw a man—it was his butler or a sommelier—open a bottle of wine and pour a little into Cole's glass, and then he tasted it. It was the first time I'd ever seen that. I got a book and found out that that's what you do. I liked him very much, but he seemed a sad and lonely man. I met him again here in Brentwood during *The Pirate* with Judy [Garland]. I'd gone out to his house to tell him that we

needed another song, and that night he wrote the verse and two
choruses of "Be a Clown" and brought it in the next day! I put it in
for the Nicholas Brothers and me. Judy liked it so much I suggested
it for her in the finale, and he did that in one night! And he had me
up to his penthouse in New York a couple of times.

DC

Why did you say he was lonely?

GK

He seemed "within himself." I never knew any of his coteries, like
Elsa Maxwell, but I do know, because Kay Thompson told me, that
she would save up all the soap operas, which were then on records
taken from the radio—there was no TV at the time—so that, when
he came back from his traveling, he could listen to them. Here was
this cosmopolite, this sophisticate, doing this! I can't do any two-bit
psychiatry about Cole and say "that's why he threw all those big
parties, because he didn't want to be alone," but I just sensed it.

DC

And what was Kern like?

GK

He frightened me at first because I was working with him and I had
heard he was the bane of all singers and musicians, but I met him
a couple of times at his home and I thought he was a charming man.
Until the fire* I had a picture of him he'd sent after we finished *Cover
Girl*. He had written "To GK who's OK from JK." *Cover Girl* is the
only film I ever made with him.

DC

You did a couple of films with Sinatra. I'm particularly interested in
your memories of dancing with him.

GK

When he first came to me, I said: "Frank, you're going to have to
take your hands off the mike. You'll have to stand up and move."

---

*The previous year a fire had destroyed Mr. Kelly's house.

DC

Could he?

GK

No. But he worked his ass off. We started with simple steps, and he was nimble. I'd played baseball with him, so I knew how he moved. I started with simple things that I had taught the children in dancing school. He did very well, and in each picture he got progressively better. He worked like a dog, though—trained like a fighter. Later on, I gather he became disenchanted with musicals. I think that happened during *Guys and Dolls*, but who knows? But when we were working together, we couldn't have had a better time.

DC

You were impelled to produce a pure dance film. Was that difficult to get on its feet?

GK

Yes, very. I made a brand new deal with MGM that I would make an experimental dance film and then, halfway through it, they decided that it had to be commercial.

DC

This was *Invitation to a Dance*?

GK

Yes. And then they kept it on the shelf for four or five years. I wanted to make a film with no dialogue, just dancing. I wanted to show the public how many great dancers there are that, outside of the big capitals of the world, audiences had never heard of. Dancers like Eric Bruhn and, from the American Ballet, Nora Kaye and Diana Adams.

DC

Why was the film shelved?

GK

Because they didn't know how to present it. There were no art theaters in those days. I suggested sending it to all the colleges. I even offered to buy it from them, but they wouldn't sell it. It was made very cheaply in England. The bottom line was $665,000. I got a consortium together to buy it for a million and a half, which would have given them a profit, but, as I say, they wouldn't sell it. Two years ago they showed it at the Radio City Music Hall in New York, and it made the most money of any film they'd ever shown there.

DC

How do you account for the enormous popularity of dance, of all kinds?

GK

I think there has been a change in the public's attitude toward dancing. That film, for instance, could never have played the Music Hall when it was made in 1953.

DC

You're a Francophile. How would you describe the typical French performers like Montand and Aznavour, as differentiated, say, from Sinatra? Is it the particular sound of the French popular chanson that gives their great performers their special signature?

GK

Yes. French music is so palpably distinctive. You hear a tune, especially by an Aznavour, who is, by the way, another close friend of mine, and you know immediately that it is a French song. And they are interesting performers who can move and embellish a song—to make it an "act." Chevalier always had that ability. When Charles [*Aznavour*] first came, nobody had ever heard of him. They asked me to present him at the Santa Monica Auditorium. And, afterwards, we went to a restaurant with four girls, and I remember sitting there the whole night not being talked to. Aznavour! He has charm and a certain je ne sais quoi that is amazing!

DC

When we talk this way about great performers, I wonder what advice you would pass on to young people who dream of a similar success in the musical theater. Should they be deterred by the negative publicity they read about what supposedly lies in the future?

GK

We are in a transitional stage. We're moving from big-scale movies to video cassettes, from Broadway to Off Broadway, and all because of money. To put on a musical these days costs as much as building the Titanic and . . . sometimes, it goes down. But nothing you say will stop anyone who truly wants to go into it. Deterrence, especially from older people, never works. You can't say, "Don't put your daughter on the stage, Mrs. Worthington," because, frankly, her daughter's going to go on the stage, anyway.

EXIT MUSIC

❧

The Future Tense:
Where Are We Going?

Ten years ago, in *On Singing Onstage*, I wrote that in some un-
foreseeable future, Broadway would not be the sole window in
which plays and musicals were presented, nor would the size of
productions be the measure of their worth. I maintained then that
regional theaters must begin to do for musicals what they had done
for the Broadway legitimate stage. This has started to happen. Almost
without exception, a successful Broadway play can now trace its
history to Off or Off-Off-Broadway or to cities as far-flung as Louis-
ville, Los Angeles, Chicago, Boston, Seattle, San Francisco, Houston,
Dallas, and London. In a mere decade, the future has become de-
cidedly foreseeable. In 1985 *Big River*, a musical based on Mark
Twain's *The Adventures of Huckleberry Finn*, became the first heavy
Tony winner that could boast a birth in Boston, an adolescence in
La Jolla, California, and a maturity to be lived in New York—and
all this for less than $3 million. Such a production must be considered
a masterpiece of cost planning when placed beside the $7 million
price tag for *Singin' in the Rain*, whose more traditional genesis did
not save it from a critical drubbing. Furthermore, by separating themselves from the conservatism that, out of necessity, backers of

289

musicals tend to practice, composers, lyricists, and librettists can pursue more iconoclastic forms and execute them in smaller, far less "spectacled" productions. One attractive aspect of the nationalization (and "internationalization") of the theater is the new practice of New York critics going wherever there is something of interest to see. Anything, everywhere will attract attention if it is worthy, and, more than likely, a good review will enhance a musical's prospects for transfer to Broadway. Equally, a "nay" can kill those prospects with the speed of a guillotine. This same critical power has been to known to stop a hit English musical from risking an Atlantic crossing.

But the cost of producing a musical on Broadway is not the only obstacle producers face. Weekly running costs are prohibitive. Union minimum contracts for the workers on stage, backstage, and in the pit, and percentages for "in-demand" members of the creative team and star(s) can mean that producers require a high-glitz musical just to break even at the phenomenally high figure of $300,000 a week. A further complication: since only one producer is understandably unable to provide the necessary millions of dollars, the roster of producers grouped above the musical's title can read like another cast list. These men and women have nothing in common with each other beyond their shared investment in the show and may very well be untutored, unfriendly, unavailable, or all three. Where once a strong executive hand could maintain order, now a Tower of Babel may likely exist. Crucial decisions are made by either the strongest willed or whoever holds the largest share of the total backing, and not necessarily in that order.

New writers and performers must be disabused of the notion that their work can only find its life on Broadway. (In Los Angeles, productions of *In Trousers*—a prequel to William Finn's *March of the Falsettos*—*Rapmaster Ronnie, Livin' Dolls, Corridos, Is There Life after High School?, Mens*, and *Color Me Dorothy* all enjoyed moderate to extravagant success.) Not hampered by yesterday's tired formulas, they may very well discover that they can create a musical theater right there in their own backyards.

Whenever I am asked if I think it wise that John or Mary chooses a career in the musical theater, I always say, "Yes, but . . ." "Yes," because no matter how black the picture may be painted today, nothing will keep incipient performers from doing what they must;

"but," because there is just too much third-rate talent that must begin to upgrade what it offers or suffer getting lost in the crowd. Anyone who has ever held auditions for a professional musical production suffers greatly from the strain of watching and listening to the long lines of shoddy performers who think of themselves as equipped and ready to go to work. It is now time for all of us to define our own gauge of excellence and, with ceaseless determination as artists, to become our own severest critics. No one is going to ask excellence of us or even take the time to explain our inadequacies to us, neither can we expect audiences, too innocent and blunted by commercial television's relentless mediocrity, to know the difference between good and bad work.

Years ago it was possible to perfect one's craft through the rough-and-tumble school of hard knocks because there was a profligacy of work to be had and work has always been regarded as the "great educator." (See "The Twenty Most often Asked Questions . . . Answered," number 20.) Today, competition is cutthroat because of the sharply diminished amount of available professional employment to be found, and, in consequence, performers must seek other ways to shape and sharpen their craft. The importance of buying a study experience now emerges as the single most valuable method of developing a proficient performing technique, but, as in the case of all mercantile transactions, the buyer must beware.

S *tudy*

Doctors and lawyers are lucky, indeed, for they know where the temples of learning are to be found and, once they are found, which should be trusted (debatable as this may appear to young doctors and lawyers). Those who aspire to the musical theater are not so fortunate. Teachers are everywhere, but they are not all to be trusted. And there is, unfortunately, no grounds for debate. All it takes to qualify as a teacher is enough money to buy an inch of advertising in a professional publication. We cannot know if they are all good or bad, but, like consumers, we should isolate what we need and not buy indiscriminately. A good rule of thumb: choose teachers whose students advertise them. If they prove to be of little to no value to you, move on. No teacher can hope to be all things to all students. Even pedagogical icons are guilty until proved innocent, although icons tend to become myths for good reason. Of course, there is equal responsibility placed on the student. Unless you are prepared to work diligently, you cannot fault teachers for what you perceive to be their failure. At the start, be very clear in your mind about what you know you do not know. Once you have identified your areas of ignorance, go about the task of discovering who teaches what you need to know. Some subjects are learned academically and, through the years that span a career, will mutate into a personal ideology that may be far removed from—and even a rejection of—those early study experiences. Other subjects must be continued beyond the point where they can be considered learned; singing and dancing are two of these, since the muscles that are trained to support both activities must be kept in shape during all of one's lifetime. Before attempting an answer, then, to "Where am I going to put it?" be certain in your mind and heart that "it" deserves to stand in good company on the professional stage.

Throughout this volume, I have used *actor-dancer-singer* as a single noun referring to a new kind of performer. The order is not without significance, for actors, dancers, and singers are not all equally compelled to learn each other's ball game.

Actors: Of the three groups, actors have realized the most broadening of their potential. In just thirty-odd years, they have learned to sing and to move with some degree of style and have, thereby, enriched both the theater and their pocketbooks. This is not to say that all actors are so impelled, but there is no question that they have turned their backs on rigid specialization and begun to affirm that a good actor must be a graceful actor with a voice capable of more than a six-note range.

Dancers: Unlike actors, but along with singers, they are the native dwellers in the country of musical theater. They are born into a land where music is a common language. But dancers have worked long and hard to erase the brand that marked them as such to their disadvantage. For a long time, Americans have been ambivalent toward them. We esteem Astaire, kowtow to Kelly, and even bow to Baryshnikov, but, at the same time, what they do is . . . well . . . not quite . . . But the picture has begun to change. (See "Entr'acte," "The Present.") Everyone is dancing, although remnants of doubt still linger. Dancers who have learned to sing and to act are often induced to dissemble or even renounce their original identity in order to be taken seriously. I have known dancers who erase from their résumés any reference to dancing because they fear it will be seen as a stigma. I do not know if this is the goad that pushes them into singing and acting classes, but their determination to be taken seriously in these fields is exemplary.

Singers: Just as dancers endure a benign second-class citizenship, singers suffer the stereotypical image of a "voice" encased in cement. This imputation is not as damaging, for, after all, singing well can be profitable, and someone who sings exceedingly well, (unlike someone who dances exceedingly well) can be paid exceedingly well. This may be why some singers display no interest in learning how to create a life on the stage. When the musical demands placed on the voice are formidable, as in the opera house, audiences tend to forgive the singer's dramatic deficiencies to the degree that his or her sound fulfills the demands of the score. In the musical theater, where the vocal tessitura is less critical, producers, writers and directors, unlike their counterparts in opera, tend to be less forgiving. After all, singers will be asked to read from the script at an audition just as actors will be asked to sing. It behooves singers, particularly now, when musical scores are more difficult to sing (a factor that places actors and dancers at a disadvantage), to demonstrate that the scenes they are asked to read are as important to them as the music they know they can sing.

Work, or "Where Am I Going to Put It?"

When you have achieved the level of proficiency that justifies presenting yourself at an audition, you are openly declaring that you are a professional, and that you wish to be so considered. I have talked about the sharp decrease in the number of musicals that are produced on Broadway each season, but it is interesting to note that, as this diminution has continued, a sharp rise in alternative marketplaces has occurred. I am not necessarily speaking here of "high-quality" productions, and in many instances the description would be considered laughable, but a performer can find a stage upon which to stand, act, dance, and sing, even though there may be little or even no payment for his or her services. The decision to go out for a job that does not pay is a personal one. I tend to place a high value on wages received for services rendered. If you hold another opinion, there are mitigating factors to support your point of view. Among them:

1. Quality of production
2. Desire to work with a particular director, choreographer, or member(s) of the cast
3. Established evidence that you will be seen to your advantage by agents and casting personnel

To perform for free in a fifth-rate production of *The Pajama Game* may sometimes do you more harm than good, especially if the chance that you will be seen in it is strong. The same damage can be inflicted in a fifth-rate professional production—one in which you are paid—but you can at least salve a nagging conscience with the thought that your wallet is thicker. The point is that there are dinner theaters, regional theaters, little theaters, and waiver theaters by the score in which you can practice your craft away from the prying eyes of those who should not yet be asked to watch and assess your work.

"Where am I going to put it?" also connotes a choice of geography. "Should I move to New York?" becomes a life question as well as a professional one and deserves to be addressed with the same serious forethought. Despite signs that can be interpreted to the contrary, Broadway (and its environs) is still the hub of the musical theater. The traditions of over a century will, for the immediate future, keep it there. Production offices, technical talent pools, dozens of allied and integral craft unions, historic theaters, all of these have trained the world to think of Broadway not only as a place but a condition, in much the same way that Hollywood is thought to be the capital of the film world. For those who are able to pull up stakes without a major uprooting of their lives, a move to New York is not without justification. For those who cannot so easily relocate, it is of some comfort to know that Broadway, though it may still be something of a hub (and for all I know, may forever remain so), cannot any longer claim to be the sole place where you will find musical theater. It is everywhere. The old formulas are changing as the business faces new economic realities. Not so long ago, a hit musical toured only after it completed its New York run. Then came a change: on the heels of a successful New York opening, a national company was cast, and it began a tour of the major cities. Following this evolution away from standard practice, second and third companies (sometimes referred to as "bus and truck companies") covered the country and were able to perform in smaller cities not on the national company's schedule. These mirror images of the original production were not pure clonings, allowances having to be made for cast, sets, and lighting modifications.

In the mid-seventies, a new wrinkle was adopted. Broadway still offers the original presentation, but the national company is now called the "west coast production" and a third company is upgraded to the position of national company. Two reasons have brought about this change:

1. The legitimate theater in Los Angeles has always had a life, but it was a parochial one contained within the city limits. Its history was, and still is, illustrious. (See Robert Preston's interview.) But it was never able to support a touring company for more than a few weeks. Today, however, productions of *Evita*, *A Chorus Line*, *Grease*, *Forty-Second Street*, *Dreamgirls*, and *Cats* can, and often do, rack up a two-year run. Other musicals may not be megahits, but they can still have "legs." Casting for these productions is, in the main, done in Los Angeles, where the likelihood of a long run works to the producers' advantage. Per-diem and touring salaries are considerably higher than those decreed by regular union contracts. Then, too, a possible two-year run in Los Angeles is as unappealing to a New

York performer—especially if he or she is married and has children—as a two-year stay in New York might be for the Los Angeleno who, in addition to a possible family, may be encumbered with a heavy real estate mortgage.

2. The cast can be selected from local talent pools already resident in California. Since the film and television industries are as much a part of the scene as Broadway is to New York, the availability of first-rate actors, dancers, and singers is a constant, and most of them are eager to get back on a stage. Perhaps the New York "leads" will transfer from the New York to the Los Angeles production, but they, in turn, want to get back on the screen. Not to be overlooked is the factor of replacements in musicals that enjoy long runs in Los Angeles. Just as in New York, cast turnovers offer a continuing audition schedule, as New Yorkers on limited-run contracts leave for home and west coast performers take their places. (An interesting afterthought: it is my personal feeling that casting west coast musical productions represents the only time theater casting in Los Angeles is taken seriously by both management and talent agencies.)

Since the west coast production settles down for a run in Los Angeles, the third, or National, company becomes the touring company and moves around the country in ritual fashion. Casting for this version may occur on either coast and often allows the interchange of cast members from one company to another. It is its own little galaxy within which shuttling is commonplace.

The choice of "where to put it," in the geographical sense of the question, is yours to make, and, as with other life questions, no one can or should be asked to make it for you.

A Move to New York

Like the West End in London, Broadway is theater. Further, the musical theater historically lives there, even though, as we have noted, the times they are a-changing. Talent agencies in New York are cognizant of the casting problems particular to the stage, while their west coast colleagues are more aware of the requirements of film and television. If you are young and free to wander, a move to New York seems, on balance, a wise one. One word of caution: New York is a rough city. It is the "most" of everything good and not-so.

Among the not-so's must be listed the difficulty of finding an
apartment—and finding one you can afford. The problem is severe,
and the expense is considerable. You must be prepared to hold down
a job that, if it doesn't support you, will require you to get another
in tandem to the first. You may have to do some elaborate juggling
to maintain the elastic timetable that scheduling interviews and auditions call for. In New York's favor is that it still offers some of the
best instruction in theater arts because professional teachers are
professionals as well as teachers. However, study makes for even
more expenses. Survival in New York takes grit, determination, and
a sense of humor.

A Move to Los Angeles

> Why be out here?
> But then, why be in there?
>
> *Philip Larkin "The Less
> Deceived," in* Reasons for
> Attendance *(1955)*

Partisans of Los Angeles, once a browbeaten lot identified by
the New York establishment as provincial lotus eaters, now have
stronger convictions about the city in which they choose to live—
and with good reason. No city in the world has altered so drastically
in the last twenty-five years. It is truly a twentieth-, if not a twenty-
first-, century town, and it still continues to change. What is wrong
with it has been well-documented by novelists and social critics and,
to a large extent, their scorn is justified. Nevertheless, there is much
to commend it. A large show business community lives and works
there. The climate is benign, and the cost of living, while not low,
is considerably less than that in New York. A good deal of peripheral
theater can be found there, and to this relatively recent source of
work must be added the ongoing television and film industries. An
interesting aspect of both coasts is the widening of work possibilities
built into show business everywhere. You can get a television series
in New York and even film it there, and you can land a musical in
Los Angeles and even play it there. You can be cast in a commercial

in Chicago, and you can play in cabarets and clubs wherever they are found. As for study, Los Angeles now boasts first-rate acting, dancing, and singing instruction on a par with what can be found in New York. The fees are the same.

In both cities the need exists to find a way to support yourself. The jobs most often sought by young performers—waiter, waitress, barman, barmaid—are still the most popular because they permit free daytime hours in which to study or to knock on important doors. Add, of late, computer word processing and, in Los Angeles, work in film studios in any number of jobs that not only pay but place you where the action is—for example, secretary, mail clerk, production assistant, and reader. But both cities need the same survival kits and the same sense of humor.

Alternatives

San Francisco, San Diego, Chicago, Seattle, Dallas, Houston, and Washington, DC are all cities where there is some show business to be found. They are even more parochial than Los Angeles was once known to be, and a career that begins to widen its targets soon feels the need to make the move to one or the other coast. This may not be true of regional theaters, for they are everywhere. But musical theater, and the expertise required to excel in it, stays mainly on the coastal plains.

*   *   *

The struggle to achieve success as a performer in the musical theater has never been easy, and today it seems even more like a Sisyphean labor. No one in his or her right mind would elect to push the rock up that steep hill, but we are not here concerned with sane behavior. The urge to perform is a wondrous insanity that I advocate to those who have ever felt the need to stand up and be heard. And, further, I praise those who, when they are heard, demonstrate beyond a shadow of a doubt why they asked for our attention.